VICTORIA FORNER

THOUGHT CRIMINALS
Truth is not defence

VICTORIA FORNER

THOUGHT CRIMINALS
Truth is no defence

CRIMINALES DE PENSAMIENTO
La verdad no es defensa
first publication by Omnia Veritas, 2017

Translated from Spanish and published by
OMNIA VERITAS LTD

OMNIA VERITAS®
www.omnia-veritas.com

© Omnia Veritas Limited - Victoria Forner – 2025

All rights reserved. No part of this publication may be reproduced by any means without the prior permission of the publisher. The intellectual property code prohibits copies or reproductions for collective use. Any representation or reproduction in whole or in part by any means whatsoever, without the consent of the publisher, the author or their successors, is unlawful and constitutes an infringement punishable by articles of the Code of Intellectual Property.

INTRODUCTION	13
PERSECUTION OF REVISIONISTS FOR THOUGHT CRIMES	17
1. MAIN VICTIMS OF PERSECUTION IN GERMANY	**20**
JOSEPH BURG, A JEWISH REVISIONIST PERSECUTED BY NAZIS AND ZIONISTS	20
THIES CHRISTOPHERSEN CONVICTED OF "BRINGING THE STATE INTO DISREPUTE".	23
WILHEM STÄGLICH, THE JUDGE WHO DEMANDED JUSTICE FOR GERMANY	26
ERNST ZÜNDEL, "REVISIONIST DYNAMO", MODEL OF RESISTANCE	29
GERMAR RUDOLF: PERSECUTION AND DESTRUCTION OF AN EMINENT SCIENTIST	49
HORST MAHLER, FROM RADICAL LEFTIST TO HOLOCAUST DENIER	64
SYLVIA STOLZ, THE UNCOMPROMISING LAWYER	75
GÜNTER DECKERT, A PERSISTENT SYMBOL OF FREEDOM OF EXPRESSION	84
UDO WALENDY, IMPRISONED FOR PUBLISHING REVISIONIST TEXTS	88
URSULA HAVERBECK. THE INDECENT CONDEMNATION OF A VENERABLE OLD WOMAN	90
MONIKA AND ALFRED SCHAEFER: "SORRY MOM I WAS WRONG ABOUT THE HOLOCAUST".	97
REINHOLD ELSTNER, THE REVISIONIST WHO BURNED HIMSELF ALIVE	105
2. MAIN VICTIMS OF PERSECUTION IN FRANCE	**110**
FRANÇOIS DUPRAT, MURDERED BY JEWISH TERRORISTS	110
ROGER GARAUDY, THE PHILOSOPHER PILLORIED FOR DENOUNCING ISRAEL	111
ROBERT FAURISSON, REVISIONISM'S ESSENTIAL ALMA MATER	121
VINCENT REYNOUARD, "HEARTS GO UP!"	135
3. MAIN VICTIMS OF PERSECUTION IN AUSTRIA	**140**
GERD HONSIK, VICTIM OF PSOE'S SURRENDER TO ZIONISM	140
DAVID IRVING, SENTENCED TO THREE YEARS IN PRISON IN VIENNA	145
WOLFGANG FRÖHLICH, THE "CANARY" STILL SINGING IN THE CAGE	150
4. MAIN VICTIMS OF PERSECUTION IN SWITZERLAND	**156**
JÜRGEN GRAF AND GERHARD FÖRSTER SENTENCED FOR WRITING AND PUBLISHING BOOKS	156
GASTON-ARMAND AMAUDRUZ, ONE YEAR IN PRISON FOR AN OCTOGENARIAN	160
5. MAIN VICTIMS OF PERSECUTION IN BELGIUM AND THE NETHERLANDS	**163**
SIEGFRIED VERBEKE, STUBBORN FIGHTER FOR FREEDOM OF EXPRESSION	163
6. MAIN VICTIMS OF PERSECUTION IN SPAIN	**169**
PEDRO VARELA, AN HONEST BOOKSELLER VICTIM OF HATRED AND SECTARIAN INTOLERANCE	170
POST SCRIPTUM	189
OTHER BOOKSELLERS AND PUBLISHERS PERSECUTED IN CATALONIA	192
7. MAIN VICTIMS OF PERSECUTION IN SWEDEN	**197**
DITLIEB FELDERER, THE MOCKING JEW USING CORROSIVE SATIRE	197
AHMED RAHMI, ARCHITECT OF *RADIO ISLAM* AND LEADING MUSLIM REVISIONIST	200
8. MAIN VICTIMS OF PERSECUTION IN AUSTRALIA	**205**
FREDERICK TÖBEN, IMPRISONED IN GERMANY, ENGLAND AND AUSTRALIA	205
9. VICTIMS OF PERSECUTION IN THE UK	**215**

ALISON CHABLOZ SENTENCED IN ENGLAND FOR THREE SONGS 215

10. OTHER VICTIMS OF PERSECUTION FOR THOUGHT CRIMES 220

ALL AGAINST CATHOLIC BISHOP RICHARD WILLIAMSON 220
HAVIV SCHIEBER, THE JEW WHO SLASHED HIS WRISTS TO AVOID DEPORTATION TO ISRAEL
.... 224
HANS SCHMIDT, THE AMERICAN IMPRISONED FOR FOUR WORDS 225
ARTHUR TOPHAM, CONVICTED IN CANADA FOR "HATRED" OF JEWS 227

11. APPENDIX ON THE RUTHLESS PERSECUTION OF NONAGENARIANS 230

LASZLO CSATARY 231
SAMUEL KUNZ 232
JOHAN BREYER 232
OSKAR GRÖNING 233
REINHOLD HANNING 234
SIERT BRUINS 234
A 91-YEAR-OLD WOMAN 234

OTHER BOOKS 237

To my friend Antonio Damas,

in the hope that this book

help you understand.

INTRODUCTION

"It is not the lie that passes through the mind, but the lie that sinks in and settles in, which does the hurting."
Francis Bacon

"Pour savoir qui vous dirige vraiment il suffit de regarder ceux que vous ne pouvez pas critiquer".
Voltaire

("To know who really leads you, it is necessary to observe those whom you cannot criticise").

Never before has a historical event become an undisputed dogma of faith for the whole of humanity. Today, however, historians, scientists and researchers in all fields of knowledge are persecuted for questioning the Holocaust. Pierre Vidal-Naquet and Léon Poliakov, two Jewish historians, are the progenitors of the universally imposed declaration of faith. It states: "It is not necessary to ask how such a mass death was technically possible. It was possible because it took place. This is the obligatory starting point of any historical research on the subject. It is this truth that we simply have to remember. The existence of the gas chambers cannot be debated". Having established this axiom, denying the existence of the gas chambers and calling into question the myth of the Holocaust constitutes a thought crime, a criminal offence in the penal codes of many countries. The mass media all over the world, always submissive, are responsible for discrediting and rejecting revisionist works. Their authors are systematically vilified and imprisoned for racial hatred or anti-Semitism. To further tighten the gag on critics in US universities, on 11 December 2019 President Trump signed an executive order banning criticism of Israel and Jews. A senior White House official explained that the new measure will interpret Judaism as a nationality and not just a religion.

On the other hand, it is very significant to note that not a single NGO has denounced the imprisonment of the revisionists or taken an interest in any of them. If one considers that the defence of human rights and freedom of expression are the raison d'être of the most prestigious NGOs, this is shameful, to say the least. To understand why this is the case, it is enough to know who is behind these "prestigious" organisations. Let's look at three cases: Reporters Without Borders has been denounced by UNESCO for receiving sponsorship from US intelligence agencies; Human Rights Watch is funded to the tune of hundreds of millions by the Jew George Soros, a Rothschild man; Amnesty International likewise receives funding from Soros' Open Society Foundations. Senior AI officials are Zionist millionaires or former members of the US State Department or CIA. Amnesty has always been conspicuously silent on Palestine, where nearly two million Gazans are subjected to subhuman conditions, while children and young people are killed with impunity every year. Curiously, however, AI has just demanded the release of several Catalan separatists convicted of sedition by Spain's Supreme Court. It is clear, then, why revisionist prisoners can expect nothing from NGOs, since most of them are at the service of deception and manipulation, i.e. they obey their masters.

The book you hold in your hands, reader, is an offprint from *Historia proscrita. La actuación de agentes judíos en la H^a Contemporánea*, a four-volume work published in 2017 by Omnia Veritas. Specifically, it constitutes the 5th part of chapter XII (fourth book). Therefore, during the reading, will find some references or allusions to the original writing from which they come, which, however, is not an obstacle to the full understanding of the text. The writing of the pages that follow this introduction was completed at the beginning of 2016. Since then, the life of our "thought criminals", heroic on so many occasions, has continued inexorably. For this reason, we have made a number of adjustments and have succinctly added the events of some of the most prominent protagonists in order to bring their vicissitudes up to date.

Having said that, it is imperative to mention at once the revisionists who have recently passed away. Prominent among them are Ernst Zündel and Robert Faurisson, two unrepeatable giants of freedom of thought, to whom we once again pay tribute of admiration. For this monograph, therefore, we have written a short paragraph at the end of the accounts of both of them to record how their deaths occurred. Two other revisionists featured in this work also disappeared in 2018. Their names should therefore appear in these introductory lines. On 7 April of that year, Gerd Honsik left us, dead at the age of 77 in Sopron (Hungary). A refugee in Spain for fifteen years, since the Audiencia Nacional had rejected his extradition in 1995 on the grounds that it was "a political crime and therefore excluded from extradition", Honsik was a victim of the submission to Zionism of Rodríguez Zapatero's socialist government and the ineffable judge Baltasar Garzón, who in 2007 authorised his extradition to Austria. The second name is that of Gaston-Armand Amaudruz, perhaps the first revisionist to question the gas chambers. Amaudruz died on 7 September in Lausanne at the age of 97.

Of necessity, what happened to Ursula Haverbeck, Sylvia Stolz and Horst Mahler has also forced us to add a few lines inside this offprint to the stories we wrote in *Proscribed History*. When we left our text on the persecution of the great lady in 2016, Judge Björn Jönsson of the Hamburg District Court, after equating the certainty of the Holocaust with the evidence of the roundness of the Earth, had sentenced her in November 2015 to ten months' imprisonment. Today, at the age of 91, she is in prison. The story of the persecution of Sylvia Stolz also ended with a new conviction, which is why this book contains a brief update of the events. As for Horst Mahler, the last thing we wrote was that, after seven years in prison, he had obtained a suspended sentence in 2015, which enabled him to leave Brandenburg Prison after an operation in which his left leg was amputated because of diabetes. We have also included what we have learned about the prolongation of his critical situation.

Among the most shameful and outrageous cases of persecution of revisionists in recent years, the names of Monika and Alfred Schaefer and Alison Chabloz stand out. Although their trials do not appear in the original pages of *Proscribed History*, we felt that their struggle to denounce the falsification of historical reality should be included. Their stories have therefore been incorporated into this book. In 2016, we wanted to conclude the list of the main victims of the thought police in Germany with the tragedy of Reinhold Elstner. We now maintain this intention and have therefore placed the account of what happened to the Schaefer brothers before the section that reproduces the political will of the revisionist who was burned alive. As for the persecution of Alison Chabloz, which is relevant because we have so far lacked convictions in the United Kingdom, it has prompted us to create a new section: Victims of persecution in the United Kingdom. "Alison Chabloz, convicted in England for three songs" is the title that heads the account of her misadventure.

Two names remain to be mentioned in this introduction. The first is Gerd Ittner. In *Proscribed History* he appears together with Dirk Zimmermann. We alluded to both of them only briefly at the time: our work had already exceeded 2000 pages in length and the inclusion of a number of German revisionists had to be dispensed with. Since Ittner's stubborn struggle has continued and his persecution does not cease, we have chosen to write a brief review of this indomitable activist, whose struggle goes back to the beginning of the 21st century, in this offprint.. The other name is Arthur Topham, who has his own space in our handbook. For this monograph we have briefly updated the information on this Canadian, whose website *The Radical Press* was an example of the will to resist.

It only remains to thank Omnia Veritas, my publisher, for the publication of *Criminals of Thought*, a book which presents together, for the first time to our knowledge, the cases of some forty revisionists who have been relentlessly persecuted by Western "democracies". Our intention is to contribute as much as possible to making their sad reality known. We also hope that the publication of this work will make readers aware of the existence of *Proscribed History*, the parent work from which it derives, which covers the historical study of two hundred and fifty years from an unpublished point of view, the common denominator of which is the action of Jewish agents in all the events of contemporary history. We will end these lines as we began them, with another authoritative argument, this time from Goethe: "None are more totally enslaved than those who mistakenly believe they are free. The truth has been hidden from their minds by masters who rule them with lies. They feed them with fallacies so that what is false appears to their eyes as true".

Persecution of revisionists for thought crimes

As a tribute to so many honest people who have risked their careers and their lives to defend freedom of expression and research in search of historical truth, we will end chapter XII of this *Proscribed History*[1] with a broad overview of the essential work of these unsung heroes of revisionism, unknown to the general public. Many of them have already been mentioned in the course of our work, but we will now introduce them more fully and thus trace the value and scope of their contributions. The persecution of revisionists for thought crimes is one of the most shameful things that can happen in self-proclaimed free and democratic societies. It is outrageous, intolerable, indecent that intellectuals from all fields of knowledge are imprisoned for exercising their right to study and research historical facts. This unjustifiable fact should be enough to make us realise that reality and history have been falsified and that the lie is being maintained at all costs

The victims of the thought police are numerous in Europe, especially in Germany, where since the end of World War II the German people have been subjected to all sorts of humiliations with the connivance of their leaders. In France and Austria, too, there are many cases of people being persecuted, prosecuted and imprisoned for exercising their right to freedom of expression. In order to facilitate the presentation and to bring together in these pages the main cases of which we are aware, we will proceed to present them by country and also try to keep a chronological order, in order to follow the process from a historical perspective. We will begin in Germany, where the ideological control that has been exercised since 1945 is not perceived to its full extent by the majority of the population, whose brainwashing, begun in childhood, has reached unprecedented levels.

---

[1] *Proscribed History, The role of Jewish agents in Contemporary History*, Omnia Veritas Limited, www.omnia-veritas.com.

We will see below how far the deterioration of civil rights has gone in Germany, a country that has accepted the censorship of its national anthem, mutilated, with banned verses that no one dares to sing in public. The idea of political correctness is the tool used by those who want to paralyse German society at all costs. Anything that does not conform to the official version of events is considered politically unacceptable. This state of paralysis is maintained by the irreplaceable support of the so-called anti-fascist movement, which viciously attacks and disqualifies those who seek to revise history, especially that of the Third Reich. Unlike anti-capitalist or anti-communist movements, which are the expression of personal convictions, anti-fascism in Germany is institutionalised, rooted and structured at all levels of society, so that those who do not express anti-fascist sentiments are morally disqualified.

It should be remembered that it was only in 1955 that Germany was granted partial sovereignty. Until then, there was neither freedom of the press nor academic freedom. To ensure that political changes could not take place, the Department for the Protection of the Constitution was set up. In addition to combating communist political parties, this department did everything necessary to legally nullify national parties and media considered to be right-wing. As a result, there are neither universities nor political parties in Germany, nor any significant right-wing newspapers or media. However, in 1968, thousands of students, incited by the teachings of left-wing, socialist and even communist professors installed in the universities by the Allies during the occupation, took to the streets with pro-communist slogans. As a result of the student revolt of 1968, the progressive entry of these leftists into the country's institutions began.

At the end of the last century, this generation with ideas ranging from socialism to communism reached the height of its power and influence on German society. Its representatives were well placed at all levels and formed a powerful political elite. In this way they can maintain extensive influence and control over public opinion and immediately silence with accusations of "fascism" those who dare to be politically incorrect. Their methods are wide-ranging and include everything from press campaigns to intimidation if necessary. The main mechanism of these leftist circles in which German Jews abound is to keep up to date the feelings of collective guilt, collective shame or collective responsibility, which have kept the German people anaesthetised for more than seventy years.

Before I begin to present the victims of the thought police in Germany and other countries, it is interesting to know that every year the German government presents the figures of its persecution of peaceful dissidents, whom it groups together with violent criminals as "enemies of the Constitution" (Basic Law that came into force on 23 May 1949). In 2011, for example, the *Report on the Protection of the Constitution (Verfassungschutzbericht)* indicated that of the 13,865 criminal investigations, 11,401 cases were for "propaganda offences". Of these cases, 2,464 were individuals who had said or written something deemed capable of "disturbing the order of the people". Most of these transgressions are attributed to "right-wing extremists". Crimes committed by radical leftists or foreigners are not lumped into the category of "left-wing extremists". Thought crimes in Germany can only be attributed to nationalists or patriots who are considered "Nazis", "right-wingers", "fascists", labels that are synonymous with "evil".

1. Main victims of persecution in Germany

Joseph Burg, a Jewish Revisionist persecuted by Nazis and Zionists

It is only fair to begin these pages on the persecution of the Revisionists with an admirable character if ever there was one, Joseph Ginsburg, better known as Joseph Burg, a German Jew of integrity and honesty like few others, who was persecuted and attacked several times by extremist thugs of the Jewish Defence League. The contempt and hatred of his co-religionists went so far as to deny him the right to be buried in the Jewish cemetery in Munich. Joseph Ginsburg was born in Germany in 1908 and was persecuted by the National Socialist regime during the 1930s. At the outbreak of war in September 1939, he was living in Lemberg, Poland, from where he fled with his family to Czernowitz in the Romanian province of Bukovina, which was occupied by the Red Army in June 1940. When Germany attacked the USSR a year later, Red soldiers fled the region and gangs of Ukrainians began pogroms against Jews. German and Romanian troops stopped these actions and prevented further violence. Ginsburg and his family were deported east to the Transnistria region, where at least they could live. The German-Romanian front collapsed in 1944, and Ginsburg and his family returned to Czernowitz, where the Red terror reigned and all was chaos and hunger.

After the war ended, in 1946 Ginsburg and his party went to Breslau and from there to an UNRRA displaced persons camp near Munich, which was run by an American Jew, whom he served as factotum. In *Schuld un Schiksal, Europas Jugend zwischen Henkern und Heuchlern* (*Guilt and Destiny, European Youth among Executioners and Hypocrites*), published in 1962, Joseph Burg recalls his experiences in the camp and tells how he organised the police, the prison, the newspaper and cultural activities. In 1949 he was living in Munich, but chose to emigrate to Israel. There he immediately rejected the sectarianism and racism of the Zionists, so in August 1950 he decided to return to Munich, where he worked as a bookbinder.

It was in Germany, therefore, that he began his struggle to establish the historical truth. His testimony in 1988 in the Zündel trial is a valuable source of information. Ernst Zündel, with whom Burg worked closely, has acknowledged that reading the book *Guilt and Destiny* was a determining factor in his life, for it prompted him to begin the struggle against the false accusations against the German people and turned him into a revisionist. Joseph Burg's courage and stature became evident when he dared to accuse the Mossad of being responsible for the burning of a Jewish old people's home in Munich on the night of 13 February 1970, a terrorist action that claimed the lives of seven people, five men and two women. Also in the 1970s, the so-called "Kreisky-Wiesenthal affair" broke out in Austria. Bruno Kreisky, a Jew persecuted by the Gestapo, was Chancellor of Austria from 1970 to 1983. Simon Wiesenthal accused him in 1975 of appointing five ministers with Nazi backgrounds. Kreisky reacted indignantly and accused Wiesenthal of being a 'racist' who had collaborated with the Gestapo and promoted anti-Semitism in Austria. Joseph Burg came to the Chancellor's support and corroborated the accusation against the notorious "Nazi hunter". Burg publicly declared that Wiesenthal had been an informer for the Gestapo.

In 1979 Joseph Burg published his second work, *Majdanek in alle Ewigkeit?* (*Majdanek in all Ewigkeit?*), in which he recounted his visits to the Majdanek camp in late 1944 and in the autumn of 1945. On this second occasion he also went to Auschwitz. In it he boldly criticised the imposture of the Holocaust and denounced the swindle of the financial reparations paid by the Federal Republic of Germany. The book was immediately banned and all copies were destroyed by order of the German judiciary, which invoked Article 130 of the Criminal Code. The accusation against Joseph Burg was as follows: "Hateful statements against Zionism and attempts to rehabilitate the criminals of the extermination camps". Burg was accused of having mental problems and was forced to undergo psychiatric treatment. When he sought refuge at his wife's grave in the Jewish cemetery in Munich, he was physically assaulted by a Zionist commando because of his testimony.

The friendship between Ernst Zündel and Joseph Burg developed over the years. Burg continued to write books denouncing the situation in Germany. In 1980, for example, he published *Zionnazi Zensur in der BRD* (*Zionazi Censorship in the Federal Republic of*

Germany). Zündel not only visited him, but also corresponded with him on an ongoing basis. In 1982, Zündel wrote to him twice for advice and help, as he was having problems with the Zionists in Toronto. Therefore, when the second trial against Ernst Zündel for "publishing false news" began, Burg travelled to Canada to testify as a witness for the defence. His testimony took place on Tuesday 29 March and Wednesday 30 March 1988.

Among other things, Burg stated that he had spoken to hundreds of people who worked in the crematoria, but that he could never find anyone who had worked in the gas chambers. About the crematoria in Auschwitz and Majdanek, he explained that they were operated in three shifts a day by prisoners who did the work voluntarily. The request for volunteers was made by the Jewish council or the Jewish police, who collaborated with the German SS. On the emigration of Jews from Nazi Germany, he charged that the Zionists made it difficult for Jews who did not go to Palestine to emigrate to other countries, since their only interest was to populate Palestine at any cost. Burg claimed to have discovered that it was German Zionist leaders who as early as 1933 asked the Nazis to force Jews to wear the yellow star. The Zionists did not see this as an insult, but as a heroic gesture, just as the SS saw it as a heroic gesture to display the swastika. In 1938, Burg said, the Zionist leaders of the Third Reich caused Jews to wear the yellow star against the wishes of Göring and Göbbels. In his statement, Burg was particularly critical of the State of Israel and the Zionist leaders, whom he accused of inventing the Holocaust in order to fleece Germany of exorbitant compensation, which was accepted by Dr. Adenauer.

A prolific writer and practising Jew, Joseph Burg was the author of more than a dozen works, today very difficult to find because more than half of them were confiscated by court orders. In *Sündenböcke, Grossangriffe des Zionismus auf Papst Pius XII un die deutschen Regierungen* (*Scapegoats, Zionism's General Offensive against Pope Pius XII and the German Governments*), he denounced Zionism's slander against Pius XII and attacks on Germany. In 1990, two years after testifying at the Toronto trial, Burg died in Munich. Considered a traitor, he was denied burial in the Jewish cemetery as he would have wished. Otto Ernst Remer and Ernst Zündel came to the Bavarian city to pay tribute and bid farewell to the remains of this self-sacrificing revisionist to whom history will never do justice.

Thies Christophersen convicted of "bringing the state into disrepute".

Few Germans dared to speak out during the harsh years of National Socialist purge and repression. One of those who rebelled against the imposed silence was Thies Christophersen, a farmer who was in Auschwitz from January to December 1944. Wounded at the beginning of the war, he was disabled for combat. On behalf of the Kaiser Wilhelm Institute, he arrived in Auschwitz as a Wehrmacht high commander with the task of cultivating vegetable rubber. As there was a large labour force in the labour camp, the plant cultivation institute was moved from Berlin-Müncheberg to Auschwitz. There, research was carried out in the laboratories of the Bunawerk plant. Christophersen was housed in the Raisko camp, and two hundred female prisoners held in the camp worked with him on his experimental farm. In addition, 100 men arrived daily from Birkenau, although civilians, mainly Russians, were also employed. Among other things, the prisoners analysed the percentage of rubber in the plants in the laboratory in order to select the plants with the highest amount of rubber for breeding. According to Christophersen, the prisoners worked there eight hours a day, with an hour's rest at noon.

After the war, Christophersen resumed his farming activities. In his efforts to defend the interests of German farmers, he edited and published a quarterly magazine, *Die Bauernschaft (The Farmers)*. In 1973 Thies Christophersen dared to publish in German the book *Die Auschwitzlüge (The Auschwitz Lie)*, a booklet of which 100,000 copies were printed, in which he denies that Germany exterminated six million Jews during World War II. At the end, he concludes with these words: "I have written my memoirs as I have experienced them and as I remember them. I have told the truth, so help me God. If I could contribute to giving our youth a little more respect for their fathers again, who as soldiers fought for Germany and who were not criminals, then I would be very happy". The book caused a sensation and was soon banned for "stirring up the people". Christophersen, who in addition to the book had published other writings that insisted on denouncing the lies against Germany, was eventually charged and sentenced to a year and a half in prison for "discrediting the state" and for "offending the memory of the dead".

He was politically persecuted and received numerous letters containing insults and threats, forcing him into exile. After passing through Belgium, he settled in Denmark, where legislation protected him, but this did not prevent him from falling victim to "anti-fascist" thugs: hundreds of them attacked his modest house in the small town of Kollund, located just across the border in Germany. The criminals stoned the house, daubed it with insulting graffiti, set fire to the storeroom where he kept his books and, using corrosive acid, smashed his car and photocopying equipment. The German authorities asked the Copenhagen government to take action against him and went so far as to suggest that the Danes review their laws on racism in order to be able to take action against Thies Christophersen. Fortunately, crimes of speech and thought were not prosecuted in Denmark and a Danish court rejected an extradition request from the Federal Republic. Finally, as the Danish police failed to prevent the constant harassment and abuse to which he was subjected, he was forced to leave Denmark in 1995. Seriously ill with cancer, he sought treatment in Switzerland, but in December 1995 he was also forced to leave the country. Finally, he found temporary refuge in Spain. Meanwhile, the printer of the *Bauernschaft* magazine in Germany was fined DM 50,000.

Despite all the tribulations, Christophersen was able to travel to Canada in 1988 to testify as a witness in Toronto in the Zündel trial. His appearance in court preceded that of Joseph Burg. The cross-examination of Doug Christie, Zündel's lawyer, took place on 8 March 1988. Months later, Thies Christophersen himself reproduced it in full, word for word, in the June issue of his magazine *Die Bauernschaft*. Lawyer Christie asked numerous questions about the prisoners, who, like the soldiers, were housed in barracks. Christophersen explained that there were bunk beds, cupboards and bathrooms with hot and cold water. Sheets, towels and clothes were changed regularly. The interrogation went on like this:

- Did prisoners receive correspondence?

- Mail was regularly delivered and parcels were opened if the contents were not very clear in the presence of the prisoners. Some things were not delivered.

- What things were not delivered?

- Money, drugs, chemicals, propaganda material...

- Were prisoners mistreated?

- No ill-treatment was allowed, and if it did occur, the perpetrators were severely punished.

- Did prisoners have the opportunity to complain?

- Yes, at all times. Even the camp commandant, Nöss, and his successor, Captain Lieberhenschel, had authorised the prisoners to speak to them whenever they wanted.

- Did you hear the complaints and grievances of the inmates?

- To tell the truth, these were not complaints, but rather requests. The greatest joy I was able to give the prisoners was when I allowed them to pick mushrooms and blackberries or to bathe in the Sula. Sometimes I would also sequester a prisoner's private letters if the contents were not very clear."

Christophersen admitted during interrogation that he did not know the capacity of the crematoria at Birkenau and that he did not see them in operation, although he had often been in the camp, where he brought material from the aircraft scrapyard and selected labour for the rubber plantations. Concerning the cremation of corpses, he claimed that medical aid was given to sick prisoners and attempts were made to save their lives, as there were ambulances and sick wards in the military hospital. As usual, Christophersen alluded to the many deaths from typhoid fever and noted that the wife of his superior, Dr. Cäsar, herself died of typhoid. As for questions about the gas chambers, he repeatedly claimed that he only heard about them after the war and that he never saw any or met anyone who had seen them.

During the last months of his life, Thies Christophersen was willing to return home to stand trial if he was allowed to present experts and witnesses of his own choosing, but the German courts treated him as an enemy of the state and refused him. His bank account was blocked. In early 1996 he applied to return to Germany to attend the funeral of one of his sons, who died in a car accident, but a court rejected the request. Despite the fact that Christophersen was suffering from cancer, the German authorities cancelled his insurance cover and stopped paying him his modest retirement pension, which had been respected for forty-five years, and his army service pension. Seriously and terminally ill, he risked returning to spend the last days of his life with his family, but was arrested for the last time. A German judge found that he was too ill to go to prison, so he was allowed to remain under the guardianship of a son. On 13 February 1997, he died in the northern German district of Molfsee, where he was denied the right to a funeral.

Wilhem Stäglich, the judge who called for justice for Germany

During the months of July to September 1944, Wilhelm Stäglich was assigned to a detachment near Auschwitz as an air defence officer. Based in the town of Osiek, some nine kilometres south of the camp, he maintained contact with SS commanders and had access to the main camp facilities. After the war, he received a doctorate in law from the University of Göttingen in 1951. For years he worked as a financial judge in Hamburg, where he wrote numerous articles on legal and historical topics. After years of silence, outraged and emotionally disturbed by the stories about Auschwitz imposed on the public, which clashed head-on with his own experience, the German judge and historian decided to undertake an investigation. When he began to express publicly what he understood about Auschwitz, he faced several legal proceedings against him as a result of his articles. Finally, in 1974, a disciplinary hearing was held against Judge Stäglich and in 1975 he was forced to retire from the judiciary. The forced retirement was accompanied by a reduction of his pension for a period of five years. There followed a series of inquiries and raids on his home in an attempt to find out his background.

Instead of shrinking back, Stäglich continued to work on the issue and in 1979 published a landmark book for German revisionism: *Der Auschwitz-Mythos: Legende oder Wirklichkeit* (*The Auschwitz Myth: Legend or Reality*), a thorough and detailed work in which he critically and systematically examined documents, testimonies, confessions and accounts that described Auschwitz as a killing centre. Stäglich denied the existence of the gas chambers and denounced the documents proclaiming the Holocaust as forgeries. In 1980 the book was banned and seized nationwide by order of a Stuttgart court. On 11 March 1982, order no. 3176 of the "Bundesprüfstelle für jugendgefährdende Schriften" (Federal Department for Dangerous Writings for Youth), listed it as harmful material which should not be distributed to young readers. In 1983 the German police confiscated all unsold copies by order of the Federal Court of Justice. On 24 March 1983, ironically invoking a 1939 law enacted in Hitler's time, the dean's council of the University of Göttingen, after a cumbersome process, withdrew Wilhelm Stäglich's doctoral degree, which it had awarded him in 1951. A judicial-administrative appeal was rejected, as were his written protests in court, which were dismissed by the Constitutional Jury of the Federal Republic of Germany.

On 23 November 1988, Judge Stäglich, with commendable fortitude and aplomb, addressed a reproachful letter to Richard von Weizsäcker, President of the Federal Republic of Germany from 1984 to 1994, enclosing the *Leuchter Report*, which for the revisionist movement was the incontrovertible ratification of its theses. We consider this document worth reproducing. *Die Bauernschaft*, Thies Christophersen's journal, initially published the text, which was also reproduced in the autumn of 1990 by *The Journal of Historical Review*, from which we have taken and translated it:

"23 November 1988

The President of the Federal Republic

Richard von Weizsäcker

5300 Bonn

Mr President:

You have repeatedly made public pronouncements on matters relating to Germany's history in this century (the first time was on the occasion of your speech of 8 May 1945 before the West German Parliament). The content and style of his statements show that they are based on what is at least a biased perspective, namely that of the victors in the two world wars. In his pamphlet *On Weizsäcker's Speech of 8 May 1945* (J. Reiss Verlag, 8934 Grossaitingen, 1985), of which you are no doubt aware, the publicist Emil Maier-Dorn convincingly demonstrated this, providing many examples of the tendentious bias. Evidently unimpressed, in subsequent years you continued, even more stridently if possible, to accuse the German people at every opportunity. Finally, you even felt it necessary to support historians by your attendance at the 37th Historians' Conference in Bamberg, whose guidelines, so to speak, included dealing with the Auschwitz problem, which had been the subject of academic discussion for at least the last decade. Is it possible that you are unaware of Article 5, paragraph 3 of the Basic Law, which guarantees academic freedom and freedom of research? The applause for your completely partisan and unreserved comments from our enemies in the world wars and from the West German media, who evidently still follow your orders, should have reminded you of a maxim of Bismarck, who once remarked that when his enemies praised him, he had undoubtedly been wrong.

Unfortunately, Maier-Dorn had to omit from his pamphlet any commentary on his statements on the issue of the extermination of the Jews, since the official version of this issue is, in his words, legally protected in West Germany. Although this is not entirely correct, Maier-Dorn's assessment hits the nail on the head in that a politically pressured, and therefore not independent, judicial system manipulates the facts and the law in order to prosecute and, if not, harass those who doubt or even refute the annihilation of Jews in the alleged 'gas chambers' in the so-called 'extermination' camps. This phenomenon is undoubtedly unique in the history of justice.

Now, however, an event that occurred about six months ago has forced a rethinking of the official story. The defence in the trial of Ernst Zündel, a German-Canadian, in Toronto presented the testimony of the American gas chamber expert Fred A. Leuchter (as is known, gas chamber executions are still carried out in certain states of the U.S.A.), according to whom those places in Auschwitz, Birkenau and Majdanek which were identified by alleged witnesses as gas chambers could not have functioned as such. This technical expertise, which has meanwhile become world famous, cannot in future be ignored by any serious historian who claims objective scholarship. In addition to the technology of the gas chambers, the Leuchter Report deals with the composition and modus operandi of the pesticide Zyklon-B, allegedly used to kill the Jews, as well as the technology in the crematoria. As early as 1979, on page 336 of my work *Der Auschwitz Mythos*, which was significantly confiscated on the orders of a court following instructions from above, I pointed out the urgent need to clarify these questions about the approach to the problem of extermination. Neither judges nor historians have bothered about this state of affairs, not to mention politicians, including yourself.

Unfortunately, the Leuchter Report, like everything else that can historically exonerate our nation, is officially ignored with a deathly silence. That is why I am taking the liberty of forwarding this important document to you in its original English, Mr. President, so that you may gain a clear understanding of things. This text differs from the original report only in the omission of the chemical analyses carried out by the American chemist Professor Roth, whom Leuchter involved in the analysis of the samples he had collected during his personal enquiries at those places in Auschwitz and Birkenau officially designated as 'gas chambers', in addition to the samples taken in the former disinfection chambers for the purpose of comparison. These analyses are included only in summary form (on page 16) in the text of the Leuchter Report intended for public distribution. Mr. President, you can now familiarise yourself with the most up-to-date and authoritative research on this subject of such importance to our nation.

I dare say that from now on, even if you do not correct your past accusations, you will at least refrain from unjustifiably imposing guilt on our nation. The high office you hold requires, in accordance with the promise you made when you assumed it, that you act as the protector of the German nation, instead of stripping it of the last shred of political self-confidence. In your speeches you have repeatedly called for 'courage to face the truth', even though the 'truth' you proclaimed was already dubious because it was so one-sided. Now is the time to show your own courage to face the whole truth, and nothing but the truth, Mr. President! Otherwise you must later justifiably face reproaches for your hypocrisy.

With greetings from a citizen,
Wilhelm Stäglich".

Wilhem Stäglich died in 2006 at the age of ninety. In February 2015, Germar Rudolf published a corrected and slightly revised edition of his book by Castle Hill Publishers, the publishing house he founded, under the title *Auschwitz: A Judge Looks at the Evidence*. This publication proves the continuing value of Stäglich's work. Robert Faurisson, who admired the magistrate's honesty, wrote these words of respect and tribute: "Dr Wilhelm Stäglich, German judge and historian, has saved the honour of German judges and historians. He has lost everything, but not his honour".

Ernst Zündel, "Revisionist Dynamo", model of resistance

The time has now come to pay our modest tribute to Ernst Zündel, the indispensable man, the revisionist of distinction, who has had the courage and fortitude to stand undaunted throughout his life against the mighty tyrants who impose the falsification of history on the world. Perhaps that is why one of the nicknames he has justifiably been given for his stellar role is "revisionist dynamo". A sketch on his life and the milestones of his unequal struggle to redeem Germany before the world will help uninitiated readers to understand and appreciate the stature of this irreplaceable figure in the history of historical revisionism.

Born in Germany in 1939, he came to Canada in 1958 and married a Canadian woman named Janick Larouche. In 1961 he left Toronto and settled with his family in Montreal, where he set up a successful graphic arts business. Zündel considered communism "a threat to our civilisation", and in Canadian politics he became involved in anti-communist activities and campaigns. One of the figures who most influenced him during these years was Adrien Arkand, a French Canadian nationalist who spoke eight languages and was imprisoned for six years during the war. It was Arkand who provided books, articles and other texts that helped the young Zündel to develop intellectually. As mentioned above, Joseph Ginsburg, who published under the pseudonym J.C. Burg, was another essential person who had a profound influence on him during the 1960s. Burg went to Canada to record with Zündel and spent a month as a guest in his home. Their love for truth and justice led to mutual admiration. Burg called Zündel "a fighter for truth for his people". But Burg was only one of the important Jewish intellectuals whom Zündel asked to collaborate with him. He also made contact with Benjamin Freedman[2], the Jewish billionaire convert to Catholicism, and with Rabbi Elmer Berger, president of the "American Council for Judaism". Zündel travelled to New York in 1967 to meet Berger, who provided him with new knowledge and information about Zionism. Later, in one of the trials, Zündel explained his relationship with Rabbi Berger in this way:

> "... I went to New York and interviewed Rabbi Berger, with whom I have been in contact ever since. He was the person who, for the first time, made it very clear to me what the differences were between Zionism and Judaism. His particular philosophy of life and of the people he represents is that they are first and foremost Americans and Jews by religion, whereas Zionists are Jews first, at least that's how I understand it, which leads them in practice to the exclusion of anything else. They reside in different countries, but their only allegiance is to the principles of Zionism, the aims of Zionism, the policies of Zionism. He felt it was a dangerous ideology because it called into question in the eyes of public opinion the loyalty of Jews living in America or Canada."

---

[2] Chapter I has already introduced Benjamin H. Freedman and discussed his famous letter to David Goldstein, edited under the title *Facts are facts*, in which he revealed the Khazar origin of Ashkenazi Jews. Freedman had personal relationships with Bernard Baruch, Woodrow Wilson, Franklin D. Roosevelt, Samuel Untermayer and other Jewish Zionist leaders, so he knew very well who was behind what he called *The Hidden Tyranny* in a booklet so titled. In 1961 Benjamin Freedman delivered at the Willard Hotel in Washington the famous speech warning America, later known as "A Jewish Defector Warns America". In it, he insisted that the Zionists and their co-religionists ruled America as if they were the absolute masters of the country and warned America's patriots of the imperative need to react.

In 1968 Zündel was denied citizenship without explanation. On 27 August 1968 he received a letter from the Canadian authorities stating: "the information on the basis of which the decision has been taken is confidential and it would not be in the general interest to disclose it". In 1969 Zündel and his family returned to Toronto, where he re-established his graphic arts company, which went on to publish books with large print runs and circulation, earning him substantial profits. This facilitated the publication of texts and interviews he had conducted with revisionist writers and historians such as Robert Faurisson and the aforementioned rabbi. Berger and Burg were not the only Jews who collaborated with Zündel in his titanic struggle to expose the falsifiers of history. Roger-Guy Dommergue Polacco de Menasce,[3] a French professor of Jewish origin, philosopher, essayist and doctor of psychology, was another honest intellectual who influenced Ernst Zündel, with whom he corresponded for years. Zündel, who received texts from Roger-Guy Dommergue in which he stated unequivocally that the Holocaust was a historical lie, would eventually travel to France to record a long interview in Professor Dommergue's house.

Ernst Zündel and his wife separated in 1975, as Zündel refused to give up his "political activities", as she herself declared, which caused the family to feel uneasy and fearful. Nevertheless, the friendship and contact between them and their children was not broken. In these years, in 1978 to be precise, Zündel founded a small publishing company called Samisdat Publishers Ltd., which produced a series of interesting films to help spread the ideas of revisionism through various testimonies. These and other resistance activities undertaken by Ernst Zündel provoked prominent columnists such as Mark Bonokoski of the *Toronto Sun* and other columnists in league with Jewish leaders such as Ben Kayfetz, president of the Canadian Jewish Congress, to launch a smear campaign to portray Ernst Zündel as a "neo-Nazi fanatic".

From this point on, the German government's attacks were joined by Jewish organisations that sought to silence Zündel with their

---

[3] Cf. *Truth and synthesis - The end of shams, Heidegger's silence and the secret of Jewish tragedy, The pain of living*, Omnia Veritas Limited, www.omnia-veritas.com.

harassment in Canada and Germany. Accusations of "incitement to hatred" and "spreading false news" became commonplace. Various Jewish lobby groups put pressure on governments and used the media to provoke public outrage. It was in this context that the JDL (Jewish Defence League), the FBI's infamous terrorist organisation, and Anti-Racist Action entered the scene and stepped up their harassment of Zundel with demonstrations outside his home. These terrorists came to besiege him by patrolling the surrounding area with dogs and, in addition, by banging on the walls of the house, shining spotlights on the windows at night and threatening him with incessant phone calls.

On 22 November 1979, the *Toronto Sun* reported that the Ontario Attorney General was going to file hate speech charges against Samisdat Publishing Ltd. In response to this threat, Zündel mailed thousands of copies of Richard Harwood's *Did Six Million Really Die?* to Canadian lawyers, politicians, journalists, professors and priests. He asked them to evaluate the information contained in the book. In the accompanying text, he insisted that he was driven only by the search for truth and that Zionists and their sympathisers were using words like "racism" and "hate" to try to suppress his freedom.

The next major setback to Ernst Zündel's rights came from Germany. In January 1981, the Federal German government seized the postal bank account he had in Stuttgart, through which Zündel received numerous donations and handled payments for books and tapes. On 23 and 24 March 1981, the German Ministry of the Interior ordered one of the largest raids in German history: some two hundred private homes were raided for the purpose of seizing books and recordings labelled as "Nazi literature". Some ten thousand police officers and three hundred judges and prosecutors were mobilised for the operation. About this Zündel testified: "the police obtained the addresses of people who had helped me monetarily by violating German banking laws, taking the addresses of the donation receipts and raiding the homes of these people". Zündel was then charged with "agitation of the people", a crime in Germany.

In Canada, raids ordered by the German Interior Ministry were reported in the press, and Ernst Zündel was publicly accused of spreading "Nazi propaganda" in West Germany from Canada. On 31 May 1981, a mass demonstration by Jewish groups took place near

Zündel's home in Toronto. The demonstration had been announced in Jewish media with the following statement: "Neo-Nazism in Canada: Why is Canada the export centre for Nazi propaganda? Why do hate-mongers freely spread the lie that there was no Holocaust? Why do war criminals move unpunished? Demonstration to protest against racism and hate speech." The organisers were the B'nai Brith Lodge of Canada and the Jewish Congress of Canada. The Jewish Defence League was not among the promoters, but its extremists were in the majority and stirred up a crowd of fifteen hundred people, who with cries of "Burn him! Kill him!" they tried to attack Zündel's house. Of course, the organisers made no attempt to restrain them,. Only the action of about 50 police officers who barricaded the house prevented further incidents. Zündel, who received bomb and death threats before and after the demonstration, recorded everything that happened and produced a tape entitled *C-120 Zionist Uprising!* in which one can hear the shouts calling for the storming and burning of the house and the killing of Zündel and all the inhabitants.

Against all odds, in unequal combat, Zündel continued to withstand all kinds of attacks. The next outrage was the ban on receiving mail. In July 1981, two months after the mass demonstration outside his home, Sabina Citron, a Zionist activist with the Holocaust Remembrance Association, complained to the post office that Zündel was spreading anti-Semitic literature and requested that his postal privileges be revoked. On 17 August 1981, postal inspector Gordon Holmes visited Zündel. He showed him some leaflets he had sent and Zündel, for his part, presented him with photos, texts and recordings of the May demonstration in front of his home and explained that he was engaged in a mail campaign to expose his views through the service. Holmes' report to his superiors confirmed that Zündel had been cooperative throughout and had provided him with books and writings. Finally, on 13 November 1981, an Interim Prohibition Order was issued against Samisdat Publishers. It was argued that Zündel's company used the postal service to incite hatred.

Zündel requested that the Interim Prohibition Order be investigated by an Evaluation Commission to see if it violated the Canada Post Corporation Act. During the hearing, held on 22, 23 and 24 February and 11 and 12 March 1982, Toronto lawyer Ian Scott, representing the Canadian Civil Liberties Association, intervened on Zündel's behalf and successfully argued that freedom of expression under the Charter of Human Rights was being violated. In his statement, Zündel showed a tape entitled *German-Jewish Dialogue*, which Benjamin Freedman had given him permission to sell. Zündel boasted of his friendship with the Jewish billionaire, whom he had known for fifteen years and with whom he had spoken on many occasions. Proving that he did not hate Jews, Zündel gave the names of Jewish intellectuals he had interviewed who had given him permission to sell the tapes. Among others, he cited Haviv Schieber, the former mayor of Beersheba in Israel; Roger-Guy Domergue Polacco de Menasce, the Jewish professor at the Sorbonne; Rabbi Elmer Berger and Professor Israel Shahak, chairman of a human rights commission in Israel.

While awaiting the final opinion of the Evaluation Commission in Canada, despite a hysterical campaign in Germany and Canada about the significance of the seized material from Samisdat Publishers, on 26 August 1982 Zündel was acquitted in Germany by a Stuttgart district court, which found that the texts in question were not hate literature. In addition, the court ordered the Federal German government to pay the legal costs of the proceedings and to return to Zündel the money seized from the accounts together with interest. Of course, the Canadian press remained silent and continued to describe Zündel as a "neo-Nazi" who sent "Nazi propaganda" to Germany. The German government reacted to the Stuttgart court ruling by refusing to renew his passport. Sarcastically, a law enacted by Hitler against Jewish refugees who published anti-Nazi materials in exile was used for this purpose.

In Canada, finally, on 18 October 1982, the Evaluation Commission recommended in its report to the Canadian government the revocation of the order suspending Ernst Zündel's postal rights. In accordance with this well-argued recommendation, Government Minister André Ouellet signed the revocation of the order on 15 November 1982, and Zündel's rights were reinstated, with the result that the Canada Post Corporation had to return numerous mailbags to him. All the cheques had expired, so that Zündel's business incurred almost ruinous losses. The Canadian Jewish Congress announced through Ben Kayfetz that they were appalled by the decision. Nevertheless, Jewish organisations immediately resumed their harassment and in 1983 launched a campaign to prosecute Zündel. The Holocaust Remembrance Association and Sabina Citron wrote to

Ontario Attorney General Roy McMurtry asking him to prosecute Zündel for incitement to hatred under the Criminal Code. On 13 October 1983, the *Toronto Star* reported that B'nai Brith was demanding that Zündel be prosecuted for racial hatred.

Zündel's lawyer in Germany had meanwhile appealed the authorities' decision not to renew his client's passport. During the appeal proceedings in 1985, the lawyer was allowed in the presence of a court policeman to study, but not copy, in the government archives various documents used in the proceedings against Zündel. It was in this way that they learned that the Ministry of the Interior, which had no competence in passport matters, had been incessantly lobbying the Ministry of Foreign Affairs since 1980 to have Ernst Zündel's passport withdrawn. The documents showed that senior officials of the German Federal Intelligence Service had travelled to Ottawa in order to get the Canadian government to ban Zündel from using the postal system. The German files also indicated that Ben Kayfetz of the Jewish Congress of Canada had written to the German Consul General in Toronto requesting copies of Zündel materials they wished to examine, but the Consul Koch initially refused. The German authorities apparently conceived the idea that if they succeeded in depriving Zündel of a passport, the Canadians would deport him. In November 1982, Consul Koch was prepared to renew the passport, but, as the files examined by Zündel's lawyer show, the Ministry of the Interior put pressure on the Ministry of Foreign Affairs to send a directive to the Consul in Toronto to do the opposite, which he did. Zündel appealed the consul's decision not to renew his passport. On 9 May 1984, the Cologne Administrative Court decided that the Federal Republic of Germany was not obliged to renew the passport. A further appeal was then lodged with the Higher Administrative Court of North Rhine-Westphalia. It was at during this appeal that Zündel's lawyer was granted access to the government archives, which showed that since 1980, the German authorities had been trying viciously to have Zündel deported.

Let us now turn to the pressure from Jewish organisations on the Canadian authorities to bring a case against Ernst Zündel, as it would eventually lead to the 1985 trial. The hate speech charge did not seem likely to succeed, so on 18 November 1983 Sabina Citron of the Holocaust Remembrance Association pressed for charges of "spreading false news" in publications such as *Did Six Million Really*

Die? and *The West, War and Islam*. Sabina Citron's charges were admitted by the Crown, which meant that the state bore all the costs of prosecution on behalf of the Zionists. Thus began Zündel's nine-year legal battle to defend his civil rights.

On 9 September 1984, a few months before the start of the trial, a bomb exploded at the back of Zündel's house, damaging the garage and two cars. Shrapnel flew out and pieces were embedded in the bedroom wall of two Jewish neighbours. On 10 September, the Toronto newspaper *The Globe & Mail* reported, "A man phoned *The Globe & Mail* last night on behalf of a group he called the Jewish Defence League (JDL) People's Liberation Movement to claim responsibility for the bombing." No arrests were made and Zündel issued a press release denouncing the escalation of violence by the JDL and related groups against him, supported by certain media outlets. He demanded a police reaction against the terrorism of this Zionist organisation, since, he argued, "the police, politicians and the media were well aware of the JDL's reputation for arson, bombings, shootings, attacks and assassinations".

Every appearance of Ernst Zündel in connection with court summons was used by members of the JDL, who were waiting for him at the courthouse gates, to threaten, insult and assault those who accompanied him. As a result, they appeared wearing construction helmets to protect themselves. Both Zündel and his lawyer Lauren Marshall received phone calls in which they received death threats. The *Toronto Sun* quoted Marshall as saying: "In a shaky voice, she said she and her client and their families were harassed daily and received death threats. She later told reporters that in one phone call her seven-year-old daughter was told: 'If your mommy goes to court, we'll kill her. Zündel addressed an open letter to members of Parliament and the media, warning that the administration of justice in Canada was in danger if it allowed intimidation and attacks by Jewish mobs.

The trial began in January 1985 and lasted thirty-nine days. The Crown sought to prove the Holocaust through the intervention of experts such as Raul Hilberg and former inmates who testified as witnesses. Since we have already reviewed Hilberg's testimony under cross-examination by lawyer Doug Christie in the *Leuchter Report* (*Proscribed History)*, we will now add that the persons called by

Zündel's defence, in addition to the well-known Faurisson and Christophersen, included, among others, Dr. William Lindsey, a chemist who had been head of research at the American chemical company Dupont; Dr. Russell Barton, who as a young man was a former head of research at the American chemical company Dupont; and Dr. Russell Barton, who as a young man was a former chief researcher at the American chemical company Dupont, among others. Russell Barton, who as a young doctor had attended the liberation of Bergen-Belsen; Frank Walus, an American of Polish origin falsely accused of being a Nazi criminal; Pierre Zündel, son of Ernst Zündel; and a hitherto unmentioned Swedish-born Austrian researcher Ditlieb Felderer, well known in revisionist circles, whose activities are worthy of recognition and will therefore have their own section below.[4]

On 28 February 1985 Zündel was convicted by a jury and on 25 March received a fifteen-month prison sentence, but was released on bail under strict conditions that prohibited him from writing, publishing or speaking publicly. Between these two dates, B'nai Brith, the Jewish Congress of Canada, the Holocaust Remembrance Association and the JDL organised a public and private campaign for the Canadian government to deport Zündel to Germany. The most

---

[4] Ditlieb Felderer testified in both trials against Zündel. In 1988 he was the first witness called to testify by the defence and his collaboration with Zündel's team was outstanding. Felderer was a conspicuous Jehovah's Witness until he was expelled when he discovered that the extermination of the sect's members was a falsehood. He did research at the Jehovah's Witnesses' headquarters in New York, as well as in the archives in Toronto, in Switzerland and in Scandinavia. He succeeded in getting it acknowledged that the figure of 60,000 Jehovah's Witnesses killed by the Nazis was false, since only 203 of them had died in concentration camps. Although the New York leadership forbade members of the organisation to speak to Felderer, a subsequent yearbook published by Jehovah's Witnesses themselves acknowledged that Felderer's figure was correct. Ditlieb Felderer was among the first to denounce Anne Frank's diary as a forgery. In his famous book *Anne Frank's Diary, a Hoax* (1979), he exposed the fraud, which was later confirmed by other researchers. Felderer, relentlessly pursued by the henchmen of the Jewish lobby, was imprisoned several times in Sweden. Recently, he has publicly accused Johan Hirschfeldt, a Jewish judge in Sweden, of being responsible for acts of terrorism against him and his Filipino wife.

prominent event was a demonstration of thousands of people, culminating in a rally. On 11 March 1985, the *Toronto Star* reported on the massive demonstration against Zündel, which culminated at Toronto's O'Keefe Centre. There, all the speakers demanded deportation amidst shouts and incessant cheers from the crowd. But not all Canadians were indifferent to the spectacle. On 21 March, four days before the verdict was made public, the *Toronto Sun* published a letter to the editor in which J. Thomas criticised the excesses of the demonstrators, whose demonstration of hatred he considered evident: "The spectacle of 4,000 Jews, very well organised," Thomas wrote, "marching from City Hall to the O'Keefe Centre and the loquacious statements of numerous speakers, all symbolically shouting 'Barabbas, Barabbas, give us Barabbas', was an appalling exhibition of mob rule.... The strident and continued demand that Zündel be deported far exceeds the bounds of justice and reveals itself as hatred of anyone who dares to question the power of a small minority of Canadians."

The *Toronto Sun* itself reported on 27 March 1985 that, following a government meeting, Flora MacDonald, Minister of Immigration, had instructed officials in her Department to begin proceedings to deport Zündel as soon as they received a report on his sentence. On 29 April 1985, without considering his legal rights of appeal, Ernst Zündel was ordered deported. On 30 April, the *Toronto Star* reported in its pages the jubilation of B'nai Brith: "We are very pleased to see that the government has acted quickly. We think it is the right procedure and the right decision". However, Ernst Zündel, a seasoned fighter, immediately appealed and the expulsion process was halted as a matter of law.

In 1987, Zündel won two very important victories that reaffirmed his will to resist at all costs. On 23 January 1987, the Ontario Court of Appeal, which had allowed the appeal against his conviction, ordered a retrial on the grounds that Judge Hugh Locke had acted in a biased and improper manner. Among other excesses, he had rejected various evidence presented by the defence and had shown the jury films about Nazi concentration camps in order to influence their decision. Half a year later came Zündel's second triumph: on 7 July 1987, the deportation order was invalidated on the grounds that it had been issued contrary to Canadian law.

And there was yet a third victory for Zündel against Sabina Citron and the usual Jewish organisations in 1987. On a CBC Radio programme, Zündel publicly told the Zionist leader that "the Germans were innocent of the charge of genocide against the Jews". Further, addressing the host, David Shatsky, she recalled that at the January trial Sabina Citron had been unable to show any document proving that there was an extermination order "because there wasn't one". Citron told the press that she was stunned by Zündel's appearance on the programme. Shortly thereafter, they sued CBC Radio for damages. On 25 August 1987, Citron sued Zündel again for spreading "false news" on the radio show. The complaint was dismissed by the Crown on 18 September 1987 on the grounds that "Zündel's statements during the broadcast constituted an opinion that did not fall within the scope of the 'false news' section of the Criminal Code".

The second trial against Zündel for "spreading false news" finally began on 18 January 1988. It lasted sixty-one days and has gone down in revisionist history for the transcendent importance of the revelation of the *Leuchter Report*. Raul Hilberg declined to return to Canada to testify, no doubt so as not to be subjected again to cross-examination by lawyer Christie, who had cornered him in the first trial. The Crown presented seven witnesses. The defence called 23 to prove that there was no "fake news" in the book *Did Six Million Realy Die?* but that its contents were true. The most striking of the statements made by the witnesses presented by Zündel was, of course, that of Fred Leuchter, who was recognised by the presiding judge as an expert on the workings of the gas chambers. Leuchter explained his inspection work at Auschwitz, Birkenau and Majdanek and asserted that the alleged gas chambers could never have fulfilled the murderous function attributed to them. The *Leuchter Report*, submitted to the court as an illustrated exposition, was subsequently translated into numerous languages and widely distributed throughout the world. Among the defence witnesses was David Irving, a British historian of Jewish origin, who was convinced that the implications of the Report would be devastating for Holocaust historiography. Significantly, media coverage of the trial was almost non-existent compared to that of the first trial.

Despite all the evidence presented, Zündel was again convicted at the end of the trial and received a nine-month prison sentence. Again, Jewish organisations were quick to call for his deportation to

Germany. Zündel, who at 1988 again requested the reasons for the rejection of his citizenship application without receiving a reply, again appealed the verdict to the Ontario Court of Appeal. Before the outcome of his appeal was known, the Consul General of Federal Germany, Dr. Henning von Hassell, wrote several letters to the Ontario Court falsely accusing Zündel of having distributed leaflets to the crew of a German ship in the port of Toronto. According to the consul, the text of the pamphlets had as its main theme Holocaust denial, which was a violation of the conditions of his bail.

On 5 February 1990, the Court of Appeal dismissed the appeal, so Ernst Zündel had to apply for leave to appeal to a higher court, the Supreme Court of Canada, which he did on 15 November 1990. At this point in the persecution, the legal battle of a single man against colossal enemies already had epic connotations. It took almost two years to hear the Supreme Court's decision, but it stood firm in its application of the law and on 27 August 1992 acquitted Zündel. The Court found that the freedom of expression protected by the Canadian Charter of Rights and Freedoms had been violated. Despite the media campaign against Zündel over the years, some editorialists eventually recognised the relevance of the Supreme Court's decision, as the right to freedom of expression of all Canadians was threatened under the guise of the "fake news" law.

As usual, organised Jewry in Canada went ballistic and did not accept the Supreme Court's verdict on Zündel's right to peacefully express his views on the "unquestionable" Holocaust. With the usual brazenness, this minority group in Canadian society arrogated to itself the right to lecture and criticise judges and the judicial system. By mid-September 1992, Jewish organisations had formed a large coalition, including some gentile groups, and began a new campaign, including posters and advertisements. The September issue of *the Covenant*, B'nai Brith's monthly publication, featured a full-page photograph of Zündel on its front page with the words: "Arrest this man, says B'nai Brith: Coalition campaigns to bring new charges against Zündel". The accompanying article said they were going to fill the streets with thousands of posters made by the Human Rights League in order to put pressure on Ontario Attorney General Howard Hampton. The Holocaust Remembrance Association took out advertisements reading: "Zündel must not escape justice! Urgent Demonstration". Evidently, the justice referred to was not the justice in Canada, but his own. The rally was held on 4 October 1992, at which Sabina Citron called for a "declaration of war" on the Canadian legal system. In its 15 October 1992 edition, the *Canadian Jewish News* reproduced Sabina Citron's words verbatim, in which she urged everyone to "continually harass the lives of politicians. Zündel must be charged and deported. We have had enough and we will not stand for any more".

In the midst of this frenzied maelstrom of anti-Zündel hysteria, a young Jewish acquaintance, David Cole, came to his aid. Cole, who had returned from Auschwitz with the film discussed above (*Proscribed History*), published a letter to Attorney General Howard Hampton in the *Kanada Kurier*, an ethnic German newspaper in Canada. For its interest, we reproduce it in full, excerpted from *The Zündelsite*:

> "Dear Mr. Hampton,
>
> I am writing to you regarding the case of Ernst Zündel and your forthcoming decision on whether to bring new charges against him. I am a Jew, and I am also a Holocaust revisionist. I am not a crackpot who comes out from under the rocks to spread hatred and anti-Semitism, quite the contrary. I have been rationally explaining to people for years that there are two sides to the Holocaust story, and that based on the available evidence, the revisionist side is simply more credible. Revisionism has nothing to do with hatred and malevolence, but with objectivity and the attempt to discern truth from falsehood. If I were trying to harm Jews, it would mean that I am trying to harm my whole family. This would be a serious accusation against me.
>
> I have been featured on a network television programme in the United States (the prime-time news programme '48 Hours' hosted by Dan Rather) and I have also debated the issue with survivors and 'experts' on a national talk show (the Montel Williams show sold to local repeaters). I have never been accused of being a racist, a Nazi or a Jew-hater (I am none of those things).
>
> The purpose of this letter is to ask you to stop the legal persecution of Mr. Zündel. I am aware that there are pressure groups trying to convince you to do otherwise, and I also realise that it must be difficult for these people to separate their emotions from what is best for intellectual freedom in Canada. It would therefore be your job, as a representative of the people and the law, to look at things objectively and do what is best for both the people and the greatness of the law. How has the continued persecution of Mr. Zündel benefited the people of Canada, except as an example of how to waste tax money, and how has the gross double standard regarding

the rights of Germans compared to the rights of other ethnic groups benefited the integrity of the law?

Please remember that the subject of the Holocaust does not only concern the Jews; the Germans were there too and, as part of their history, they have as much right to study it as the Jews. In future years, perhaps many years, perhaps only a few, when sanity has prevailed and the Holocaust can be reviewed objectively, and we see that the world as we know it does not disappear as a result, the hypocritical and miserable persecution of Ernst Zündel will in retrospect seem quite pointless and history will not look favourably on those who were involved in it.

Yours sincerely,

David Cole".

For months, the media were used to put pressure on the authorities and to tighten the noose around Zündel, who, unwavering in his will to resist, even sent letters to London newspapers, the effect of which was the opposite of the desired one, provoking angry and irrational reactions from the Jewish communities. However, on 5 March 1993, for the umpteenth time, the Jewish organisations failed in their attempt to break the stubborn resistance of the "revisionist dynamo". The police forces involved in the investigation did not understand that he could be charged. The Hate Literature Section of the Ontario Provincial Police reported that no charges could be laid under the hate propaganda law, as Zündel's comments did not constitute the crime of hate speech. Zündel issued a press release reiterating his position:

> "The facts are: my material, my ideas, my appearances on radio and television do not generate anti-Semitic incidents, because they are not anti-Semitic. My material is trying to counter anti-German hate speech in the media, in films and in textbooks. There is a simple solution to the problem: stop telling untruths, half-truths and outright lies about Germans and their role in history and I won't have to retort with uncomfortable and unpopular truths. Simple! Remember: a lie does not become the truth just because it has been repeated millions of times."

Ernst Zündel's legal successes and his persistent fighting spirit could only further inflame his enemies, who saw how a single individual stood up to them without them being able to finish him off as usual. Sabina Citron and her cronies stepped up their campaign with all kinds of pressure that reached the highest levels of political power. Citron threatened again: "He must be indicted; if not, we will lose our respect for the law in Canada". A signature campaign was launched among university students: all student federations were asked to take a stand against Zündel, including the African Students' Association. Jewish agitators arrived on university campuses, lecturing young people with fierce diatribes. In addition, the petition was extended to the gay, lesbian and bisexual community, women's centres and other social organisations. Further demonstrations were called in various cities and in May 1993 the Jewish Student Network organised a sit-in in front of the Ontario Attorney General's building.

B'nai Brith and the Canadian Jewish Congress extended their tentacles and decided to use leftist and anarchist groups. The aim was to mobilise all sectors of Canadian society to put an end once and for all to "the largest international purveyor of Holocaust denial materials". In the summer of 1993, Zündel launched an international shortwave programme via radio and satellite television. His programmes, entitled "The Voice of Freedom", touched on revisionist issues and general historical interest. These programmes expanded and gained access to public television in the United States, where Zündel's supporters and sympathisers sponsored the programme in various American communities.

On 24 October 1993, Zündel opted to apply for Canadian citizenship for the second time. Of course, if he had been granted citizenship at the time when the campaign against him was at its height, it would have been a humiliating defeat for his persecutors. The Department of Citizenship and Immigration made him aware that his activities constituted a threat to Canada's security. The Canadian Jewish Congress (CJC) and B'nai Brith put pressure on the government. The Jewish Masonic Lodge issued a statement in the *Montreal Gazette* on 28 July 1994 calling for his extradition to Germany instead of citizenship: "This man does not deserve the privilege of Canadian citizenship. Not only would it be an affront to Canada's minorities, but it would be tantamount to a message to those who spread hatred around the world that Canada is a haven for racism."

A detailed account of the attacks on Zündel would take up too much space. Since what has been written gives a full picture of his titanic struggle, we will only list the most brutal ones at. On 24 November 1993, a group called ARA (Anti-Racist Action) gathered in front of Zündel's house with hundreds of posters to throw eggs and paint it. Since Zündel's house had police protection, the same group had months earlier set fire to the unprotected house of a friend named Gary Schipper. On 7 May 1995, however, Zündel's house was also burned down. An arsonist threw flammable liquid on the porch: the fire destroyed the front of the building and completely consumed the third floor. A JDL henchman named Kahane Chai claimed responsibility. Two weeks later, Zündel received a package that he found suspicious. He took it to the police, who found it to be a bomb containing shrapnel and nails. Once exploded, the device left a crater half a metre deep. Police confirmed that it would have killed anyone who opened the package and could have injured, if not killed, anyone within ninety metres of the explosion.

More interesting is the appearance of *The Zündelsite* on the Internet, also in 1995. Interested readers can find further information on this website. This breakthrough into cyberspace came about thanks to the collaboration of his friends in "American Free Speech". In September 1995 Jamie McCarthy, co-webmaster of *The Nizkor Project*, a project of websites promoting the Holocaust and debunking revisionist arguments, sent an e-mail to Zündel inviting him to connect or link the two sites so that users could have a view to determine who was telling the truth. McCarthy wrote: "Since you maintain, time and again, that 'truth needs no coercion', I trust you will not insult the intelligence of your readers by withholding an alternative point of view." Surely contrary to expectations, Zündel gratefully received the offer: "Thank you wholeheartedly for your proposal to make the internet the open forum in which we can discuss, in a sensible and civilised manner, what is of such importance to all of us." After explaining that since in the early 1980s he had already offered a public debate to the Canadian Jewish community, he said he would "be delighted if the offer was genuine and shared by the people who supported *The Nizkor Project*, as it was precisely what I had been waiting for a long time. It did not take long for the two sites to become connected (linked).

On 5 January 1996, Zündel invited the Simon Wiesenthal Centre to link its website to *The Zündelsite*, but received no response. Two days later, on 7 January, Zündel announced a global electronic debate on the Holocaust on his site. In preparation, the webmaster of *The Zündelsite* started uploading all texts and documents, including the *Leuchter Report* and *Did Six Million Really Die?* to the File Transfer Protocol (FTP). Almost immediately the files, even the restricted ones, were downloaded by someone unknown, which led Zündel to believe that there had been continuous surveillance of his site and his activities. In an editorial on the website he later asked: "Who has the money, the ability, the equipment and the staff to do that? Two days later, the Simon Wiesenthal Center sent hundreds of pages to internet providers and university presidents asking them to refuse to transmit messages promoting "racism, anti-Semitism, chaos and violence". *The Zündelsite* began to be attacked, its mail stolen, tampered with or destroyed. E-mail "bombs" even came from Russia. Falsified messages from Zündel began to circulate on the net in order to damage his reputation. On 25 January 1996, the media reported that German prosecutors were preparing charges of hate speech against those Internet providers in Germany who helped distribute Ernst Zündel's site. Zündel made a desperate call for help: "If there are any patriotic Internet experts anywhere who can help us defend ourselves through technical or legal means, please call. Surely we can use your help!"

Patriots or not, advocates of freedom of thought, regardless of whether they believed in the Holocaust or not, reacted against any attempt to censor the internet. At universities in the United States, supporters of free speech, understanding that freedom was at stake for everyone, began to set up electronic clones (called "mirror pages") on their own initiative. These electronic safe havens were set up at the universities of Stanford, Pennsylvania, Massachusetts, among others. Dean McCullagh, a graduate student at Carnegie Mellon University (CMU) wrote: "If the German government forces Deutsche Telekom to block access to the web servers of CMU, MIT (Massachusetts Institute of Technology) and Standford University, it will be cutting off communications with three of the most respected universities in the United States". One of the mirror pages contained this statement by the webmaster: "This is a mirror file of most of Zündel's revisionist page. My reasons for this mirror are not my agreement with Zündel's political ideas. I do not agree..., but I think that the questioning of any creed deserves some space. Therefore, I think Zündel's project is good for our society". On the battle to maintain *The Zündelsite*, it remains to add that the webmaster of the site was Ingrid Rimland, whom he met in January 1995. Born in Ukraine and naturalised US citizen,

Rimland, a woman of great intellectual stature, has been an irreplaceable support for Zündel ever since.

After more than four decades in Canada, where two applications for citizenship were rejected, Ernst Zündel decided to settle in the United States, where Ingrid Rimland managed his website. In January 2000, they married in Tennessee, making Ingrid, who had also been married before, Zündel's second wife. Being married to an American citizen, one might have thought that he would finally be able to live without being permanently harassed, and so he was initially. For two years he lived peacefully in a mountainous region of East Tennessee, but on 5 February 2003 he was arrested at his home in the presence of his wife. Three Immigration and Naturalisation Service agents and two local agents handcuffed him and took him away. Thus began an ordeal that was to end in Germany seven years later, on 1 March 2010 to be exact.

Ingrid asked for help from her husband's friends and supporters to publicly denounce his arrest, as he had committed only a minor violation of immigration laws: he had allegedly failed a procedural hearing and was therefore technically illegal in the US. On 10 February 2003, Ingrid explained on a radio programme all the efforts and unsuccessful efforts she had made to have her husband released and expressed her fear that if Ernst was deported to Germany he could be imprisoned for years because anti-Holocaust views were a crime there. Mark Weber, director of the Institute for Historical Review, also participated in the programme at Ingrid's request. Weber was honoured to be a friend of Zündel, whom he described as a civil rights activist who had fought costly and endless battles in Canada for basic freedoms. Days later, on 14 February, it was reported in the newspapers that the US authorities planned to deport Zündel in the coming weeks, but it was unclear whether he would be sent to Germany or Canada. Finally, after two weeks behind bars, Ernst Zündel was deported to Canada on 19 February 2003.

Zündel applied for refugee status, but on 24 February 2003 the Department of Citizenship and Immigration Canada notified the Refugee Protection Division to suspend consideration of the application, as it was considering whether Ernst Zündel constituted a threat to national security. Finally, on 1 May 2003, the Canadian authorities issued a certification stating that Zündel could not remain in Canada for national security reasons. On 6 May, Zündel's lawyer Barbara Kulaszka filed a constitutional challenge in the Federal Court of Canada and subsequently challenged his detention in the Ontario Superior Court of Justice. All to no avail: on 21 January 2004, a magistrate ordered Zündel's continued detention on the grounds that he posed a danger to national security. On 1 March 2005, Ernst Zündel was deported to Germany, where he was arrested for publicly denying the Holocaust. A lifetime of patriotic struggle to defend the honour of his country and demand justice for Germany ended in the most depressing way. The Simon Wiesenthal Centre, the Canadian Jewish Congress, the Holocaust Remembrance Association, the Human Rights League (equivalent to the JDL in Canada) had finally won: Ernst Zündel was at the mercy of the judicial terrorism of his native country.

Locked up in Mannheim prison, Zündel, who had already spent more than two years incarcerated in Canada, was to face the bitterest years of his heroic life. Due to the conditions of prolonged solitary confinement, without being able to speak to other prisoners, Zündel was already suffering from depression when he entered the German prison. As Barbara Kulaszka complained in a submission to the UN Human Rights Committee, the most basic human rights were violated during the Canadian period of detention: she was not allowed to have a chair in her cell, whose lights were on 24 hours a day and dimmed only slightly at night; she was not allowed to take her natural herbs for arthritis and high blood pressure; her request to be seen by a dentist was refused; she was not allowed to exercise physically; she was not allowed to have a chair in her cell, whose lights were on 24 hours a day and dimmed only slightly at night; she was not allowed to take her natural herbs for arthritis and high blood pressure; her request to be seen by a dentist was refused; he could not exercise physically or even walk; the cold in the cell in winter forced him to cover himself with blankets and sheets, which were only changed every three months; he had no pillow; he could not wear shoes; the food was always cold and of poor quality. Barbara Kulaszka reported that Zündel had a lump in his chest that could be cancerous, but she had no right to a diagnosis.

On 29 June 2005, the Mannheim public prosecutor formally charged him with "inciting hatred". According to the text submitted by the prosecutor's office, some of Zündel's writings "condoned, denied or minimised" genocidal actions by the German regime that "denigrate the memory of the dead Jews." Thought criminals in Germany cannot plead not guilty. If the defendant's lawyer proclaims the innocence of his defendant, he runs the risk of being arrested for "Holocaust denial" or "hate speech". In the height of absurdity in the German judicial terror for thought crimes, the judge can prohibit the presentation of evidence in favour of the accused. Sylvia Stolz, Zündel's lawyer in Mannheim, was herself sentenced to three and a half years in prison for Holocaust denial during her client's defence and five years of disbarment. Since Sylvia Stolz is a major victim of the thought police in Germany, we will comment on the details of the trial below, where she will have her own space, for she has suffered and continues to suffer a disgraceful persecution for the honest practice of her profession, degrading for any judicial system worthy of the name.

For his part, Zündel insisted before the "court of justice" that the alleged murder of millions of Jews was a falsification of history. In his final words before the court, he called for an independent international commission to investigate the Holocaust and promised that if it was proven that Jews had been gassed, he would "call a press conference to apologise to the Jews, to the Israelis and to the world". Finally, two years after he was imprisoned in Germany, the Mannheim court convicted him on 14 February 2007 of incitement to racial hatred and Shoah (Holocaust) denial and sentenced him to five years in prison. In Canada, Jewish organisations that had persecuted him welcomed the court's ruling. Bernie Farber of the Jewish Congress said the sentence sent a strong message to the world and would serve to "comfort" Holocaust survivors.

When he was released from prison on 1 March 2010, exactly five years after his deportation, Ernst Zündel was seventy years old. His face was a poem of infinite sadness and pain. A disturbed look, undoubtedly the result of prolonged suffering, was visible in his visionary blue eyes, which, wide open, gazed raptly, illuminated by a strange, unsettling light, bordering on madness. A group of twenty people were waiting for him on the other side of the iron prison gates and took their first photos of him at liberty. They welcomed him with applause, bouquets of flowers and shouts of "bravo". His first words were: "I am free again after seven years, three weeks, three prisons and three countries".

Five months after the publication of our *Proscribed History*, Ernst Zündel, the indispensable man, the "revisionist dynamo", left this world in the Black Forest, at his home in Bad Wildbad (Baden Württemberg), where he was born. His sister Sigrid, who was with him, found him unconscious and called an ambulance, but his heart stopped beating shortly afterwards. After a life devoted to denouncing lies and defending the honour and dignity of the German people, Ernst Zündel died on 5 August 2017, aged 78, of a heart attack. We emotionally subscribe to the words of Ingrid Zündel (Ingrid Rimland), who referred to her husband's demise with these words: "A glow, he has left this world". Only two months later, on 12 October, Ingrid herself, our hero's companion in so many battles for freedom of speech and thought, passed away.

Germar Rudolf: persecution and destruction of an eminent scientist

Germar Rudolf, a brilliant graduate in chemistry from the University of Bonn, received a government scholarship that enabled him to do doctoral research at the prestigious Max Planck Institute in Stuttgart. He was working on his doctoral thesis when in 1991 he agreed to prepare a forensic study for the defence of Otto Ernst Remer, accused in a trial for "Holocaust denial". He was asked to study various documents, take samples, analyse them and issue a report. Rudolf was particularly interested in verifying the assertions made in the *Leuchter Report* and in proving that traces of cyanide remained stable for a long time and could therefore be found in the murder gas chambers if Zyklon B had been used in them. "Initially," Rudolf wrote, "I was only interested in finding out whether the resulting mixture, ferrocyanide or Prussian blue, is stable enough to survive forty-five years in harsh environmental conditions.

Germar Rudolf travelled twice to Auschwitz and for eighteen months worked with the intention of compiling his report. He tested some of the Auschwitz buildings for residues of hydrocyanic acid, i.e. chemical traces of the famous Zyklon-B. He also tested some of the Auschwitz buildings for residues of hydrocyanic acid. The result of his investigations was recorded in an expert report entitled *Technical Report on the Formation and Detectability of Cyanide Compounds in the "Gas Chamber" of Auschwitz* (*Gutachten über die Bildung und Nachweisbarkeit von Cyanidverbindungen in den "Gaskammern von*

Auschwitz), which was used as evidence by Remer's defence. Years later, Rudolf wrote in *Resistance is Obligatory* that the purpose of the expert opinion was to correct the omissions and deficiencies of the *Leuchter Report*. Between 1992 and 1994 this report was presented as evidence in seven or eight criminal trials in Germany. In all cases it was rejected because according to German jurisprudence, the facts that took place in the Auschwitz camp during the Third Reich are considered obvious and therefore do not require proof or demonstration. Since 1996 it has been a criminal offence to try to argue otherwise. Thus, as unheard of as it may seem, the technical analyses were roundly rejected.

Otto Ernst Remer, one of the defendants for whose benefit the report had been prepared, published the results of Germar Rudolf's research in July 1993. The pamphlet of some 120 pages became known as the *Rudolf Report*, a chemical study on the formation and detection of hydrogen cyanide in the alleged Auschwitz gas chambers, an apt complement to the *Leuchter Report*, since both documents agreed that hydrocyanic acid murders never took place in the camps of the Auschwitz complex. This led to the indictment of Germar Rudolf. The German press, which consistently supported the decisions of the courts of law, reacted angrily and associated the young chemist with the accused Remer.

The result of the whole affair was catastrophic for Germar Rudolf, who was refused by the Max Planck Institute in 1993 to submit his thesis for the final doctoral examination. In late spring of the same year, the Institute issued a memorandum informing of Rudolf's expulsion for his research at Auschwitz. The Max Planck Institute, disdaining that forensic examination is a moral obligation in any criminal investigation, argued that it was repugnant to discuss the specific way in which the Nazis had murdered Jews. In 1995 Germar Rudolf was sentenced to fourteen months in prison and was additionally charged with new charges for continuing his forensic research activities. Copies of *Grundlagen zur Zeitgeschichte* (*Foundations of Contemporary History*), in which Rudolf had published under the pseudonym Ernst Gauss an up-to-date collection of research papers on the problem of the Holocaust, were seized and destroyed by court order.

In connection with the persecution of Germar Rudolf and revisionists in general, it should be known that the West German government, following the example of the Israeli Parliament (Knesset), passed a law in 1985 according to which "denying the systematic annihilation of the majority of European Jews perpetrated by Nazi Germany" constitutes a criminal offence. That said, it can be said that the persecution of Germar Rudolf is the story of an infamy, the story of a blatant insult to intelligence, cynically consummated by the authorities of the Federal Republic of Germany. There is no better source of information on the life, work and persecution of this intellectual than *Germar Rudolf's Site*. There, the interested reader will find everything he could wish for and more. The site contains, for example, all the essential and complementary documents of his case: reports, verdicts, asylum applications, expert statements, affidavits, lawsuits, appeals and other texts of various kinds. Much of what follows is therefore drawn from this source, but also from Germar Rudolf's books and IHR publications.

In one of the texts on his website, Rudolf reflects on the semantic nuances of the terms "prosecution" and "persecution". Prosecution is legal - explains Germar Rudolf - if it takes place in accordance with internationally recognised civil rights and freedoms; but it becomes persecution if these are not respected, as in his case. During the trial of Ernst Zündel, a magistrate ordered that Sylvia Stolz be replaced by a public defender while she was acting as counsel for her client. Stolz was sentenced to three and a half years' imprisonment and five years' disbarment for questioning the Holocaust in court. Naturally, a judicial system that not only prevents lawyers from working freely but also prosecutes and persecutes them does not meet international models or benchmarks. Section 130 of the German Criminal Code allows for the removal of civil rights of disruptive citizens, who are usually those who question the Holocaust or oppose multiculturalism. These undesirables commit an offence that can lead to five years' imprisonment. This aside, we can continue the story of the persecution of Germar Rudolf.

In addition to the indictment that brought him before the Stuttgart District Court, which sentenced him to fourteen months, three other indictments on charges brought against him were in progress. One of them concerned an exchange of correspondence with the Kraków Institute for Forensic Research, which Rudolf had approached, as discussed in the fourth part of Chapter XII of our *Proscribed History*, in order to clarify technical questions related to the research of this Polish institution at Auschwitz. As a result, Rudolf's house was searched three times and on each occasion books, files, correspondence and computers were seized, which ruined his work and his scientific research. When in March 1996 the Federal German Supreme Court confirmed the sentence of fourteen months imprisonment, Rudolf decided to leave Germany with his family. Initially they settled in southern Spain, but their stay was short-lived, because in May 1996 Rudolf was informed that the Spanish government was also planning to enact an anti-revisionist law. After consulting with his wife, he decided to settle with his family in the South East of England, where he hoped that freedom of thought and speech would be more than just talk. His contact was David Irving, who in 2006, as will be seen below, would also end up imprisoned in Austria.

Once in the UK, problems began as early as 1997: the *Telegraph* reported that German embassy officials in London were working on the extradition of Germar Rudolf, a fugitive from justice. In 1998 his wife began to feel uncomfortable with the new situation: life in exile was not fulfilling her expectations: she was homesick for her family and friends and could not find new friends. In addition to homesickness, the constant fear of extradition hung over her head like a sword of Damocles. She decided to leave her husband and return with her two children to Germany, where she began divorce proceedings against Germar, who was left alone in exile.

In June 1999 Rudolf, after a few moments of uncertainty at Heathrow airport, was able to travel to the United States to give a series of lectures there. It must have been on this occasion that he gauged the possibility of emigrating there. At the end of September he made his second trip to the United States and received an offer from a small publishing house called "Theses & Dissertation Press". In the autumn of 1999, a campaign against the "neo-Nazi fugitive" began in the British media, which led to a halt in his family's visits. Since there was no longer anything tying him to England and in order to avoid persecution in Europe, he finally decided to emigrate to the USA, even though he did not have a "green card" (work permit). One of the most important events of his English period was the founding of a modest publishing company called "Castle Hill Publishers", now famous in revisionist circles.

Once in the United States, his hopes of obtaining the longed-for work permit were dashed in July 2000. To avoid problems with the immigration authorities, he settled temporarily in Rosarito, Baja California (Mexico), where he rented a small house near the home of Bradley Smith, the visible head of CODOH (Committee for Open Debate on the Holocaust). During the ten-week stay in Rosarito, a close friendship between the two revisionists was born. In August Rudolf learned from his mother that his parents had decided to disinherit him in favour of their children. Previously, his father had asked him to be sterilised so that he would no longer be able to procreate. On 29 August 2000, increasingly depressed, Germar Rudolf sent out a distress call to several friends. He finally decided to fly to New York via Iceland and in October 2000 he applied for political asylum in the United States. At the end of the month, he received a notice from the Immigration Service announcing that his application had been formally accepted and that he would have to attend an interview with Department officials at the end of November 2000. The interview took place on the 29th.

On 4 April 2001, a date of 24 September 2001 was set for an immigration court to hear the case. Rudolf therefore had almost half a year to prepare documents on the deterioration of civil rights in Germany and get them into the hands of a specialised lawyer. Days before the big day, the attacks of 11 September had occurred and the immigration judge, after a brief discussion, decided to postpone the hearing until 18 March 2002. The asylum application process thus dragged on and on for years. In the meantime, Rudolf married a US citizen named Jennifer in 2004 and applied to have his immigration status upgraded or changed to permanent resident status. At the end of 2004, the US Immigration Service informed him that his application had been rejected and shortly thereafter he was informed that he was not eligible to file a petition for permanent residence because of his marriage. Consequently, Germar Rudolf filed an appeal with the Federal Court in Atlanta. In early 2005, he became the father of a baby girl.

Despite the fact that the Immigration Service had said that he was not eligible for permanent residence because he was married to a

US citizen, almost a year later, on 19 October 2005, the couple was summoned by the Immigration and Naturalisation Service for an interview. It was supposedly intended to verify that the marriage was "bona fide" (genuine, in good faith). The couple confidently went to the appointment with their baby in the pram. Within seconds of returning the certificate of recognition, Rudolf was told by two officials that he was under arrest. The reason for this arbitrary decision was his failure to keep an appointment that was supposed to have taken place five months earlier. Rudolf's lawyer tried to convince the officers that the arrest was unjustified and the police officer seemed willing to accept the arguments, but claimed that he needed to consult with someone in Washington. After an hour of phone calls back and forth, the order came down from Washington that the arrest was final and that deportation proceedings to Germany were to be initiated without further ado. With shackles on his hands and feet, Rudolf was added to a chain of criminals being taken to the Kenosha County Jail. There he awaited deportation. According to the identification bracelet he was given at the jail, he was the only inmate in the entire facility who was not a criminal, a fact that surprised guards and prisoners alike.

Neither his marriage nor the clear evidence that he was politically persecuted by legal publications in the United States were sufficient considerations for the Federal Court in Atlanta to prevent his deportation. It should be noted that Rudolf had filed an appeal in the Atlanta Federal Court against the decision to deny him the right to asylum and that the decision had not yet been rendered and was therefore still pending. Although the Fifth Amendment to the Constitution guarantees due process for all persons - not just US citizens - present on US soil, the Federal Court rejected the request to postpone deportation until a final decision on the asylum claim had been made. The Supreme Court did not even bother to examine an emergency claim, which was dismissed without explanations. The question Germar Rudolf asks himself is: "What is the point of a political asylum application, if the government deports the applicant before the court examining the case has decided whether there are grounds to grant it?"

On 14 November 2005 Germar Rudolf was deported to Germany. He was immediately arrested to serve his outstanding sentence of fourteen months and transferred to Stuttgart prison, where he was informed that new proceedings had been initiated against him for his publications in England and the United States. It is incomprehensible how the German Criminal Code can be applied to activities carried out in other countries where they are perfectly legal. Thus, the new trial against Rudolf began in Mannheim on 15 November 2006. Accused of "inciting the masses", which theoretically would have been done through the publication of the results of his historical research, summarised in the book *Lectures on the Holocaust* (2005), Rudolf was sentenced in February 2007 to 30 months in prison. According to the prosecution, the aforementioned book was the main reason for the new conviction, since all reprehensible opinions were set out in it in an exemplary manner.

Germar Rudolf published in 2012, now legally residing in the United States, the book *Resistance is Obligatory*, which contains the presentation he made in his defence before the Mannheim District Court. All motions submitted by the defence team to prove that their defendant's writings were of a scientific nature and therefore protected by the German constitution were rejected by the court, which also prohibited academics willing to testify on the scholarly nature of Rudolf's texts from testifying. During the trial, Rudolf's defence lawyers were prohibited from making submissions in support of their client's views under threat of prosecution.

Faced with this Kafkaesque situation, Germar Rudolf gave a speech to the court that lasted for seven full sessions. For days on end, Rudolf brilliantly presented in a perfectly structured text a dissertation on what science is and how its manifestations can be recognised. Furthermore, although jurisprudence was not one of his specific fields of expertise, he demonstrated that German laws designed to repress peaceful dissidents are unconstitutional and violate human rights. It explained in detail why it is everyone's obligation to nonviolently resist a state that throws peaceful dissenters into dungeons. The Mannheim court did not bat an eyelid and, in addition to sentencing him to thirty months in prison, ordered all copies of *Lectures on the Holocaust* to be confiscated and burned under police supervision.

We will now look at some faint glimpses of this defence speech by Germar Rudolf, the text of which forms the core content of the book *Resistance is Obligatory*. Rudolf tried to publish his dissertation in court while serving his sentence, which prompted a new criminal investigation by the prosecutor's office. On 10 August 2007, already months after the end of the trial, the Mannheim court issued a warrant to search Rudolf's cell for documents showing that he was in the process of publishing his defence speech. On 25 September 2007, he was visited by several Mannheim police officers who confiscated all the documents he had used during the trial. The reasons given to him were that his plans to publish the speech were once again evidence of his intention to disseminate the contents of *Lectures on the Holocaust*, for which he was serving a sentence. He was made aware that he could incite the masses with the use of adjectives such as "alleged", "pretended", "supposed" or "claimed".

Faced with the evidence that few lawyers were willing to take on his defence for fear of being charged, and convinced that those who would take the risk would try to convince him during the trial to recant, which was tantamount to hiring them to waste time and money, Germar Rudolf decided to approach the trial as an opportunity to expose the Kafkaesque legal conditions prevailing in the Federal Republic of Germany. His intention was to write a book after the trial was over. For seven sessions, Rudolf delivered a lengthy speech that was exhausting for the judges, the audience and himself. Aware of this, Rudolf writes: "I prepared these lectures not primarily for the listeners, but rather for posterity and for the whole world, for you, dear reader, who are now holding the book in your hands". For this to be possible, Rudolf acknowledges that it depended on the judges, despite their constraints, being rational enough to authorise such a defence, which they were. The presentation to the court began with a principled clarification of his position throughout the trial, headed "General remarks on my defence", which, because of its relevance, is reproduced in full:

> "1. Statements on historical matters shall be made only for the purpose of
>
> a. Explain and illustrate my personal development;
>
> b. Illustrate by examples the criteria of a scientific nature;
>
> c. Put the prosecutor's charges about my exposures in a broader context.
>
> 2. These statements are not made to back up my historical views with facts.
>
> 3. I will not formulate proposals asking the court to consider my historical theses for the following reasons:

a. Policy: German courts are prohibited by superior orders from accepting such requests to present evidence. As stated in Article 97 of the German Basic Law. Judges are independent and subject only to the law'. Please excuse my sarcasm.

b. Timeliness: Point a) above does not prohibit me from submitting proposals for evidence. However, since they would all be rejected, would be a wasted effort. We will all be spared the waste of time and energy.

c. Of reciprocity: Since current law denies me the right to defend myself historically and on the basis of the facts, I for my part deny my accusers the right to accuse me historically and on the basis of the facts, in accordance with the maxim of equality and reciprocity. Thus, I consider the historical allegations of the accusation to be non-existent.

d. Legal: In 1543, Nicolaus Copernicus wrote:

'If perchance there should be stupid speakers, who, together with those who are ignorant of everything about mathematics, should dare to make decisions in relation to such things, and by some page of the Law twisted in bad faith for their purposes, should dare to attack my work, they do not deserve the least importance, so much so that I despise their judgment as foolhardiness.'

No court in the world has the right or competence to rule authoritatively on scientific questions. No Parliament in the world has the power to use criminal law to dogmatically prescribe answers to scientific questions. It would therefore be absurd for me as a publisher of science books to ask a court of law to determine the validity of my published works. Only the scientific community is competent and authorised to do this".

Germar Rudolf, Stuttgart, 4 November 2006".

On the basis of this statement before the court that was to try him, Rudolf put together a coherent discourse arranged around four axes: scientific considerations, legal considerations, specific considerations, resistance to the state. On the first of these axes, he reviewed his academic training. The demonstration of scientific and technical knowledge was considerable: biochemistry, chemistry in electronics, nuclear chemistry, theoretical chemistry, quantum mechanics, organic and inorganic chemistry, physical chemistry, mathematics, were some of the optional subjects that he did not want to give up, until, overloaded with work, he ended up studying nuclear chemistry and electrochemistry in depth. Rudolf tried to make the court understand the importance of curiosity for any self-respecting scientist. When a state tries with all the means at its disposal to suppress certain research and declare its results illegal, "automatically," he told the judges, "it exposes itself to the suspicion that it is trying to conceal something extraordinarily interesting and important. Then no sincerely passionate scientist can resist any longer". Rudolf said he was convinced that the need to know the truth is part of human dignity.

As a contrast to the lack of scientific rigour and the desire to conceal the truth and impose lies, Rudolf brought up before the Mannheim court the study on the Auschwitz crematoria by the French pharmacist Jean-Claude Pressac, which appeared in 1993 and was constantly used by the media and official historians as a refutation of the revisionist theses. He denounced that at no time had Pressac had the capacity to confront, let alone refute, a single one of the revisionist arguments. Rudolf reminded the court that he and other researchers had analysed and criticised Pressac's work in a book published in 1996 (*Auschwitz: Nackte Fackten*). For the specific reason that our book, in contrast to Pressac's book," Rudolf reminded the judges, "was in accordance with scientific procedure, the German government ordered it to be seized and destroyed and initiated a new criminal case against me". In his eagerness to contrast the attitude of the exterminationists and revisionists, Rudolf insisted that the attitude of any scientist worthy of the name is to examine any attempt at refutation and to discuss it rationally, as the revisionists do. He regretted that the official historiography and the German and international courts support their theses almost exclusively on witness statements instead of presenting conclusive documents and evidence, and deplored the attacks on researchers who ask for something more.

The judicial considerations in Rudolf's exposition take up half a hundred pages. Without being a lawyer, he demonstrated his ability to study and analyse the German judicial system, which he compared with the Soviet judicial system, using quotations from Alexander Solzhenitsyn's *Gulag Archipelago* to show that in both, political prisoners are treated as criminals. He acknowledged, however, that at least in Germany detainees are not tortured, for which he was grateful. The definition of a political prisoner and the progressive deterioration of civil rights in German law were addressed by criticising the heavy-handed application of certain articles of the Basic Law of the Federal Republic of Germany. "The present trial," he said, "is taking place only because the prosecutor alleges that a conflict has arisen between my scientific freedom and freedom of expression on the one hand and the human dignity of a particular group of the population on the other." Germar Rudolf insisted in court that the law recognises that there can be no conflict between the publication of the results of scientific research and human dignity, however much one might want to put the human dignity of a certain group above that of the rest of the citizenry. Of course, he did not accept the charge that he had violated the Youth Protection Act, through which freedom of expression in Germany is limited.

Of particular interest in the judicial remarks was the consideration of the arbitrary interpretation of certain terms systematically made by judges and prosecutors in Germany, "an illegitimate tactic," he said, "of immunisation against criticism. The expressions, taken from his own indictment, used to charge researchers, writers or publicists were: "incitement to hatred", "in a manner capable of disturbing public order". In relation to the writings, they are interpreted as "insulting", "maliciously disseminated to belittle", "denigrate" and/or "despise", and, among other things, "deny" historical facts or present them "knowingly untruthfully". On the latter assertion, Rudolf told the judges that the claim of consciously going against the truth "was the most absurd expression of German jurisprudence, which seriously thinks that it can determine historical truth and knowledge through verdicts. History - he added - cannot be treated in this way in courts of law". Rudolf insisted once again that it cannot be established that a piece of writing is "insulting", "contemptuous", "repudiatory", "defamatory", "denigrating" or "toxic to the mind" just because a reader subjectively interprets it in this way. His presentation on the dangerous arbitrariness of the terms used against dissidents in courts of law concluded with quotes from jurists such as Dr. Thomas Wandres and Dr. Florian Körber, who in different dissertations had expressed the opinion that Germar Rudolf's books should enjoy the protection of Germany's Basic Law, which protects freedom of speech and scientific research.

Dr. Körber had published in 2003 *Rechtsradikale Propaganda im Internet -Der Fall Töben* (*Radical right-wing propaganda on the Internet - the Töben case*), a monograph on an Australian revisionist, Dr. Töben, whom the German authorities wanted to prosecute (his prosecution will be discussed later). Rudolf quoted verbatim before the court several theses from Körber's work:

"The protection of historical truth through the criminal code harbours the danger of removing or withdrawing parts of history from an essential social discussion.

Despite its neutral wording, Section 130 III of the German Criminal Code grants problematic special protection to the Jewish part of the German population by means of a 'privileium odiosum'. There is a danger that, in the eyes of the people, one group appears to be more protected than the majority, which strengthens the perception of antipathy towards the protected group...".

After citing these and other theses, Rudolf endorsed before the court the views of Dr. Körber, who was in favour of the complete repeal of Section 130 of the Criminal Code, and supported the idea that "special protection" for Jews could end up being "counterproductive for them", which should be avoided. Rudolf ended this part of the speech on judicial considerations with these words:

"What is certain is the fact that my writings and those I have published do not, if objectively considered, contain content that 'incites hatred', 'disparages or insults', etc., nor can they be considered to 'disturb the peace'. That the accusation uses such terms - for lack of any other explanation - only shows what it really intends: to shock, to create taboos and to ostracise me by making false assertions."

"Specific considerations" is the heading of the third major block of content in the defence speech before the court. In it, Rudolf referred to specific issues contained in the indictment, among which he alluded to his theoretical sympathies with National Socialism and, above all, to his famous book *Lectures on the Holocaust*, considered by all, including himself, to be his main work, in which, over five hundred pages, he gives readers a comprehensive overview of revisionist research and its results in relation to the Holocaust. After recalling that the indictment called for the seizure and destruction of the book, and after comparing this attitude to that of the Nazis themselves, he asked that, before handing the book over to the flames, the members of the court should at least be aware of its contents. To this end, he submitted a request that the book be read during the court proceedings. The court decided that the judges should read it in private, so the proceedings were interrupted for three weeks to allow the judges to read the book.

We will devote a few more lines to the fourth block of the speech, entitled "Resistance", which begins with quotes from various authors, including our own Ortega y Gasset and his work *La rebelión de las masas (The Rebellion of the Masses)*. Ortega warns that when one renounces a shared life based on culture, one returns to the everyday life of barbarism. In accordance with this idea, Rudolf said: "That you do not try to persuade me to change my mind with arguments, but on the contrary reject any discussion and try to send me to prison, is exactly this return to barbarism". He then singled out the German state as the main target of non-violent resistance, advocated among others by Gandhi, because it restricts the freedom of peaceful citizens from whom it claims to protect itself. Rudolf, drawing on texts by authoritative intellectuals, recalled the Cuban missile crisis, the Vietnam War, the attempt by NATO to deploy nuclear missiles on German soil and the social rejection of nuclear energy as examples of resistance and/or civil disobedience in the Federal Republic. "In the case of revisionism or in my case," he said, "disobedience or resistance is directed against an unconstitutional law and consists only in deliberately ignoring and violating this, and exclusively this, law." Rudolf turned to a quotation from the Basic Law, specifically Article 20 paragraph 4, to legitimise his right to resistance: "All Germans have the right to resist against anyone who tries to eliminate this order, if there is no other remedy." Hence, the accused eventually declared in court that he was in fact fulfilling his constitutional duty by resisting and fighting to reverse a situation in which the state is acting in an unjust and totalitarian manner.

Germar Rudolf ended this fourth part of his defence speech by completely rejecting any kind of violent resistance, because violence begets violence. He did, however, appeal to collectives and institutions capable of remedying the situation. In particular, he appealed to parliamentary and legal initiatives, social organisations, intellectuals, the media and the German people as a whole to demonstrate in defence of freedom of expression. With regard to the latter means of protesting against injustice, he noted that, unfortunately, the remedy through public protests was proving impossible, since in April 2006, while awaiting the start of his trial, a demonstration in Mannheim had been banned on the grounds that prohibited opinions could be expressed during the course of the demonstration. "Well, you know," Rudolf commented, "if it wasn't so deeply sad, one should really write a satire about it."

After seven days of gruelling sessions, it was time for Rudolf to formulate his own "Conclusion" before the judges. He began by recalling the principles he had upheld as a publisher and insisted that none of the books he had published denied human rights to others, proposed or justified it, which did not rule out that he had edited texts with which he disagreed. He claimed to have acted along the lines of an idea attributed to Voltaire, who would have written: "I detest what you say, but I will defend to the death your right to say it". It appears that the attribution of the quote to Voltaire is erroneous, as acknowledged in a footnote in *Resistance is Obligatory*. We will, however, take the opportunity to quote another thought also attributed to Voltaire, which Rudolf himself could perhaps have used: "To find out who dominates you, simply find out who you cannot criticise". On his vital need to express himself in freedom, we highlight this fragment of the Conclusion:

> "Professor Faurisson once said that he is like a bird whose nature is to sing. Even if he were locked up in a cage, he would still sing. And this is also my way of being. It is part of my character, my personality, yes, it is even in my genes that I cannot keep my mouth shut, that I have to express my opinion, in particular if I think I discover an injustice. In this case nothing will shut me up. Just as a black man can't help being black, I can't help speaking my mind. Punishing this is as unjust as punishing a black man for the fact that he is black".

Addressing the presiding judge, Matthias Schwab, he reminded him that a retired colleague of his, Günther Bertram, former president of the District Court, had expressed in an article in a legal weekly, *Neuen Juristischen Wochenschrift*, all the problems related to paragraph 130 of the Criminal Code. Rudolf read the text in full before the court, since, he said, it was an article written by an expert who "clearly emphasised the unconstitutional nature of the law under which he was being prosecuted." He expressed, however, his disagreement with Bertram's opinion on the Shoah, which he said justified the German taboo on Auschwitz, and also disagreed with Federal Interior Minister Wolfgang Schäuble, who had not only justified the taboo, but, unlike Bertram, had supported its judicial implementation. Schäuble, who had been interior minister twice: from April 1989 to October 1991 and from November 2005 to October 2009, was appointed by Angela Merkel as finance minister of the Federal Republic of Germany on 28 October 2009, a position he held until 24 October 2017. Since he is a key figure in the economic policy of the European Union, it is of interest to know the text of Minister Schäuble that Rudolf quoted before the magistrates who were trying him, published in the *Frankfurter Allgemeine Zeitung* on 24 April 1996 in the context of an exchange with Ignatz Bubis, then president of the Central Council of Jews in Germany:

> "With regard to whether lying about Auschwitz is a criminal act and with regard to the banning of National Socialist symbols, I will only say this: in an abstract place we could have wonderful discussions about whether it is nonsense or not, from a legal point of view, to repress the expression of opinions. Nevertheless, this is what must be done, because we are simply not acting in an abstract place, but we have had concrete historical experiences. I do not believe that these legal provisions will remain in force for all eternity; but here and now it is right to say, through laws that could be considered problematic from purely legal considerations: there are limits and barriers in this regard and this is where the joke ends."

Rudolf obviously found the text unacceptable and called it "absurd mental censorship". In order to highlight the pseudological nature of the reasoning, he used a text from his book *Kardinalfragen*, published in 1996, which he also read out to the judges:

> "Now everybody knows: the persecution of revisionist historians does not take place for legal reasons, since laws created for the punishment of those who hold fastidious opinions can be qualified as problematic nonsense. On the contrary, some alleged 'historical experiences' must serve as an excuse so that an open debate on precisely those historical experiences can be outlawed. Or to put it another way:
>
> Art. 1: The party is always right.
>
> Art. 2: If ever the party is not right, Article 1 shall automatically apply".

After the appointment, Rudolf indignantly addressed the court, declaring that "the imprisonment of dissident historians was not a problematic nonsense but an outright crime" and asked the judges to review the passages in the Criminal Code which spoke of the persecution of innocent people and of illegal imprisonment. He then recalled that on 3 May 1993, after the publication of the *Rudolf Report*, the director of the Max Planck Institute, Dr. Arndt Simon, informed him of the following in a personal conversation:

> "Every era has its taboos. Even we researchers have to respect the taboos of our time. We Germans must not touch this issue (the extermination of

the Jews), others have to do this. We have to accept that we, Germans, have less rights than others".

Drawing parallels between his situation and that of Galileo Galilei occupied the final part of his speech. One was born in 1564, the other four hundred years later, in 1964. Neither was able to take his final university exam. Both had had two daughters and a son. Both were scientists and authors. In both cases the main work was a 500-page volume that had been banned, confiscated and burned for the same reason: to reject a dogma of their time that subverted the claim of infallibility of powerful groups. Both had been tried and convicted for denying the dogma and both had lost their freedom. Germar Rudolf's lengthy speech ended with the following words:

> "In my opinion this trial is not really about me and my books. This trial is a turning point. It will be decided here whether it will be possible in the future to maintain or regain a leading position in Germany on the intellectual, cultural and scientific level, or whether Germany will remain on a second- or third-rate level. It is up to you to decide. Therefore, all I can do at the end of my statement is to call upon you:
>
> Gentlemen, grant us freedom of thought!' (from Schiller in *Don Carlos*)
>
> And following Martin Luther, I must conclude:
>
> I say all this; I can't do anything else, so help me God!'
>
> Thank you for your attention.

After forty-four months in prison, Germar Rudolf was released on 5 July 2009. When, in 2011, he was finally granted a "green card", the unrestricted permission to join his family in the United States, Rudolf was able to publish *Resistance is Obligatory* there.

Horst Mahler, from radical leftist to Holocaust denier

The case of lawyer Horst Mahler is, like those of Zündel and Rudolf, extraordinary in itself. Mahler began to be persecuted in 2003 for denouncing the hidden lie behind the attacks of 11 September 2001. Years later, in 2006, the first sentences for denying the systematic extermination of the Jews began. Now seventy-three years old, he was sentenced in 2009 to six years in prison, a sentence that was later extended to eleven years. While in prison, probably in 2010, Mahler married the much younger lawyer and close friend Sylvia

Stolz, who was serving time for questioning the Holocaust while defending Ernst Zündel. Sick with diabetes, Horst Mahler's condition steadily worsened in prison due to lack of movement, poor nutrition and inadequate medical treatment, a fact denounced by his son in an open letter. On 29 June 2015, close to his eightieth birthday, he was hospitalised in a critical condition due to septicaemia, a severe infection that can spread throughout the body. To avoid the worst, his foot had to be amputated.

The son of a dentist, Horst Mahler was born in 1936 in Haynau/Schlesien. His father, a convinced National Socialist, committed suicide years after the Americans released him from captivity. With the head of the family gone, in 1949 his family settled in Berlin, where Mahler studied law at the Free University of Berlin. When he managed to set up on his own, he began defending defendants from the left-wing student movement and the extra-parliamentary opposition, APO (Außerparlamentarischen Opposition). In 1969 he defended Andreas Baader and Gudrun Ensslin, accused of setting fire to a department store. In the early 1970s, Horst Mahler was to become the father of the RAF (Red Army Faction), as it was apparently he who persuaded Baader and Ensslin to form a "guerrilla". In March 1970, the West Berlin District Court sentenced him to ten months in prison for his connection with riots outside the Axel Springer building in Berlin. He was granted parole, but in June he was ordered to pay a fine of 75,800 marks for damages to the Axel Springer publishing house. He then decided to flee to Jordan with Ulrike Meinhof, Gudrun Ensslin, Andreas Baader, who had escaped from prison with violence, and other sympathisers of the "Rote Armee Fraktion" (RAF), to join the Palestinian guerrillas. There they intended to train for the armed struggle. On 8 October 1970 Mahler was caught in a trap and arrested in Berlin's Charlottenburg district. He was accused of having planned and participated in the violent escape of Andreas Baader from prison.

It is clear that at this point in his life Horst Mahler had not discovered the true nature of communism and was at the antipodes of understanding the falsification of history and reality. In May 1972, the court trying him could not prove his involvement in Andreas Baader's escape from prison and acquitted him, but he remained imprisoned for other crimes. In October of the same year came the trial in which he was charged with organising and participating in a criminal organisation. On 26 February 1973, he was convicted of founding the RAF, also known as the Baader-Meinhof gang, and for his involvement in some of its violent actions. The sentence of twelve years' imprisonment was much discussed and considered inconsistent in legal circles. In July 1974, Mahler's licence to practise law was withdrawn.

It was in these stormy years that the scandal of the alleged suicide in their cells of the RAF leaders occurred. Andreas Baader, Gudrun Ensslin, Jan-Carl Raspe and Ulrike Meinhof had been arrested in 1972. Meinhof, who had testified at the trial of Horst Mahler, faced very harsh conditions of imprisonment: after her arrest she spent 236 days in total isolation. After two years of preliminary hearings, she was sentenced to eight years' imprisonment on 29 November 1974. On 19 August 1975 Meinhof, Baader, Ensslin and Raspe were jointly charged with four counts of murder, fifty-four counts of attempted murder and forming a criminal organisation. Before the trial was over, on 9 May 1976, Ulrike Meinhof was found dead in her cell in Stammheim prison: she had allegedly hanged herself. At the request of her lawyer, an international enquiry in 1978 tried to get access to the first autopsy report, but the authorities refused. The international commission issued a report stating that "the initial claim that Meinhof had committed suicide had no basis in fact". On 18 October 1977, Andreas Baader and Jan-Carl Raspe had also been found dead in their cells from gunshot wounds, while Gudrun Ensslin had hanged herself by a rope made of speaker wire.

With this overview of Horst Mahler's circle of friends, we can now turn to the transformation that was to turn him into a stubborn Holocaust denier. In July 1979 Mahler was granted an open regime for the remainder of his sentence, and finally in August 1980, after ten years in prison, he was released on parole after condemning terrorism and publicly declaring that he repudiated the methods of the RAF. Interestingly, his lawyer was Gerhard Schröder, who later became Chancellor of Germany. In 1987, his application to be allowed to practise his profession again was rejected; however, again thanks to Schröder's good work, the matter was reconsidered in 1988 and his rights as a lawyer were reinstated.

Over the next ten years, Horst Mahler's thinking underwent profound transformations. Already in 1997 his political ideology had changed. One of the people who most influenced his evolution was Günter Rohrmoser. On 1 December 1997, at Rohrmoser's seventieth birthday celebration, Mahler gave a speech in which he denounced that Germany was an occupied country and that it had to free itself from debt slavery in order to re-establish its national identity. A year later he published an article in the weekly *Junge Freiheit* entitled "Zweite Steinzeit" (Second Stone Age), in which he explained his conversion to the "Völkisch" ideology (anti-materialistic romantic idealism based on the concepts of people, fatherland, blood and tradition). In 2000 he joined the National Democratic Party of Germany, NPD, of which he became an advocate.

By March 2001, he was already well identified with revisionist ideas. Proof of this is that he was among the participants in a conference entitled "Revisionism and Zionism", held in Beirut from 31 March to 3 April 2001. Horst Mahler's name appeared among speakers such as Robert Faurisson; Frederick Töben, PhD, director of the Adelaide Institute in Australia; Mark Weber, director of the IHR; Henri Roques, author of the doctoral thesis on Gerstein's "confessions"; Oleg Platonov, Russian historian; and Roger Garaudy, the French philosopher who like Mahler came from the Marxist camp and who in 1998 had been sentenced by a Paris court to pay a fine of $45,000 for the publication of Gerstein's "Confessions".45,000 for the publication of *The Founding Myths of the State of Israel*. Three of the most powerful Jewish organisations - the World Jewish Congress, the Andifamation League (ADL) and the Simon Wiesenthal Center - with the support of the US government and some members of Congress, lobbied the Lebanese government to ban the meeting. Predictably, the "friends" of freedom of speech and thought succeeded in their aim and the Lebanese authorities announced nine days before the conference was due to start that the conference was cancelled.

As mentioned above, Mahler's persecution in Germany began because of his denunciation of the attacks of 11 September 2001. In 2003 he was charged with "disturbing the public order" and "inciting the people". Mahler testified in court that it was not true that Al-Qaeda had anything to do with the attacks. In 2004 he was charged with disseminating videos and other documents denying the Holocaust. In 2006 the German authorities withdrew his passport to prevent him from attending the "International Conference for the Global Review of the Holocaust" in Tehran, about which we will report more when we discuss the persecution of Professor Faurisson. In 2007, new charges were brought against him as a result of a lengthy interview for *Vanity Fair* magazine on 4 October at the Kempinski Hotel at Munich airport. It was published on 1 November 2007 and the author of the interview, Michel Friedman, former vice-president of the Central Council of Jews in Germany, denounced Mahler on the grounds that he had given him a Hitlerian arm wave and shouted "Heil Hitler, Herr Friedman! Friedman portrayed the interviewee as a demented Nazi who inspired the German far right with his anti-Semitic theories and who had prevented the banning of the NPD when he was its lawyer. During the interview, Mahler told the Jewish journalist that the alleged extermination of the Jews in Auschwitz was a lie. As a result of Friedman's complaint, Mahler was sentenced to six months in prison without bail on 23 November 2007.

In February 2009, the international news agency Associated Press reported that Horst Mahler, a seventy-three-year-old neo-Nazi who in 1970 had been the founder of the Red Army Faction, an extreme left-wing terrorist group, had been sentenced to six years in prison. He had been charged with publishing Holocaust denial videos on the internet and distributing CDs inciting anti-Jewish hatred and violence. Mahler, whose experience as a lawyer meant that he knew he could expect nothing from the court, did not waste time during the trial trying to excuse himself or seeking mitigation, but began his intervention by filing a lawsuit against himself. Upon hearing him, Judge Martin Rieder, who presided over the court in Munich, described his words as "nationalistic squawking". According to the Associated Press, Judge Rieder accused him of "using the court to spread his message of hate." In his hour-long address, Mahler reaffirmed that "the Holocaust was the biggest lie in history" and had words of admiration for English Catholic Bishop Richard Williamson, who in a recent interview on Swedish television had denied the extermination of the Jews.

Rieder's indignation at Mahler's arrogance and defiance caused him to increase the sentence by one year over the statutory maximum of five years in his sentence of 21 February 2009. To justify himself, the judge explained that the defendant was "stubborn and impossible to re-educate". Of the verdict, the Simon Wiesenthal Center in Jerusalem said, "It reinforces the message that there is no tolerance for Holocaust denial and seriously reminds the courts that they must not allow themselves to be used by deniers to propagate their lies." Three weeks later, on 11 March 2009, the sentence was extended by four years and nine months by a court in Potsdam, which, considering Mahler's advanced age, amounted to a life sentence. Once again Mahler had denied the Holocaust and questioned many of the war crimes attributed to Germany.

Horst Mahler had chosen to bring charges against himself before the Munich court in order to set an example to the civil disobedience movement that was forming in Germany. Many of his supporters, however, understood that he would be more useful out of prison. "Why are you doing this?" they had asked him, unable to understand what they disapproved of. To answer them, Mahler managed to write a text for public opinion before his imprisonment. In it, which is considered a kind of political testament, he tried to make it clear that it was not only the right to express an opinion that was at stake, but also the right to survival:

> "If one realises, as I do, that the religion of the Holocaust is the main weapon for the moral and cultural destruction of the German nation, then it becomes clear that what is at stake here is nothing more and nothing less than the collective right to self-defence, i.e. Germany's right to survive. Does the world really believe that we Germans will submissively allow ourselves to be destroyed as a People, that we will passively allow our national spirit to be extinguished without a fight? What jurists can argue that self-defence is a criminal act? As a People and as a collective entity we have a national and spiritual nature. The surest way to end Germany as a spiritual entity is to destroy our national soul and our identity, so that we will never know who or what we are. Destroying our national spirit is precisely the purpose of our enemy in demanding that we unquestioningly accept his Holocaust dogma and give up emphasising that his fantastic Holocaust never happened. There is no evidence of it! Once we grasp the fact that we face the threat of annihilation, we will have no doubt who our enemy is: it is the old nation-killer. If we understand this, we will no longer passively accept his lies and misrepresentations."

As can be seen, Mahler resolutely called for resistance as an existential necessity for Germany. Part of the text was devoted to explaining the years of armed struggle of the Rote Armee Fraktion (RAF). Mahler explained that he and his comrades intended then to fight against "the System" and that they believed what "the System" had taught them in schools about the Holocaust. He admits that they even "bought" the anti-German propaganda spread by the Americans. His realisation, it transpires from this writing, came in 2001 when he had to defend as a lawyer Frank Rennicke, a patriotic singer-songwriter who had been charged and convicted of Holocaust denial. As a result of taking on Rennicke's defence, he began an investigation that set him on the path to a new understanding of the historical facts. Let us look at another excerpt from Mahler's political testament:

> "It is clear that the victors or the victor of World War II (the only real victor was international Jewry) went to great lengths to ensure that the basis of Jewish domination, primarily the religious cult of the Holocaust, would be legally irrefutable. This was their goal when they created the Federal Republic, and it is clear that the Supreme Court long ago adopted a judiciary designed to perpetuate the Holocaust. The mission to protect the Holocaust underlies both the Basic Law and the Federal Republic. This is the basis of Germany's domination by its enemies. German Foreign Minister Joschka Fischer explained this very clearly when he referred to the Holocaust and the support of Israel as the raison d'être of the Federal Republic."

In his writing, Mahler appealed to his compatriots to resist and to regain a sense of pride in being German. He reaffirmed his conviction that what he had done was the best he could do, and acknowledged that fighting alone and depending on himself, he could do nothing but "repeat the truth over and over again", since he had left a promise on the internet that he would "never cease to repeat this truth". As for the eleven years in prison he was about to face, he admitted that with his seventy-three years behind him anything could happen, a fact he took on board with a phrase from the Gospel of St. Matthew: "Whoever is not willing to take up his cross is not worthy of me." Mahler finally showed his hope in the power and strength of the Church. Despite lamenting that its leadership had been corrupted and undermined by the Jews, he was confident that it "could be the rock on which the ship of the Great Lie could crash and disappear." The text ended with the conviction that only truth would bring freedom:

> "I wanted to give an example. I have often said that ours is the easiest revolution that could ever be made. We need only a few thousand people to stand up and speak the truth clearly as Bishop Williamson has done and as I have tried to do, along with others who have suffered prosecution for speaking the truth and distributing Germar Rudolf's *Lectures on the*

Holocaust. The ultimate victory of truth is inevitable, as is the defeat of the global Zionist empire."

Having examined the absolute control of nations and peoples through the economy, the media and co-opted politicians, and having seen what is happening in the courts of justice in Germany and other European countries, the idea of a revolution, the "easiest ever", of thousands of people shouting the truth does not seem right. It must be admitted that only by means of absolute power can the courts of a country be forced to proceed as they do in the Federal Republic of Germany. Whichever way you look at it, it is aberrant for a defendant to say in court that he is not lying, that he has proof that he is telling the truth, that he wants to show it, and for the judges to reply that they do not want to see this proof, because he has denied the Holocaust. The perversion reaches delirious heights when you consider that when the defence lawyer tries to prove that his client is telling the truth, he is warned that his actions are illegal, that he will be incapacitated and that he will go to prison. Specifically, the judge who removed Sylvia Stolz from Ernst Zündel's defence told her that he could understand a defendant behaving as Zündel did, but that it was then the lawyer's duty to tell his client that what he was doing was illegal. This is the monstrous formula for Holocaust justice.

Two years after Horst Mahler's imprisonment, Kevin Käther, a young German revisionist who wanted to follow his example, and his lawyer Wolfram Nahrath organised a demonstration outside the Brandenburg prison, some eighty kilometres from Berlin, where Mahler was incarcerated. The aim was to demand his release, that of Sylvia Stolz and the repeal of Article 130 of the Criminal Code. Käther, too, had pleaded guilty in court and, despite having received a 20-month sentence in 2010, had surprisingly been granted parole. On 26 March 2011, around three hundred people gathered in the prison car park, including revisionists who had travelled from France, Belgium, Great Britain, Austria, Switzerland, Japan and elsewhere in Germany.

Lawyer Nahrath addressed the demonstrators to let them know that the event was authorised from noon until 4 p.m. He then read out a moving text in which he described Mahler as an idealist, a freedom fighter. He then read a moving text in which he described Mahler as an idealist, a freedom fighter. Wolfram Nahrath denounced the hypocrisy of so-called democracies, which condemn the repression of human rights in China while imprisoning their own dissidents for thought crimes. As an example of double standards, he recalled that while Horst Mahler was serving an inhuman sentence for a man of his age, the Nobel Peace Prize had been awarded to the Chinese dissident Liu Xiaobo. Dr Rigolf Hennig and Ursula Haverbeck, both of "Europäische Aktion", also spoke. Haverbeck, recently sentenced to eighteen months despite being almost ninety years old, said with extraordinary lucidity that Germany "had been deeply wounded" and that the BRD (Bundesrepublik Deutschland) "was not the state of the German people". British politician Richard Edmonds spoke on behalf of a group of British revisionists and described what was happening not only in Germany but in the European Union as "scandalous" and "cynical". Lady Michèle Renouf, a well-known English revisionist model who runs the website *Jailing Opinions*, was the last to speak.

In January 2013 Horst Mahler had finished writing in prison a book that will never be published, but which can be read in German in PDF format, *Das Ende der Wanderschaft. Gedanken über Gilad Atzmon un die Judenheit (The End of the Walk. Reflections on Gilad Atzmon and Jewry)*. The work had been born after reading a book sent to the prison by a friend, *The Wandering Who?*, a work published in 2011 by Gilad Atzmon, an anti-Zionist Jewish dissident exiled in London [5]. Mahler's book consisted of a series of historical

---

[5] We could write a long article about Gilad Atzmon, for he deserves to be known and recognised. Born in Tel Aviv in 1963, after living through the war in Lebanon in 1982 as a Tsahal soldier, Atzmon became a friend of the Palestinian people and an activist for their cause. In 1994 he emigrated to the UK and became a British citizen in 2002. After studying philosophy at the University of Essex, he became known for his activities as a jazz saxophonist. Because of his criticism of Zionism and his revisionist views on the Holocaust, he is considered an anti-Semite and many of his Zionist enemies accuse him of being "a Jew who hates himself for being Jewish". His discography now consists of more than a dozen titles, including the CD *Exile*, released in 2004 and considered album of the year by the BBC. It is a moving work in which almost all the tracks, including *Jenin, Al Quds* and *Land of Canaan*, refer to the suffering of the Palestinian people. Two Palestinians, musician Dhafer Youssef and singer Reem Kelani, collaborated with Gilad Atzmon on this album. Before publishing *The Wandering Who*, Atzmon had already written two other books. The present work is an investigation of contemporary Jewish identity politics and ideology. Among the many topics

considerations on the contents of Atzmon's book, to whom in the foreword dated 3 January 2013 he expressed his heartfelt thanks for his honesty and courage: "May God grant him long life, health and creative strength. The world needs Gilad Atzmon - and know: not only one Gilad Atzmon, but many Gilad Atzmons are needed. Two years later, on 11 June 2015, the Federal Department for Materials Harmful to Young People in Germany included Horst Mahler's book on the list of harmful books. Among the people who at 11.30 a.m. on 11 June appeared before the Department's board to argue that Mahler's work should not be banned were the parish priest Friedrich Bode and Gerard Menuhin, son of the famous Jewish-born violinist Yehudi Menuhin and author of *Tell the Truth and Shame the Devil*, in which he considers the Holocaust to be a huge historical lie.

At the end of June 2015, only a few days after the book was banned, Horst's son Axel Mahler wrote a letter to the parson Friedrich Bode to inform him that his father was in a critical condition in the ICU. Four years had passed since the demonstration in Brandenburg in favour of Horst Mahler, and the "revolution of thousands of people shouting out the truth" had still not taken place. Of course, a few hundred meant nothing to the German authorities, who were also oblivious to the desperate prison situation of the revisionist dissident. Axel Mahler explained to Bode in his letter that his father's diabetes had not been adequately treated and that he was suffering from a severe infection which made him fear for his life. Therefore, he said, they were considering "taking legal action against the judicial authorities for keeping him imprisoned".

On 4 July 2015 Ursula Haverbeck wrote to Prof. Dr. Andreas Voßkuhle of the German Supreme Court, demanding in a very severe and critical tone that he consider the suffering of the lawyer and philosopher Horst Mahler and that the German judiciary no longer submit to the dictates of Israel, represented by the "Zentralrates der Juden in Deutschland" (Central Council of Jews in Germany). With great courage and risk-taking, she referred to the Holocaust as "the biggest and most persistent lie in history" and wrote: "Eine Untat ohne

---

critically examined are the hatred of Jewish racists towards gentiles and the role played by the religion of the Holocaust.

Tatort ist keine Tatsache" (A crime without a crime scene is not a reality). Ursula Haverbeck concluded by pleading for swift action before it was too late. On 14 July 2015, the press reported that Horst Mahler's left foot had been amputated and that he was in a stable condition after the operation. After the operation, Mahler remained incarcerated. Increasingly distressed, in October 2015 he finally decided to ask for help in a desperate note:

> "Dear friends, for a long time I have doubted whether I should ask for help. But now my life is in danger. My left leg has been amputated and the doctors are trying to prevent further amputations. Finally, a lawyer has agreed to defend me in court. However, since I am financially ruined, I cannot afford it. Moreover, the implementation of my parole has to be financed. If I were to get out of prison, some renovations to my house would be necessary to allow for the life of an invalid.
>
> Please help! Thank you in advance!
>
> Horst Mahler."

A few days after the publication of this petition, on 6 October 2015 some media outlets published the news that Horst Mahler, who was about to turn eighty years old, had been released from Brandenburg prison, where he had spent almost seven years incarcerated for a thought crime.

On 6 April 2017, at the age of 81, Mahler received notification from the public prosecutor's office that he was to return to prison on 19 April to serve the remaining three and a half years (1,262 days) of his sentence. Faced with this prospect, Horst Mahler gave a lecture on 16 April in which he denounced the Jewish plot for the last time. On 19 April, after recording a short video explaining why he was unwilling to return to prison, he took a risky decision: he fled to Viktor Orbán's Hungary in order to seek "asylum in a sovereign state". There, he was arrested in Sopron on 15 May. The Budapest public prosecutor cited an EAW (European Arrest Warrant) to justify the arrest. On 6 June a Budapest court ordered that he should be handed over and a week later the police of the "sovereign state" put him on a plane to Germany. We have learned from a report by Lady Michèle Renouf that at the end of October 2018 Mahler's life was in danger. After collapsing in his cell, he was in the detention section of the Brandenburg Municipal Hospital, admitted with pneumonia and a process of necrosis.

Sylvia Stolz, the uncompromising lawyer

What happened to the lawyer Sylvia Stolz has become clearer as we have narrated the vicissitudes of Zündel and Mahler. In any case, what happened to this brave woman is worthy of a proper place in our *Proscribed History*. We shall begin her unhappy "adventure" in December 2005, when she was a defence lawyer in the trial of Dr. Rigolf Hennig, a medical colonel in the reserves accused of having disparaged the "Bundesrepublik" in the newspaper *Reichsboten*, which he himself published. Hennig was accused of denying the legitimacy of the Federal Republic. On Monday, 12 December, prosecutor Vogel arrogantly threatened a defence lawyer, Sylvia Stolz. Vogel warned her that if she continued in her line of defence she would risk being charged with incitement and contempt for the "Bundesrepublik" and that he would not hesitate to prosecute her. Instead of being intimidated, the lawyer expressed gratitude to Vogel because, she told him, "by his attitude he was reinforcing his thesis that the trial was a show trial". Stolz expressed her opinion that it was not German law that was being applied, but the will of a foreign ruling power.

In the course of the trial, which lasted until almost the end of December 2005, Sylvia Stolz demonstrated commendable competence, citing texts by Jewish intellectuals such as Harold Pinter, who had just been awarded the Nobel Prize for literature, and Gilad Atzmon, whom we introduced earlier. Atzmon had just given a lecture in Bochum on 2 December 2005, in which he had publicly stated that the history of World War II and the Holocaust was "an absolute falsification initiated by the Americans and the Zionists". Stolz also quoted texts from Germar Rudolf's *Lectures on the Holocaust* and predicted that this work would "nip the Holocaust religion in the bud". In the end, Dr. Hennig was sentenced to six months in prison for denigrating the Federal Republic.

Almost simultaneously with the trial of the medical colonel Rigolf Hennig, the Mannheim court that was to try Ernst Zündel had already begun preparatory preliminary hearings. Sylvia Stolz, whose experience and expertise in matters of nationalism and the persecution of revisionists were well known, was part of the team of lawyers chosen to defend Zündel, which also included Jürgen Rieger and the Austrian Herbert Schaller. Sylvia Stolz was assisted by the lawyer

Horst Mahler. The first hearing took place on Tuesday, 8 November 2005. More than thirty journalists and about eighty Zündel supporters, some from Canada, France, the United Kingdom and Switzerland, gathered at the Mannheim courthouse, famous for its anti-revisionist fervour.

As soon as he had pronounced the name, date of birth, profession and address of the accused, the presiding judge, Ulrich Meinerzhagen, proceeded to attack the team of lawyers from the defence. He read out the decision of a local Berlin court prohibiting Horst Mahler from practising his profession. Meinerzhagen quoted at length from Mahler's revisionist statements and comments relating to the Jewish question and the Reich. He then demanded that he be replaced as assistant to lawyer Stolz, who immediately pointed out that there was no reason. The judge insisted that he understood Mahler's influence on the defence to be considerable, to which Stolz replied that it was up to him to determine which writings he would use in his defence and that this was all his responsibility. The judge threatened to forcibly remove Mahler and detain him for a day. Lawyer Rieger then intervened to tell the judge that such attacks on the defence did not occur even in the Gulag. Sylvia Stolz insisted that she would not give up the assistance of lawyer Mahler; but without further words the judge ordered the policemen to take him away. Seeing that she could do no more, Stolz opted to take the decision to remove her assistant herself, which made it possible for her to sit in the audience, which was clearly shocked. Meinerzhagen then threatened to clear the room.

Further intimidating warnings for the team of lawyers followed: the presiding judge made it clear that any "incitement to hatred" would be vigorously dealt with and directly threatened the lawyers with the application of paragraph 130 of the Criminal Code. He then pointed out that he would not listen to "pseudo-scientific views, since the Holocaust was a historically verified fact". This statement provoked uproar and laughter from the audience. It did not end there, as Judge Meinerzhagen was just warming up. He immediately went back on the attack and said that he was not sure that Sylvia Stolz was suitable for Zündel's defence, as she would probably end up being guilty of the violation of paragraph 130. Zündel made it clear that he wished to be represented by Ms. Stolz. The court then decided to adjourn to deliberate on the matter.

After deliberation, the court annulled the appointment of Stolz as Zündel's first lawyer. Dr. Meinerzhagen then added that Jürgen Rieger was not a suitable lawyer for the defendant either, since his revisionist views were well known and it was to be feared that he might proceed inappropriately in this matter. In order to give the entire defence team its share, the judge then turned to Dr. Schaller, whom he also considered unsuitable because of his age, which did not guarantee his suitability for the job. It became clear to everyone that the presiding judge intended to eliminate Ernst Zündel's brilliant team of lawyers in order to appoint others of his own choice. Naturally, the lawyers tried not to be intimidated. After Sylvia Stolz had been reproved as Zündel's lead counsel, Judge Meinerzhagen asked how the defendant was going to settle the case. Zündel declared that he would dispense with his third lawyer of choice (Ludwig Bock, who was not attending the hearing) and Sylvia Stolz would take his place[6]. On this occasion, the lunch break served as a pretext for interrupting the session.

In the afternoon, lawyer Rieger read a text in which he asked the court to abandon the discriminatory attitude. This was followed by Sylvia Stolz, who stated that the defence was being publicly threatened not to say anything forbidden by the court and that this was an outrage that could only be the result of a sick mind. Stolz then requested that the public be excluded from future sessions, arguing that the court was threatening to prosecute the defence for violation of paragraph 130 of the Criminal Code (this paragraph is only applicable when the "crime" is committed in public. By excluding the public, the defence intended to be able to express "forbidden thoughts" before the court without running the risk of prosecution). The lawyer added that if the court wanted the trial to be public, the defence team would be in grave danger of persecution. The court's

---

[6] Since we are not lawyers, we are not competent to explain the functioning of German courts. It appears, in any case, that in regional courts German law requires the defendant to have a lawyer with specific powers authorised by the court and may have three more lawyers of his choice. In the case of the trial against Ernst Zündel, it was Sylvia Stolz who had these specific legal powers, which were overruled by the presiding judge.

response was to adjourn the proceedings until Tuesday 15 November 2005.

For the objective press and the public there was no doubt that presiding judge Meinerzhagen had tried to destroy Ernst Zündel's defence. Moreover, by threatening the lawyers before they had even begun their defence, the judge had violated basic rules of judicial procedure. Sylvia Stolz had developed a brilliant strategy, maintaining a calm attitude and a perfectly proper demeanour throughout. If the court decided that the trial should not be public, the judges would be confronted with the evidence contained in Germar Rudolf's *Lectures on the Holocaust* and Horst Mahler's request to "hear evidence on the Jewish question", which could be burdensome for the court, which would have to explain why a secret trial was being held. In the event of an open trial, the defenders had been threatened with prosecution, thus embarrassing the Mannheim court in the eyes of public opinion and jurists around the world.

At 10.00 a.m. on 15 November 2005, a hundred or so supporters of Ernst Zündel had gathered outside the building. However, there were fewer journalists and only two cameras. At 10.40 a.m., access to the hall was granted and it was packed. Zündel's entrance was greeted with a round of applause. As soon as the judge appeared, he said he would tolerate neither applause nor rumours and warned that he had ordered the police to remove those who broke his rules and take their names. He then found the claim that the court had adopted a discriminatory attitude to be unfounded and stated that there was no reason for the accused to have any doubts about the judges. Secondly, he corroborated his disapproval of Sylvia Stolz and repeated the reasons given in the previous session. Meinerzhagen insisted that Ms. Stolz was not suitable because she could not guarantee an orderly procedure, which would lead to conflicts between the defendant and the defence. The presiding judge rejected Ms. Stolz's request to exclude the public from the hearings. He stated that the public could only be excluded if it posed a threat, which was not the case. On the contrary, he claimed that it was the defence that posed a threat to the trial because of its intention to incite the public. Meinerzhagen added that it was to be expected that, if the public were absent, the defence would make inciting applications and submissions. Without giving any choice, the magistrate's next move was to announce that he was suspending the trial, as the court had to replace Ms. Stolz and the new lawyer would need time to familiarise himself with the materials. In the meantime, the defendant should remain in prison, which he considered fair, given the magnitude of his crime. To top it all off, Dr. Meinerzhagen claimed that the trial had been adjourned because of the defence.

At this point, Jürgen Rieger expressed his disagreement and stated that the judge had not informed the defence of his intention to suspend the court proceedings, which he was obliged to do. Rieger claimed that the defence had not had the opportunity to prepare a statement on this decision. The judge replied that the defence had indeed been informed, which was a blatant lie. After a procedural battle over what decisions to make, Sylvia Stolz found the time to ask the court to allow her to make a statement about her substitution; but Meinerzhagen replied that this was not appropriate. Stolz retorted by telling the judge that his attitude was improper and out of place. "The trial is adjourned," the judge insisted. "I haven't had a chance to make my statement," the lawyer complained. "I don't care! The trial is adjourned!"

In little more than an hour the presiding judge had settled the matter. Naturally, the public reacted with indignation and shouts of protest and disapproval were uttered, such as "this is a carnival", "scandal", and the like. Outside the courtroom, Zündel's lawyers and close friends met to assess what had happened and came to the conclusion that the trial would resume in February or March 2006 and that the judge would pursue the defence as soon as he began his proceedings. These events coincided with Germar Rudolf's arrival at Frankfurt airport, where he was arrested and immediately taken to Stuttgart prison.

As the lawyers had predicted, the trial resumed in February 2006. On Thursday, the 15th, Ulrich Meinerzhagen rejected three defence motions to exclude himself on the grounds of biased or tendentious views. As for Sylvia Stolz, he threatened to charge her if she questioned the Holocaust. The session on the 16th saw a serious confrontation between Stolz and Meinerzhagen. The lawyer interrupted on several occasions and raised a battery of objections and new requests. He denied that she had insulted the court and tried to sabotage the trial, accusations made by the judge. Specifically, Meinerzhagen said she suspected that Stolz "intended to make the judicial process impossible by causing the trial to collapse". He further announced that he would file a complaint with the relevant bar association requesting that action be taken against her. Instead of submitting, Stolz replied that she was "not prepared to bend to his will" and, turning to the room full of Zündel supporters, accused Meinerzhagen of wanting to "gag" her. The situation became extremely tense when the lawyer ignored the judge's demand for an apology. Meinerzhagen fined three Zündel supporters for singing banned verses of Germany's national anthem and sent another to jail for four days for insulting him. Lawyer Ludwig Bock then intervened, telling the court that he needed to study the authorship of dozens of statements and texts, mostly from *The Zündelsite*, submitted by the prosecutors. The presiding judge adjourned the trial again for three weeks so that the lawyers could analyse the publications in *The Zündelsite*.

On 9 March 2006, the sessions began again and the confrontation that was to be the ruination of Sylvia Stolz and the end of her career as a lawyer finally took place. At the height of her outrage, Stolz declared that the court "was an instrument of foreign domination" and described Jews as "enemies of the people". The judge requested the withdrawal of Silvya Stolz's trial and adjourned the hearing again. On 31 March, a higher court in Karlsruhe removed Sylvia Stolz from the case for her illegal obstruction of the proceedings "with the sole aim of sabotaging the trial and making it a farce". Despite this verdict, on 5 April, Stolz disregarded the Karlsruhe ruling, which she considered to be without legal force, and appeared at the Mannheim court of justice. Judge Meinerzhagen ordered her to leave the courtroom, but she refused to obey. Two policewomen had to force her out, at which point the lawyer shouted, "Resistance! The German people are revolting!" Some of Zündel's supporters also left the courtroom. For the umpteenth time, the presiding judge suspended the trial, which was not to resume until June 2006.

The sentence of three and a half years' imprisonment and five years' disqualification from practising her profession came in January 2008. Sylvia Stolz was convicted by a Mannheim court, which found that she had incited racial hatred during the defence of Ernst Zündel. The verdict stated that the defendant had denied the Holocaust and declared that the extermination of European Jews during World War

II was "the biggest lie in history". Sylvia Stolz served her imprisonment in three different facilities. When three hundred people gathered on 26 March 2011 in front of the Brandenburg prison where Horst Mahler was serving his sentence, most of the banners showed the same solidarity for Sylvia Stolz, whose imminent release was eagerly awaited at the time.

When she left Aichach prison in Bavaria at 9.00 a.m. on Wednesday 13 April 2011, a large group of international freedom of expression lawyers and supporters from France, Italy and Great Britain were waiting for her at the main gate to celebrate her release with flowers and gifts. Among them was Michèle Renouf, who had once again travelled from England to show solidarity with the revisionist lawyer. Sylvia Stolz emerged to applause, laden with a large number of written documents, carefully accumulated and organised during her years of captivity. After loading the material into a van, they all went together to a nearby tavern, where Günter Deckert had reserved the main room for the celebration.

On 24 November 2012, twenty months after her release, Sylvia Stolz gave a lecture in Chur, capital of the Swiss canton of Graubünden, entitled in German: *Sprechverbot-Beweisverbot-Verteidigunsverbot. Die Wirklichkeit der Meinungsfreiheit* (*Prohibition of expression-prohibition of evidence-prohibition of legal defence. The reality of freedom of thought*). This was the 8th Conference of the "Anti-Zensur-Koalition" (AZK). The conference organiser, Ivo Sasek, introduced Sylvia Stolz as a person uniquely qualified to speak on the subject and referred to her experience of the trial of Ernst Zündel, his arrest in the court of justice and his conviction. The presentation ended with these words: "Welcome Sylvia Stolz. If you were not allowed to speak there, we will let you speak here. We trust that you know your limitations. I am sure you do.

After thanking Ivo Sasek and the audience of more than two thousand people for their warm welcome, Stolz delivered a well-structured, calm speech without reading at any point, appropriately seasoned with eloquent silences. His voice, extremely warm and as soft as a child's, maintained a calm and serene tone throughout his speech, which was rigorous in its legal terminology, extremely sensible and entirely convincing. The lecture, delivered in German, can be viewed on You Tube with English subtitles. Of course, for reasons of space we cannot reproduce it in its entirety, but we will give a few outlines. In her presentation, Sylvia Stolz gave the audience a very beautiful thought by Johann Gottfried von Herder, which in her opinion embodied the essence of all human beings: "To believe in truth, to feel beauty and to love what is good".

The principles that should govern the functioning of any court of law worthy of the name took up the first part of the lecture: the rights of the accused and the obligations of the court to avoid their defencelessness and to establish the truth at through evidence. In relation to the need to present evidence, he drew a comparison with the evidence that courts usually require in murder cases, i.e. where it took place, when it was committed, what weapons the criminal used, possible fingerprints, where the victim's body was found, forensic analysis to determine the cause of death, etc. However, Stolz insisted, in none of the "Holocaust denial" cases has any of this specific evidence ever been proven or presented:

> "There are no details regarding the crime scene, the method of murder, the number of victims, the time period of the crimes, the perpetrators, the bodies. We have no physical traces of the murder. The testimonies do not specify, there are no documents or similar evidence. The intention to exterminate all or part of Jewry during the National Socialist regime has not been proven anywhere. There are no documents proving prior decisions, plans or orders. When there are trials of Holocaust deniers, we do not find these things specified. Nor do we find references to other verdicts in which these things are specified. This is the problem. As long as the court does not record the crime scenes where the alleged mass killings are supposed to have taken place; as long as the court does not claim at least one specific piece of evidence; as long as this is the case, these mass murders simply cannot be proven."

At another point, Sylvia Stolz read out to the audience an embarrassing excerpt from the verdict of the Auschwitz trials that took place in Frankfurt. In it, the lawyer said ironically, one might expect some specification of details of the Holocaust. These are the words of the court:

> "The court lacks almost all the means of evidence of a normal murder trial, necessary to get a true picture of the facts at the time of the crime. There were no bodies of the victims, no autopsy reports, no expert reports on the causes and time of death, no evidence on the murderers, on the

murder weapons, etc. Verification of the witnesses' testimonies was only possible on rare occasions..... Therefore, in order to clarify the crimes of the defendants, the court relied almost exclusively on the testimony of witnesses...".

Drawing on her own experience, Stolz complained that, by contrast, when evidence was presented on behalf of a Holocaust denier and the court was asked to establish that such and such was true because it had been corroborated by expert reports, then the court would not admit the evidence and the lawyers were accused of Holocaust denial. Sylvia Stolz lamented that the European public knew nothing about the treatment of defendants, about the threats and punishments that lawyers suffered just for doing their job, and about the way in which the administration of justice in German courts was aborted. He gave as an example his own case, when a Bavarian court decided to withdraw his licence:

"I presented evidence in relation to the alleged 'obviousness' of the Holocaust. Once again the evidence was not admitted and the reason given was that the court, in the light of available books and photos, had no doubt about the 'obviousness' of the Holocaust. Both I and my lawyer asked the court to point out which books and which photos gave them such certainty as to the 'obviousness' of the Holocaust. These requests were rejected because: 'the Holocaust and the violent crimes of the National Socialists against the Jews were obvious'. Therefore, we were given no answer as to what materials formed the basis of the court's finding. All we got were general references to 'newspapers, radio and television, encyclopaedias, dictionaries and history books'."

After recalling the most disappointing moments of her experience with Judge Meinerzhagen during the trial against Ernst Zündel, Sylvia Stolz ended the lecture by returning to the sentence from Herder with which she had begun her speech. These were her final words:

"I will now return to the phrase with which I began this lecture. Believing in truth, feeling beauty and loving what is good' implies the ability to identify and label lies, the ability to identify the inhuman, the ability to identify and label injustice. It also involves character traits, which is of particular importance at our age. The knowledge of our immortality, of our constancy and incorruptibility. With this character we should be able to shape a world for the many children who were here earlier today. A world in which we are allowed to tell the truth without punishment."

In January 2013, a Jewish lawyer from Bern, Daniel Kettiger, filed a criminal complaint against Sylvia Stolz with the public prosecutor's office in Graubünden. Kettiger accused Stolz of having violated Article 261 of the Swiss Criminal Code, which relates to a Swiss racial law. Ivo Sasek, the organiser of the AZK event, was also denounced by this lawyer, an uncompromising guardian of censorship. The fact that during the conference Stolz had said that the Holocaust had never been proven in a court of law because the evidence had never been presented was sufficient grounds for criminal charges to be brought against her. On 25 February 2015, a Munich court rejected the arguments of Sylvia Stolz and her lawyer Wolfram Nahrath on the right to exercise freedom of speech in Switzerland and sentenced the lawyer to twenty months in prison for the lecture delivered in Chur in November 2012. Stolz and her lawyer appealed and appealed to the Federal or Constitutional Court (Bundesverfassungsgericht), which issued a final and binding judgment on 15 February 2018. Details of the appeal to the Constitutional Court are explained below in the section on the Schaefer brothers which we have incorporated into this edition. On the morning of 23 May 2019 Sylvia Stolz was arrested at her home and remanded in prison to serve a final sentence of eighteen months. At the time of writing, she is still in prison, and we hope that this admirable woman will regain her unjustly taken freedom for the second time.

Günter Deckert, a persistent symbol of freedom of expression

Günter Deckert, leader of the NPD (National Democratic Party of Germany), lost his job as a high school teacher in 1988 because of his political activism. In November 1990 he took part in an event to present Fred Leuchter, at which he declared that the Holocaust was a myth perpetrated by an exploitative group that was using a historical lie to muzzle Germany. In 1991, he also shared a table with historian David Irving at a lecture in Weinheim, Germany. These events earned him a criminal complaint and in 1992 he was sentenced to one year in prison. Deckert was forced to appeal against the verdict, and in March 1994 the Mannheim District Court, which at that time was not yet the court we have seen in the persecution of Ernst Zündel and Sylvia Stolz, ordered a retrial on the grounds that the lower court had failed to prove all the necessary facts.

In the summer of 1994, the trial began again, in which two of the three judges on the tribunal, Wolfgang Müller and Rainer Orlet, had words of sympathy for Deckert. Müller described him as "an intelligent man of character", who acted out of deep convictions. For his part, Judge Rainer Orlet declared that Deckert had "expressed legitimate interests" in questioning the Jews' endless political and economic claims on Germany fifty years after the end of World War II. In a sixty-six-page report, Orlet recalled that while people in Germany were being persecuted for expressing opinions, "mass criminals of other nations remained unpunished." The judge added that Deckert was "not an anti-Semite" and that he had made a good impression on the court as a "responsible person of good character." Nevertheless, the court found Deckert guilty and upheld his one-year prison sentence, but he did not have to go to prison because he was given the opportunity to remain on probation as long as he did not reoffend.

As usual, the howls of protest from Jewish lobby groups were automatic. At the centre of the target was Judge Rainer Orlet, whose opinions were considered Holocaust deniers. Justice Minister Thomas Schäuble was quick to acknowledge that the judge's statement was "a slap in the face of the victims of the Holocaust." On the other hand, the Association of German Judges considered it "a blunder". A parallel trial then began which was to lead to Judge Orlet's voluntary retirement, a decision he took to avoid forced removal from office. On 23 January 1995, Ulrich Maurer, the Baden-Württemberg parliamentary leader of the SPD (Social Democratic Party of Germany), called for Judge Orlet's dismissal for having written a scandalous verdict on Günter Deckert in June 1994. This disciplinary measure was the only way to remove Orlet from the 6th Grand Criminal Division of the Mannheim District Court. Minister Schäuble had to listen to accusations from the CDU (Christian Democratic Union) of double standards and double standards.

On 9 March 1995, the *Berliner Zeitung* published a report that Judge Rainer Olmert himself could end up in the dock. The newspaper commented that the dismissal of Rainer Orlet before the German Constitutional Court would be the first case of the dismissal of a judge in the history of the Federal Republic of Germany. In addition to the judge's voluntary retirement, the campaign led to the retrial of Günter Deckert in April. In December 1995, Deckert was sent to the Bruchsal

Detention Centre in the state of Baden-Wurttenberg with an effective two-year prison sentence for "dangerous political arson".

While serving this two-year sentence, Günter Deckert was again brought to trial because of a letter he wrote from prison to Michel Friedman, vice-president of the Central Council of Jews in Germany. He allegedly asked him to leave Germany. This letter led to a new charge of incitement to racial hatred. A new trial was held in Mannheim and on 12 April 1997 Deckert was sentenced to an additional two years and three months in prison. His lawyer, Ludwig Boch, was fined 9,000 marks for basing his defence on the idea that the Holocaust was a "legend" invented by Jews. David Irving was quick to write a protest text to *The Daily Telegraph*, declaring himself a friend of Deckert's and denouncing the ongoing assault on freedom of expression in Germany.

After spending two years behind bars, instead of being released, Deckert began serving his new sentence on 31 October 1997. The international outcry was barely visible to the public, although letters were received by German embassies in several countries calling for the release of political prisoner Günter Deckert. On 10 December 1998, for example, Rainer Dobbelstein, a senior German official in London, justified in a letter of reply to an outraged Londoner, Milton Ellis, that the tapping of Günter Deckert's correspondence was justified by law because of his extremist views.

In October 2000, the "dangerous neo-Nazi" was released from Bruchsal prison, where he had spent almost five years. Just when it seemed that the revisionist fighter was past the worst, in 2012, at the age of seventy-two, he was once again sentenced to prison. What was Günter Deckert's crime this time? In 2007 he had translated *Auschwitz* into German. *The First Gassings, Rumours and Reality*, a book by Carlo Mattogno published in 1992 in Italian and in 2002 in English. In 2008, on the orders of Mannheim prosecutor Grossmann, the thought police raided his house. It was the twelfth "special visit", as she told a friend in a letter of March 2012. They took her computer and two copies of Mattogno's book. In the summer of 2009, a court in Weinheim, the town where Deckert lived, accepted the indictment. The charges were "promotion and incitement of the public by means of Holocaust denial and defamation of the memory of the dead." On 28 July 2010 Deckert went to trial without a lawyer. A single judge sentenced him to four months, but granted him probation, to be put on probation for a period of three years, and a fine of 600 euros. In addition, he had to pay costs. Both public prosecutor Grossmann, who had asked for six months, and Deckert himself appealed against the verdict. Once again, the case came before the famous Mannheim district court. The retrial began on 14 November 2011 and ended on 2 February 2012 with a verdict sentencing Deckert to six months in prison. In the aforementioned letter, Deckert explains the following to her friend

> "The trial lasted so long because I changed my tactics to make the court understand why I was in favour of revisionism. I offered all the arguments and evidence that could be presented in court without being charged again. At first it seemed that Judge Roos was hesitant about the problem of convicting a person for publicising and disseminating a book. But in the end he seized on the suggestion of prosecutor Grossmann, who said that the possibility of accessing the book via the internet fulfilled the requirements of paragraph 130."

On 2 February 2012, the verdict was delivered and on 6 February the six-month prison sentence was announced. Upon receiving it, Deckert courageously declared: "A prison sentence will not force me to believe." He announced that he would appeal to the court in Karslruhe; but the appeal was dismissed. Finally, on 23 November 2012, the Mannheim Public Prosecutor's Office informed him that at 3 p.m. on 17 December he was to be remanded in prison. Deckert protested vehemently, as he wanted to spend Christmas with his family. For once there was understanding, and his admission was postponed until 2 January 2013. This confirmed a shameful fact: with hardly anyone protesting and without the media denouncing it, an honest and decent person in Germany could be sentenced for translating a history book. Here are the words of Günter Deckert:

> "Friends, comrades and fighters for the truth about the history of World War II, the time has come! Although my constitutional appeal has not yet been decided, I must soon enter prison to serve my five-month sentence. I have to report to prison on 2 January 2013. My release will take place on 2 June.... 'What doesn't kill me makes me stronger!' With this thought in mind, my best regards and comradely loyalty to our relatives and our people. I wish everyone a very good 2013 full of success and the best possible health."

When Sylvia Stolz was released from Aichach prison on 13 April 2011, Günter Deckert had organised a celebratory meal for her in a Bavarian tavern. In February 2013, Stolz, who must surely have known that a Jewish lawyer had denounced her for her lecture in Switzerland, wanted to show solidarity with her friend and published a long article, the English translation of which could be *El terror de opinar (The terror of giving an opinion)*. In it, he broke down the text of the sentence and technically demonstrated all the inconsistencies of the legal process that had been followed against Deckert, whose defencelessness was exposed by the procedural abuses that are common in all Holocaust denial trials.

Udo Walendy, imprisoned for publishing revisionist texts

Born in Berlin in 1927, Udo Walendy, who is approaching his 90th birthday, had time to serve in his country's army before the end of the war. After the war, he studied journalism and political science in Berlin, where he became involved in the publication of revisionist books. In 1956 he graduated in political science and for a time worked as a lecturer at the German Red Cross. As early as 1964 he published his own book *Wahrheit für Deutschland - Die Schuldfrage des Zweitens Weltkriegs* (*The Truth for Germany - The Question of Guilt for the Second World War*). In 1965 he established his own publishing house, "Verlag für Volkstum und Zeitgeschichsforshung" (Publishing House for Contemporary History and Folklore Research). In 1974, ten years after the publication of *Wahrheit für Deutschland*, Udo Walendy founded the journal *Historische Tatsachen* (*Historical Facts*), a serious journal focusing on the rigorous investigation of facts about National Socialism and the Third Reich that official historiography prefers to ignore. In issue 31 of the magazine, for example, he investigated the first Soviet reports on Auschwitz printed on 1 and 2 February in *Pravda*, in which nothing is said about burning pits, gas chambers, piles of shoes and spectacles, piles of dentures or piles of hair.

Udo Walendy's legal problems began in 1979, when the government blacklisted his book as dangerous or harmful material for young people. Walendy engaged in a lengthy legal battle that was to last fifteen years. Finally, in 1994, the Federal Constitutional Court ruled that the author's rights were being violated, since the book was defensible from an academic point of view. Proof of the value of this work is that *The Barnes Review* republished it in 2013 and a year later, on 1 September 2014, Castle Hill Publishers, Germar Rudolf's publisher in the UK, published an updated and corrected reprint of the book, again translated from the German. Also in 1979 Walendy delivered the first lecture of the Institute for Historical Review (IHR), which had been founded in 1978. From 1980 he was a member of the Editorial Advisory Board of the *Journal of Historical Review*, the Institute's prestigious publication. In the United States, he became personally acquainted with Arthur R. Butz, whose landmark work he translated into German and then edited. The book was soon banned by the German authorities. In 1988, Udo Walendy testified in Toronto at the second trial of Ernst Zündel. His revisionist activities also include his close association with the Belgian online magazine *VHO* (*Vrij Historisch Onderzoek*), where many of the books he has published in German can be found.

The persecution of this veteran publicist and revisionist historian took a qualitative leap forward when on 7 February 1996 a squad of twenty policemen raided his residence and his company. Without respecting the "data protection law", they seized documents, disks and downloaded copies of computer files and took Udo Walendy away for fingerprinting. Shortly afterwards, two German courts found that articles in *Historische Tatsachen*, the magazine he edited and published, incited hatred. On 17 May 1996, the Bielefeld District Court sentenced Walendy to fifteen months' effective imprisonment, despite the fact that he had no previous record. The court rejected any consideration of the academic value of the works in question. Half a year later, in November 1996, a Dortmund court fined him 20,000 marks for possessing twelve copies of *Mein Kampf*. Without any evidence, the court found that Walendy was preparing to distribute these copies of Hitler's book, which was banned in Germany: "The planned distribution of the books," the court declared, "manifests an extreme and therefore particularly dangerous mentality. The books are propaganda for the dismantling of the legal and constitutional system of the Federal Republic of Germany and the establishment of a National Socialist injustice system.... This must be judged with all severity."

A year later, in May 1997, another court in Herford finished the job off and sentenced Walendy to an additional fourteen months' imprisonment. Judge Helmut Knöner found that Walendy had not knowingly published lies, but had not offered alternative interpretations. The court quoted a passage from an issue of *Historische Tatsachen* in which Walendy reported approvingly on Fred Leuchter's research on the "gas chambers" at Auschwitz. The judgment said that the quotation from Leuchter's text "lacked critical sense and repeated the alleged findings of the 'expert'. The defendant endorsed them." The court also criticised Walendy for having reproduced in issue No. 66 of the magazine an article published on 13 June 1946 in the Swiss newspaper *Basler Nachrichten*, the title of which was "How high is the number of Jewish victims", discrediting the imposed figure of six million. The Herfod court did not want to take into account that this was not the editor's point of view, but that of the authors of the texts. As is well known, many newspapers warn in their opinion section that the editor is not responsible for the opinions expressed in the articles published. Walendy explained to the court that in order to ensure that the articles he published in *Historische Tatsachen* did not violate the law, he routinely submitted the texts to the supervision of four lawyers. The court rejected the opinions of the four lawyers as irrelevant.

In 1999, already in the midst of a campaign of legal harassment, the ownership of his publishing house was transferred to his wife. As if imprisonment were not enough, in 2001 there was a new attempt to censor *Wahrheit für Deutschland*, Walendy's book which had received a favourable ruling from the Federal Constitutional Court in 1994. With little chance of the Constitutional Court's ruling being overturned, the government authorities eventually abandoned the plan.

Ursula Haverbeck. The indecent condemnation of a venerable old woman

Ursula Haverbeck was sentenced to ten months in prison in 2015 for denying the Holocaust, without any consideration for her 88 years of age. This aberrant and shameful conviction exposes the servitude and misery of the Federal Republic of Germany to anyone who cares to look at it. Surely any honest person must condemn this abuse by a state that has long since lost its sense of decency. However, the media, instead of criticising the revolting condemnation, served up the news to their readers as if it were logical, since it was about "a Nazi grandmother". In reality, as the sentencing magistrate said from an obscene moral superiority, "there is no point in having a debate with someone who cannot accept the facts." However, even if the judge could not perceive it because of her limitations and short-sightedness, Ursula Haverbeck is a great lady and is recognised as such among revisionists. Despite her venerable old age, she expresses herself with astonishing intelligence and lucidity. There is not a single inconsistency to be found in her texts, speeches or interviews, which are perfectly cohesive.

Ursula Haverbeck was born in Berlin in 1928. When the World War ended in 1945, she was a seventeen-year-old teenager. As a result, she lived through the air terror, the barbaric rapes perpetrated by the communist armies, Eisenhower's death camps, the pogroms and ethnic cleansing of Germans throughout Europe, the famine brought about by the Morgenthau Plan... Her husband, Werner Georg Haverbeck, who died in 1999, was a professor, intellectual and historian, who wrote numerous works of all kinds. He had participated in the leadership of the NSDAP and fought as a soldier on the Eastern Front. Ursula Haverbeck is also a woman of great erudition who studied pedagogy, philosophy, history and linguistics, and thus holds several university degrees. In 1963, the two of them founded the "Collegium Humanum", which was a pioneer among the environmental movements. In the last decades of the 20th century they were very active in the defence of the German language and culture and in the struggle for the preservation of nature. Between 1983 and 1989, Ursula Haverbeck was president of the German section of the World Union for the Protection of Life.

In 2000, Ursula Haverbeck and other researchers, who had already focused on her revisionist activities, gained access to original National Socialist government documents on Auschwitz, which had been confiscated by the USSR at the end of the war. These are now in the hands of the Institute of Contemporary History and can be consulted by the general public for 124 euros. She and other historians have supplied some of these relevant documents to various German government ministries and the judiciary. Although they have asked for an official investigation, they have never received a response. It is clear from these papers that Auschwitz was not an extermination camp but a work camp for the defence industry and that there were orders to preserve the health of the prisoners as far as possible.

During these years she met Horst Mahler and on 9 November 2003 she took part in the founding of the Society for the Rehabilitation of Those Persecuted for the Refutation of the Holocaust ("Verein zur Rehabilitierung der wegen Bestreitens des Holocaust Verfolgten"), of which she was the director. Zündel, Faurisson, Rudolf, Töben, Stäglich, Honsik, Graf and other prominent revisionists joined this society, which was banned by the Ministry of the Interior in 2008. The first sanctions for its revisionist activities came as a result of articles published in *Stimme des Gewissens* (*The Voice of Conscience*), a publication of the Collegium Humanum: in 2004 it was fined 5,400 euros and in 2005 a further 6,000 euros. On both occasions the publication was confiscated by the authorities.

In 2008 the Collegium Humanum was outlawed: Charlotte Knobloch, chairwoman of the Central Council of Jews in Germany, had publicly called for the banning of the Collegium Humanum and its publication *Stimme des Gewissens*. Haverbeck's response came in the form of an open letter, in which he indignantly asked Knobloch "not to interfere" in matters that did not fall within her competence. Alluding to the Ashkenazi Jews' Khazar origins, he invited Knobloch to return to Asia if he did not like life in Germany. These words and others like them led to the filing of a criminal complaint. In June 2009, the Bad Öynhausen District Court fined Haverbeck a further 2,700 euros for insulting Charlotte Knobloch.

Ursula Haverbeck took an initiative that may explain the harshness with which she was subsequently treated. On 20 November 2014 she filed a criminal complaint, an unprecedented event in post-war Germany, against the Central Council of Jews in Germany, which she accused of persecuting innocent people. The complaint was based on paragraph 344 of the Criminal Code and concerned prosecutions of innocent Germans for Holocaust revision. The crime of false prosecution is punishable by up to ten years in prison; however, as early as December 2014, the complaint was dismissed and the investigation dropped. In contrast, the public prosecutor's office examined the possibility of prosecuting Haverbeck for false accusations.

On 23 April 2015, the astonishing event occurred that led to Ursula Haverbeck being sentenced to ten months in prison. Incomprehensibly, ARD, the German public broadcaster founded in

1950, broadcast during its *Panorama* magazine slot a historical interview recorded in March with the grand dame of revisionism. The broadcast was one of the most disconcerting events in Germany since World War II. It should be noted that after the BBC, the ARD, a consortium of public broadcasters with 23,000 employees, is the second largest television station in the world. Millions of viewers were shocked at home by Ursula Haverbeck's unprecedented statements. Never before had a German public broadcaster allowed anyone to even hint at the truth about World War II. It is clear that the ARD ran the risk of a multimillion-dollar lawsuit for broadcasting a programme in which it committed the crime of denouncing the Holocaust as a lie sponsored by the Bonn regime in the hands of the criminal transnational Jewish financial occupation. We do not know what consequences the broadcast of the interview had for the *Panorama* journalists and the ARD management. In any case, this is of lesser concern to us, as it is the content of the statements that is of interest. Angela Merkel had declared in January 2013 that Germany "bears eternal responsibility for the crimes of National Socialism, for the victims of World War II and above all for the Holocaust." On the basis of these words, no moderately educated person can deny that the Germans have been subjected since the end of the war to the iron grip of Zionism. This is exactly what the great lady denounced.

The interview, an excerpt of which follows, is available on You Tube with English subtitles. It begins: "You have claimed that the Holocaust is the biggest and most persistent lie in history". After citing the works of Professor Faurisson, Haverbeck reaffirms himself and points out that it is a universal lie operating all over the world. He then mentions evidence of the non-existence of gas chambers, that Zyklon-B was a disinfectant and insists that the Holocaust is the biggest lie that has ever been imposed. The interviewer reminds him that this is a slap in the face, as everyone has learned that the Holocaust happened and resulted in the deaths of six million people. "Can you briefly explain once more why the Holocaust is for you the biggest lie in history?" Haverbeck reiterates that it is the most persistent and the one that has had and still has the greatest impact. He explains that instead of answers you get sentences and adds, "When you need a law that imposes the Holocaust and threatens punishment if someone freely investigates there is a problem, isn't there? The truth doesn't need any law.

The interview goes on to consider the terrible suffering of the generation of Germans to which Ursula Haverbeck belongs. She recalls that fifteen million Germans, including herself, were driven from their homes. She denounces the murders, rapes and other criminal acts that no one in Europe remembers. In this thematic context, the great lady categorically denies the figure of 25,000 dead in Dresden offered by the authorities and gives a verified figure of 235,000 victims. She concludes with the statement that only the truth can reconcile everyone. Paragraph 130 of the Penal Code adopted in 1994, which is irreconcilable with Article 5 of the Constitution on freedom of expression and freedom of enquiry, is the next topic. Haverbeck reviews the known absurdities and mentions Germar Rudolf's chemical study, his conviction and Mahler's: "This must deeply outrage any decent person," she concludes in growing excitement.

Despite the octogenarian's obvious emotion, the interviewer insists: "So you maintain publicly that the Holocaust never existed?" "Yes, of course, that's right," replies Haverbeck, who immediately recalls that the orders in the concentration camps were strict, that the commandants could not overstep their bounds, and that two of them were even executed. "I understand, then," the journalist interrupts, "that concentration camps existed, but that there was no mass extermination programme as we understand it today." Haverbeck then explains the importance of industrial activity at Auschwitz and provides evidence, including the Leuchter and Rudolf Reports, which allow her to conclude that there were never any gas chambers because "Auschwitz was not an extermination camp, but a labour camp." The old woman wields texts and documents proving that she is not lying, which prompts another question: "If there are so many documents, why don't you talk about them?" Answer: "You could answer that yourself. Because it is not desirable. "For whom?" "For those who have set up the lie". There follows a conversation about the publication and concealment of materials and banned or censored texts, culminating in the lament that reversing the teaching received by Germans in schools for half a century is a serious problem. Haverbeck explains that there was no extermination of the Jews, but there was persecution, deportation and resettlement. The Zionists themselves wanted this," he adds, "and that's why they even collaborated. The Zionists wanted to have a state.... They had the same goal: they wanted their own state, and above all they wanted the

German Jews because they were the smartest. The fraud of Anne Frank's diary, the falsehood that Germany was the cause of the two world wars, Eli Wiesel's hoaxes about the concentration camps, the realisation that the piles of bodies in Bergen-Belsen had died of typhus, starvation and disease, are other topics of the 49-minute conversation. At this point, Haverbeck recalls: "At the end of the war we were all starving. My mother weighed only 40 kilos. We were all skeletal..." The interviewer insists: "Do you think you could convince the majority of Germans that the Holocaust, as we know it, did not happen, that it never happened?" Haverbeck replies that someone has to do it "because otherwise they will suffer uselessly for eternity. And suffer they do. And they are told they have to. This guilt complex is deeply rooted. And then on top of it all there are the demands: give us more submarines, give us more of this, do that, and so on and so forth. It's all a function of our past..."

The interview takes place in Ursula Haverbeck's huge library. The subject of hatred comes up. Then the great lady mentions the *Talmud* as an example of the ultimate expression of Jewish hatred of gentiles: "All you have to do is read the *Talmud*. I have there," she says, turning her head, "all twelve volumes in the most recent and authoritative translation, a 2002 edition...". The dialogue ends with a warning, "The things you say that you believe, specifically, that the Holocaust did not take place, as you claim, could cost you prison." Response, "Well, then, if people think that's the best thing to do, that's just a risk I have to take.... It's the price to pay. I always think of Schiller, the Field of Waldstein: 'Get up, my comrades, to the horses, to the horses!.... And if you do not risk your lives, you will never receive life as a prize.'"

As a consequence of the expression of the ideas just summarised, in June 2015 the grand dame of revisionism was arrested. The public prosecutor's office ordered the Lower Saxony State Criminal Police to enter the home of Ursula Haverbeck and three other historian colleagues in search of evidence of her thought crimes. The operation took place at night. An armed group of political police kicked in the door and stormed in. It can be said that the house was razed to the ground, as most of the books and other objects ended up on the floor during the search for documents or other evidence that could be used to incriminate Ursula for incitement to hatred and Holocaust denial. The same scene also took place at the homes of the other three revisionists, whose books and documents were seized by the police. What is puzzling about the whole affair is that the ARD programme management allowed the interview to be broadcast, especially since the journalist warns the revisionist historian that she could end up in prison for what she has said. Ursula Haverbeck's arrest was foreseeable from the start.

On 11 November 2015, the Hamburg District Court sentenced her to ten months in prison for questioning whether Jews were gassed at Auschwitz. The defendant appeared at the trial without a lawyer and defended herself in good spirits. About fifty people who accompanied her tried to sit in the courtroom, but a group of "activists" had previously occupied the seats in order to keep out Ursula's friends, many of whom had to remain outside due to lack of space. She was accused of having given an interview to the television magazine *Panorama* in which she stated that Auschwitz had not been an extermination camp, but a labour camp, and that the mass murder of Jews had not taken place. Haverbeck's words to the judge were, "I stand by everything I said." Turning to the prosecutor, he asked: "How do you as a lawyer prove the accusation of that Auschwitz was an extermination camp?" His request for a revisionist historian to testify and provide evidence that no one had been gassed in Auschwitz was rejected by Judge Jönsson, who said it was useless to argue with someone who does not accept the facts.

This magistrate, in the height of his arrogance, blithely disregarded the fact that the non-acceptance of the facts went the other way, given that it is the German courts that systematically refuse to examine them and reject proof and evidence of the crime on trial. Judge Jönsson equated the certainty of the Holocaust with the evidence that the earth is round: "I don't have to give evidence that the world is round either". Finally, after hypocritically expressing his sadness that the old woman used all her energies in "fomenting hatred", the judge ruled that "it was a lost cause." The state prosecution maintained that the defendant had not changed her "fanatical delusional thinking," so that, despite her advanced age, she should be sentenced to ten months' effective imprisonment. The judge agreed.

In 2016, therefore, we abandoned our account of the persecution of the grand dame when she was sentenced in November

2015 to ten months' imprisonment by the Hamburg District Court Judge Björn Jönsson. We will now add that this was followed by two more convictions: one in 2016 for writing letters to a mayor and a newspaper denying the Holocaust and another in August 2017 for incitement to hatred. She was scheduled to be sentenced to prison on 23 April 2018. Ursula did not show up. At the urging of the International Auschwitz Committee, which pressed the police to "search intensively" for her, she was arrested at her home in Vlotho on Monday 7 May. Despite being 89 years old and under medical treatment, she was incarcerated in Bielefeld-Senne prison to serve a two-year sentence. The cruelty and immorality of the Federal Republic, a "democratic" state that imprisons nonagenarians for their ideas, is unprecedented. In March 2019, our heroine, now 90 years old, was preparing to head the election poster of Die Rechte for the European Parliament. On 8 November of the same year, Ursula Haverbeck was in prison for 91 years in the hope that the German judiciary would consider her request for a remission of the remaining months of her sentence, a concession that is customary for most prisoners in Germany. On 12 December 2019, the Associated Press reported that a German court had decided that the elderly woman should not be released. Unless circumstances prevent it, Ursula Haverbeck will remain in prison until 7 May 2020.

Monika and Alfred Schaefer: "Sorry Mom I was wrong about the Holocaust".

It is necessary to return to the Sylvia Stolz trial to recount the persecution and imprisonment of the Schaefer brothers, another shameful and regrettable affair. When we left the case of the irreducible lawyer, we wrote that the Munich Regional Court (Landgericht) had sentenced her on 25 February 2015 to twenty months' imprisonment for the lecture she gave in Chur (Switzerland) in November 2012. The sentence contained the terms "incitement of the people" (Volksverhetzung) and "abuse". The latter referred to the fact that, despite her exclusion from the bar, Sylvia Stolz had signed the trial documents under the name "Rechtsanwältin" (lawyer). On 3 May 2016, the Bundesgerichtshof (Federal Court) overturned the Munich court's ruling with regard to the consideration of "abuse". However, it upheld the entirety of the Munich Landgericht's conviction. Accordingly, the Munich Regional Court was, in accordance with the decision of the High Court (BGH), to consider the entire sentence as a whole, but not the sentence. On 15 February 2018, the Munich Regional Court announced the outcome of its review process, which resulted in a reduction of the sentence by two months to one and a half years.

In January 2018, the hearings to complete the trial of Sylvia Stolz had begun at the Munich Landgericht. Among the audience were the siblings Alfred and Monika Schaefer, who had travelled to Germany to visit relatives. On 3 January, barely an hour into the session, the prosecutor surprisingly called for a recess, which was used to arrest Monika Schaefer. The same prosecutor entered accompanied by three allegedly armed police officers, who handcuffed her and dragged her out of the courtroom against her will. B'nai Brith Canada had alerted the German authorities and they had been watching her since she entered the country. Evidently, Monika protested. She said that she was a free person, a Canadian citizen who had done nothing wrong. Then the prosecutor said to her, and I quote: "If you wanted to remain free, you should have stayed in Canada". Without further explanation, she was held in a high-security prison in Munich, where she remained for six months without trial, in isolation, initially unable to receive correspondence or visits from family and friends. In our opinion, such a scandalous action confirms once again the intrinsic perversion of the German judicial system and its blatant submission to Zionism and the Holocaust lobby (jewdicial system).

If we now consider the motive for Monika Schaefer's abrupt arrest in Munich, the shock and bewilderment increases. A year and a half before her arrest, in June 2016, Monika, a cultured woman who speaks languages and plays the violin with virtuosity, posted online a video recorded by her brother that has become famous in revisionist circles. Its title: "Sorry, Mom, I was wrong about the Holocaust". In it he apologised to his mother for having mortified her with guilt, instilled in all Germans from childhood through education and propaganda. After saying that her parents emigrated to Canada (her mother in 1951 and her father in 1952), where she was born, Monika explains in the video that, as a child, she felt ashamed of her origins and recalls that when she went to school one day dressed in Tyrolean costume she was teased and shouted "Heil Hitler". She then expressed her desire to apologise to her parents, now deceased, for having reproached them for her past and blamed them for their inaction. Monika recalls in the video that her mother looked at her saddened and promised her that they never knew anything. She finally explains that it was in 2014 that she began to understand why her mother knew nothing, as she discovered that the Holocaust is, as she put it, "the biggest, most pernicious and persistent lie in all of history". The video ends by highlighting the incoherence of having a hospital in an extermination camp and denying the existence of the gas chambers. Before saying goodbye, playing a lively melody on his violin, he turns to the spirit of his mother and apologises again. That is all. Undoubtedly, a horrendous crime.

Until 2014, Monika Schaefer had held positions that were considered left-wing politically. Specifically, she had been a candidate in Yellowhead County (Alberta) for the Green Party. It appears that she ran unsuccessfully on the Green lists in the 2006, 2008 and 2011 elections. Of course, as soon as Monika's views on the Holocaust became known, the Green Party of Alberta (GPA) was quick to condemn them "in the strongest terms" and began proceedings to expel her from the party as soon as possible, which was consummated in August 2016. In her letter in response to their expulsion, Monika Schaefer reproached them for their silence on the attacks of 11 September 2001 and let them know that she had realised that "the Green Parties seem to be controlled by the same hidden power that controls the other dominant parties." Among other recommendations, he invited them to learn about the *Leuchter Report*, to care a little about the Palestinian people and to respect freedom of expression.

After the arrest and imprisonment of his sister, Alfred Schaefer, armed with courage, could not contain his indignation and began an international campaign of denunciation. In January 2018, he gave an extensive interview to Jonas E. Alexis for the online publication *Veterans Today. Journal for the Clandestine Services*, in which he was at ease. Among other things, he explained that in order to understand what is happening today, it is necessary to go back in history. Here is a quote from one of his comments: "The primary reason for creating the Holocaust myth was to divert attention from the genocides that Jews have engineered, instigated and perpetrated behind the Iron Curtain under the guise of communism and Bolshevism". He went on to say, "The Jews know why they must control all the media. They are the window through which we work out our perception of reality and of the world. They are the instrument through which we interpret everything. People are fed the ideas that serve the plan laid out in their agenda. This is as true today as it was in the past for fomenting wars and revolutions." Naturally, with public statements such as these, Alfred Schaefer was exposed and placed in the crosshairs of Holocaust propagandists, who were quick to launch their persecution. This did not bother him at all, and he continued to produce videos and to denounce his sister's situation. The lawsuits against Alfred Schaefer, who had German nationality and instead of returning to Canada chose to remain in Germany, were a foregone conclusion. At the end of January 2018, searches began at his home. On 23 January, around ten police officers came to his home and seized his and his wife's computers and mobile phones.

On 1 February 2018, barely a month after his sister's arrest, Alfred Schaefer received a summons to report to a police station on the 25th of the same month. He was supposedly to be questioned about a speech he had given on 25 November 2017 in Bretzenheim on the occasion of a memorial service for the one million German soldiers killed in Eisenhower's nineteen death camps (in the third volume of *Proscribed History*, Chapter X, we devote ten pages to the events in the death camps in 1945). Aware that they intended to arrest him in order to imprison him like his sister Monika, Alfred sent a letter to the police. In it he said that his words in Bretzenheim were published in English on the internet and that if they needed a German version he would provide it himself. As for the content of his speech, he explained that he had spoken about his father, Otto Schaefer, a prisoner of war in one of the Rhine camps. In the letter, he recommended the police to read *Other Looses*, the book by James Bacque, which, as we have already said in the aforementioned chapter X of our work, is an indispensable source for learning about the genocide of the PWTE (Prisoners of War Temporary Enclosures). We reproduce verbatim the words that allude to his father and the accusation against the Jews: "He had to watch every day as young men who were healthy when they were abandoned in the camps died in the most terrible way. They were penned up like cattle in a huge camp with no protection from the elements, no food, and not even water. The mass starvation of those Germans was a deliberate plan. The Jews wanted to exterminate as many Germans as possible. Their intention to do exactly that is well documented by themselves in publications such as *Germany must perish*, written by the Jew Thedodor Kaufmann. My father, who was awarded the Order of

Canada in 1976, owes his life to a camp guard who helped him escape...".

Although it was clear that Alfred Schaefer was accumulating "crimes" and would be tried in Munich together with his sister Monika for incitement to hatred, he previously faced a trial at the Dresden District Court, where he was tried in April 2018 for having attended a rally together with Gerd Ittner on 11 February 2017 in Zwingerteich, a town where some 200 people gathered to commemorate the 72nd anniversary of the bombing of Dresden. According to the indictment, Schaefer had claimed that Dresden was not a military target for the Allies and that there were only women, children and refugees from the eastern territories in the city. In court, Schaefer said he was grateful for the indictment because it would allow him to expose the truth. Among other things, he denounced before the judges the criminalisation of the German people and the power of the international bankers. He also denied the crimes attributed to National Socialism. The court sentenced him for "incitement" to a fine of 5,000 euros. In May, the verdict was made public, arguing that, although the defendant made no mention of the Holocaust, he had minimised the crimes of the Nazis. Gerd Ittner and a third speaker in Zwingerteich were also charged.

Alfred Schaefer's arrests were continuous, but he was released on his own recognisance not to leave Germany, although he had to report to a police station twice a week. On 6 July, when the trial against him and his sister Monika, in which Alfred had managed to project a series of videos, had already begun, five armed policemen arrived at his home at 2 p.m. There they handcuffed him in front of his wife and Lady Michaels. There they handcuffed him in front of his wife and Lady Michèle Renouf, who was with them, and took him into custody. The trial in Munich had finally begun on 2 July 2018. The charges had been brought for videos that both brothers had produced and posted on the internet, in which they denied the Holocaust. Monika, a 59-year-old Canadian citizen, was charged with six counts of "incitement to hatred", while her brother Alfred, 63, was charged with 14 counts of "incitement to hatred".

Lady Renouf was in Munich to accompany and encourage the Schaefer brothers. In a chronicle of the first day of the trial, she herself explains that her lawyer Wolfram Nahrath, who was also defending Monika Schaefer on that day, advised her not to enter the court building, let alone the courtroom, as she feared that the same strategy used to arrest Monika could be used against her. In February 2018, Lady Renouf had attended the 1945 genocidal bombing memorial in Dresden and was under investigation in Germany for her speech, with a view to being charged with "incitement of the people" (Volksverhetzung). Lady Renouf, who obtained the following information from Sylvia Stolz's lawyer, reports that Alfred managed to embrace his sister when she appeared in handcuffs in the courtroom. She waved her arm in the Roman style and adopted a defiant attitude. Judges Hofmann and Federl considered it an offence and a contempt of court; but he told them that he considered them and the Federal Republic of Germany illegitimate. He was then warned by the judges that he would be severely fined if he persisted in his offensive attitude. When Alfred Schaefer began his opening statement, Judge Hofmann asked him to summarise it, which prompted the defence lawyers to ask for a two-hour interruption to draft the judges' rejection, as they considered that the defendant's rights were clearly infringed by attempting to prevent his right of defence,. Alfred and Monika Schaefer's lawyers requested that Judge Hofmann, who presided over the court, be removed from the trial because of his prejudice towards Alfred Schaefer. The presiding judge himself decided that the trial would continue under his authority until 4 July, when the matter would be considered. Naturally, the request was rejected.

In the afternoon session, the judge complained about the breadth of the topics Alfred Schaefer intended to address in his brief, so he deleted twelve pages. Despite this, the reading lasted four hours. Schaefer used historical and current accusations to argue for the dismissal of the case against him and his sister. No sooner had he finished than the judge announced that the defendant was to remain in police custody for two days because of his contempt for the court's authority. The hearing was already over when Sylvia Stolz, who was in the audience, shouted: "This is terror! The judge asked her what she meant when she described the court's rules as "terror". She replied: "I am ruined by words". Lawyer Wolfram Nahrath had already taken off his robe, as the session was over. Even so, the judge, instead of understanding that the protest had been made after the public hearing was over, insisted that Sylvia Stolz had interrupted the court proceedings and, instead of imposing the usual fine, ordered her to be placed in a cell for two days for contempt of court.

The trial lasted throughout the summer of 2018 and concluded in the autumn at the end of October. Readers interested in following the trial sessions in more detail are referred to the Adelaide Institute's Newsletter for a wealth of information. We will highlight only a few significant ideas from the final plea speeches that the Schaefer brothers delivered before the Munich court, so we are already in the final days, when the verdict was handed down.

As lawyer W. Nahrath denounced in his final speech on 22 October, Alfred Schaefer had been treated by the public prosecutor as an "enemy of humanity". Alfred intervened on 25 October. He immediately reaffirmed his convictions. He considered that it would be undignified to give up expressing opinions when one was morally certain that one was right. He then went through the charges against him, at which point he was interrupted by the judge to warn him that he had no right to commit further affronts in his statement. In any case, the possibility of accruing further offences for his words hung in the air, as for example when he referred to the *Protocols of the Elders of Zion*, a taboo subject that prompted the judge to rush to make emphatic notes.

Nevertheless, in his four-hour speech Alfred Schaefer did not refrain from making the accusation that some Jews had organised 11 September 2001, the consequences of which were the attacks on Afghanistan, Iraq and the so-called "war on terror". He regretted that the *Leuchter Report*, presented during the trial, had been ridiculed. He alluded to Benjamin Friedman's famous speech, *A jewish Defector Warns America*, which had also been presented to the court. He charged that it was all based on lies that were inexorably imposed as truth. He also had a moment to remember Ursula Haverbeck and asked the court how an 89-year-old woman could be imprisoned. "All this is happening," he said wryly, "on behalf of the human rights organisation B'nai Brith." When he tried to argue the immigration issue, the judge again warned him that what he said could be damning. The session was adjourned shortly afterwards, so Alfred Schaefer concluded his presentation on the morning of the 26th. He immediately recorded his and his sister's disappointment with the figure of Noam Chomsky, who had initially been an icon for them.

Towards the end of his speech, he said he was ready to sting like a bee and die for his people. He said that he was prepared to go to jail for what he had said and that he was not afraid to stand up for the truth. At this point Alfred looked towards the seats in the room where his wife was sitting and the emotion was evident, so much so that for a moment he seemed to be trying to hold back tears. He concluded by calling for solutions to the world's problems and expressing his desire for peace. His final plea was: "Let us think of future generations".

At 12.35 p.m. on 26 October it was the turn of Monika Schaefer, who wanted to make her plea speech standing up. She recalled her arrest in the same building and the words addressed to her by the public prosecutor. She then gave a brief outline of her past. He pointed out that in 2011, when he was a Green Party member, he had sent a report to the Canadian Parliament with his research on 11 September 2001, which was ignored. He pointed out that the Greens demanded in 2014 that he withdraw a letter on the Zionist attack on the Gaza Strip that caused thousands of deaths and injuries, and stressed that they also asked him to publicly apologise. She told the court that this "was impossible" because she "could only be guided by the truth". After this disappointment, she told the court, she came to understand why the Green Party defended Zionism. She also realised that the people she had to apologise to were her parents, and so she decided to record "Sorry Mom...". He then experienced, he said, the defamation and exclusion suffered by "people who break the taboo". She alluded to a passion for the violin, her great companion during the months of incarceration, and recalled playing and teaching in schools, at weddings and, voluntarily, in old people's homes. Monika told the court that it was precisely because she was so well known that she should be socially destroyed. She denounced the hate campaign against her and gave many examples: she was beaten in the street, had her car tyres slashed, had gravel thrown at her, was spat on in the street by youths, was excluded from the Alberta Fiddlers' Union... After these facts she asked the court: "Who incites hatred against whom?" Monika deplored the fact that the Canadian government had forbidden the consul to attend the trial to find out what was happening to a Canadian citizen. She ended by assuring that she was no longer ashamed of her German origin, that she was proud of her parents and her ancestors. Instead of a world based on lies," she concluded, "we need enlightening education.

After a recess, at 5.30 p.m. on the evening of the same day, the judge pronounced the verdict, in which it was stated that both brothers had spread hatred. They were considered to have committed the crime of sedition against people of the Jewish religion and also against foreigners. Alfred and Monika Schaefer were found guilty. Alfred was sentenced to three years and two months in prison for eleven offences of "incitement to hatred". Monika was sentenced to ten months' imprisonment for four offences of "incitement to hatred". The magistrate concluded: "the videos are made with criminal intent, knowing that pseudo-scientific evidence is capable of disturbing the legal peace and inciting hatred against minorities". As for the defendants' pleading speeches, they were found to have nothing to do with the facts. In the defendant Alfred Schaefer," the sentence said, "hatred must have already devoured the soul. He may claim to be interested in the history of Germany, but it must not degenerate into such hatred". The judge implied that Alfred Schaefer might have to face a new trial, since some of the things he had said or done (the Roman salute) could be punishable under the Criminal Code.

Since Monika Schaefer had already been imprisoned for ten months, she was able to regain her freedom and finally return to Canada, where her daily life would no longer be the same. In January 2019, for example, in a photocopy shop where she was a regular customer, the owner refused to serve her, pointed to the door and asked her to leave the shop. After a brief discussion in which Monika asked for explanations, the woman told her that she did not want to serve a person she hated. As for her brother Alfred, who is imprisoned in a Munich jail, the last we heard before concluding these lines is that on 28 January 2019 he was set to face a new trial on additional charges brought against him.

Reinhold Elstner, the revisionist who burned himself alive

In the Federal Republic of Germany about two thousand people are arrested annually for crimes of opinion and nobody cares about it because they are only "neo-Nazis". We could go on to with other honest revisionists who, for no other crime than thinking freely, ended up behind bars, such as Dirk Zimmermann, who in 2007 sent copies of *Lectures on the Holocaust* to three local figures: the mayor of Heilbronn, a Lutheran clergyman and a Catholic clergyman. After sending the books, he filed a lawsuit against himself and in 2009 was sentenced to nine months in prison. Another case is that of Gerhard Ittner, sentenced in 2015 by a Munich court. Previously, in 2005, he had been sentenced to two years and nine months, which led to his flight to Portugal, where he was arrested in April 2012 and extradited in September. Three years later, in November 2015, the Nürnberg-Fürth Court again sentenced him to eighteen months for the habitual offences. At the time of sentencing, he had already been remanded in custody for a year and was released. In February 2017, together with Alfred Schaefer, he participated in the anniversary of the genocidal bombing of Dresden, for which he was again investigated for "incitement". On 12 May 2018, his 60th birthday, three policemen arrested him in Bretzenheim without a warrant and without identifying him. A few days later he was remanded in Nuremberg prison, where he spent six months in custody without being brought before a court. On 10 November of the same year he was released. Everything indicates that the persecution of Gerd Ittner will continue. These few lines, written for *Thought Criminals*, are a tribute to his courage.

To give more examples would unnecessarily lengthen our work. We will therefore end with an extreme, generally unknown case, that of Reinhold Elstner, to whom we have reserved the last place as the culmination of the persecution of revisionists in Germany. On 25 April 1995, this 75-year-old retired chemist, engineer and Wehrmacht veteran went to the stairs of the "Feldhermhalle" (Hall of the Heroes) in Munich, doused himself with flammable liquid and set himself on fire. The people who saw him tried to rescue him to save his life, but twelve hours later Elstner was dead. The reasons for such an unfortunate action are explained in a text written before he committed suicide, in which he explains his sacrifice. We reproduce it in memoriam.

> "Germans in Germany, in Austria, in Switzerland and in the world, please wake up!
>
> Fifty years of endless defamation, of continuous hateful lies, of demonisation of an entire people are enough.
>
> Fifty years of unbelievable insults to German soldiers, of permanent blackmail costing billions, and of 'democratic' hatred are more than one can bear.
>
> 50 years of Zionist judicial vengeance is enough.

Fifty years of trying to create a rift between generations of Germans by criminalising parents and grandparents is too long.

It is unbelievable that in this anniversary year we are inundated with a flood of lies and slander. Since I am already 75 years old, I can no longer do much more; but I can still take my own life by immolating myself, a last action that can serve as a signal to the Germans to come to their senses. If by my act a single German should wake up and find the way to the truth, then my sacrifice would not have been in vain.

I felt I had no choice after realising that now, after 50 years, there is little hope that reason will prevail. As someone who was expelled from his home after the war, I always had one hope, the same hope that was granted to the Israelis after 2000 years, namely that the expelled Germans would have the right to return home. What happened to the right of self-determination enacted in 1919, when millions of Germans were forced to live under foreign rule? To this day we have had to suffer for these mistakes, and I can say that the Germans cannot be held responsible for them.

I'm a German Swede, I have a Czech grandmother, and on the other hand Czech and Jewish relatives, some of whom were imprisoned in concentration camps such as Buchenwald, Dora and Theresienstadt. I never belonged either to the Nazi party or to any other group that was in the least connected with National Socialism. We always had the best relations with our non-German relatives and, when necessary, we helped each other. During the war, our grocery shop with bakery was responsible for the distribution of food to French prisoners of war and workers from the East who lived in the city. Everything was done correctly and this ensured that at the end of the war our business was not looted because the French prisoners of war guarded it until their repatriation. Our relatives who had been detained in the concentration camps returned home as early as 10 May 1945 (two days after the end of hostilities) and offered their support. Particularly helpful was our Jewish uncle from Prague, who had seen the bloodbath of the remaining Germans in the Czech capital caused by the partisans. The horror of these cold-blooded murders could still be seen in the expression in his eyes. Obviously, a horror that he himself as a former prisoner of the Reich had not experienced during his imprisonment.

I was a soldier in the Wehrmacht of the great German Reich, fighting from day one on the eastern front. To this I must add a few years of slave labour in the USSR as a prisoner of war.

I remember well Kristallnacht (Night of Broken Glass) in 1938 because on that day I found a Jewish girl crying, a girl with whom I had studied. But I was much more shocked when I saw in Russia how all the churches had been desecrated, how they were used as stables and gun shops; I saw pigs grunting, sheep bleating and the clattering of guns in holy places. The worst for me was when I saw churches turned into museums of atheism. And all this happened with the active connivance of the Jews, that small minority of which so many members were Stalin's criminal thugs. The most prominent of these were of the Kaganovich clan, seven brothers and sisters, who were such mass criminals that the alleged SS murderers can be considered harmless by comparison.

After the return from the Russian prison camps to my "homeland" (what a mockery to speak of "homeland" to a prisoner who has been expelled from the land of his ancestors!) I heard for the first time about the brutalities of the concentration camps, but at first I heard nothing about gas chambers or the murder of human beings by the use of poison gas. On the contrary, I was told that in concentration camps like Theresienstadt and Buchenwald (Dora) there were even brothels for the inmates in the confines of the camp. Then, on the occasion of the 'Auschwitz trials', Mr Broszat of the Institute of Contemporary History stated that the famous figure of six million is only a symbolic number. Despite the fact that Mr. Broszat also declared that there were no gas chambers for the murder of human beings in the camps set up on German soil, for years the alleged chambers were shown to visitors in Buchenwald, Dachau, Mauthausen and others. Lies, only lies to this day.

It all became very clear to me when I read dozens of books written by Jews and so-called anti-fascists. In addition, I could draw on my own experience in Russia. I lived for two years in the hospital city of Porchov, where already in the first winter the danger of a typhus epidemic arose and all hospitals and primary care centres were deloused with what we called then 'K.Z. Gas', specifically 'Zyklon-B'. There I learned how dangerous it was to handle this poisonous gas even though I was not part of the teams that fumigated the buildings. In any case, since then I have had no choice but to study all the works about the concentration camps that tell fabulous tales about the gas chambers. This must be the real reason why all the victims' reports about the concentration camps are regarded as the truth by the courts and do not need to be proven.

In 1988 German television broadcast a report on Babi Yar (a ravine near Kiev) where it was reported that the SS had stoned 36,000 Jews to death. Three years later a lady named Kayser wrote a report for the Munich newspaper *TZ* in which she said that these Jews had been shot and their bodies burned in deep ravines. Asked about this, Ms Kayser pointed to a bookshop in Konstanz that sells the book *The Shoah at Babi Yar*. The day the book arrived at my house, German television showed a report from Kiev on the findings of a Ukrainian commission: at Babi Yar were the bodies of 180,000 human beings, all murdered on Stalin's orders (before 1941). The Germans were not responsible at all. However, Babi Yar memorials blaming the Germans for the massacres can be found all over the world (Clinton visited Babi Yar on 10 May 1995 and in front of a Menorah alluded to the Germans as the slaughterers).

Because, as Mr Broszat said, we have been deceived about what happened in dozens of concentration camps. I am not prepared to believe the stories that are being told about what allegedly happened in the camps in Poland. Nor do I believe the post-war accusations that paint the Germans as particularly aggressive. After all, it was Germany that kept the peace from 1871 to 1914, while England and France, the leading democracies, conquered most of Africa and expanded their colonies in Asia. At the same time, the United States fought Spain in Mexico, and Russia waged war on Turkey and Japan. In these matters I consider the US Government to be particularly cynical, since it was the country that twice in this century crossed the ocean to attack Germany and bring us to 'democracy'. It must be considered that this was a government whose nation exterminated the original inhabitants, and which to this day treats its coloured population as second-class citizens.

During my years I found kind and helpful Jews not only among my relatives, but also among prisoners of war in Russia. In Gorky a Jewish teacher helped me back to health when I suffered from pleurisy and serious eye problems. But I also heard a lot of bad things about this small minority. Didn't Churchill write the following in the *London Sunday Herald* (8 February 1920)?

From the days of Spartakus Weishaupt to Marx, Trotsky, Bela Kun, Rosa Luxemburg and Emma Goldmann, there is a world conspiracy engaged in destroying our civilisation and changing our society by events of appalling greed and by the implementation of the impossible dream of the equality of all. This conspiracy, with its relentless undermining of all existing institutions, was able to employ a gang of unscrupulous people from the underworld of the great cities of Europe and America to seize power in Russia and make themselves masters of this vast empire. It is not necessary to overestimate the part which these atheistic Jews played in the establishment of Bolshevism.'

I believe I am entitled to quote the recipient of the prestigious Karls Prize. In the 18th century, Samuel Johnson wrote: 'I do not know which we should fear more, a street full of soldiers ready to plunder or a room full of writers accustomed to lie'.

Considering our experience after 1918 and after 1945, we Germans know who we have to fear the most!

Munich, 25 April 1995
Reinhold Elstner".

2. Main victims of persecution in France

François Duprat, murdered by Jewish terrorists

The law that prohibits Holocaust revisionism in France is the Gayssot Law, also known as the Fabius-Gayssot Law, passed on 13 July 1990. Two Jews, the communist MP Jean Claude Gayssot and the wealthy socialist Laurent Fabius, were the fathers of the invention that since then has made it possible to prosecute those who question the existence of certain crimes against humanity, namely those defined in the London Charter, which was used as the basis for convicting Nazi leaders in the infamous Nuremberg trials. As usual, the Jewish lobby, using the supposed defence of human rights as a cover, succeeded in ensuring that in France, as in Germany, investigators are harassed for thought crimes and deprived of freedom of expression. Prior to the existence of this law, revisionists had already been subjected to coercive measures. It has been said (*Proscribed History*) that Paul Rassinier, one of the fathers of historical revisionism, had to endure from the publication of *The Lie of Ulysses* until his death in 1967 all kinds of slander and exclusion, as well as several legal proceedings.

Another precursor of historical revisionism in France was François Duprat, who in June 1967 published an article in *Défense de l'Occident* entitled 'The Mystery of the Gas Chambers'. Later, Duprat read *Did Six Million Really Die?*, the book by Richard Harwood whose publication was to cause Ernst Zündel so much trouble, and became involved in its publication and distribution in France. François Duprat, born in Ajaccio in 1941, is considered one of the ideologues of French nationalism and the creation of the National Front. One of his mentors was Maurice Bardèche, a propagator of Holocaust revisionism alongside Paul Rassinier. Influenced by Bardèche, Duprat suggested the dissolution of the Zionist state and supported the Popular Front for the Liberation of Palestine. Duprat promoted the translation and publication of fundamental Holocaust revisionist texts. Thanks to him, Thies Christophersen's *Die Auschwitz Lüge* (*The Auschwitz Lie*) and Arthur Robert Butz's *The Hoax of the Twentieth Century* were circulated in France.

At 08:40 on 18 March 1978, a bomb killed François Duprat, who at the age of 37 became the first person to be murdered for his support of Holocaust revisionism. His wife Jeanine, who was with him, was seriously injured and, although she was able to save her life, she lost her legs and was paralysed. Duprat was driving his wife to school in Caudebe-en-Caux, where she was teaching. The car stopped at a petrol station to buy newspapers and the criminals took the opportunity to plant a bomb in the underbody of the vehicle. When they resumed driving, the car was blown up. The investigation showed that the device used was sophisticated and could only have been the work of skilled experts. Two groups claimed responsibility for the attack as a way of rejecting 'Shoah denialism': the self-styled Commando of Memory and the Jewish Revolutionary Group; however, Zionist organisations in France condemned the murder in the public eye and an intoxication campaign was spread to attribute the crime to ultra-left and/or rival nationalist groups. Duprat's funeral in the church of Saint-Nicolas-du Chardonnet in Paris was a massive event.

No one was arrested and the crime went unpunished. Today there is little doubt that Duprat's murder was the work of the Mossad. Thanks to the publication in 1990 of *By Way of Deception*, the book by former agent Victor Ostrovsky, international public opinion gained access to revealing details of how the Israeli Secret Service trains and arms so-called "Jewish defence groups" in different countries. Ostrovsky explains in his controversial book that young people from other countries are brought to Israel for various intelligence-related training. In Europe, the "Tagar", a branch of the Zionist Betar movement, is the most important terrorist group. Tagar/Betar, headquartered in Paris, has close ties to the Israeli government and is therefore used in Mossad covert operations. It is more than likely that this Tagar was linked to Duprat's assassination, as it has been credited with numerous criminal attacks against people considered "enemies", including Holocaust revisionists.

Roger Garaudy, the philosopher pilloried for denouncing Israel

As we begin to write these lines on the philosopher Roger Garaudy, we are plagued by a few doubts. His life, a paradigmatic example of eclecticism, was so rich and varied that one is tempted to explain something of it to those who do not know this scholar, who wrote incessantly during his long life of almost a hundred years. Our limitations, of course, are imposed by the contents we have been dealing with. What basically interests us in his extensive oeuvre of more than fifty essays is what concerns historical revisionism. For this reason, we will focus mainly on the book that was to provoke the so-called "Affaire Garaudy", *Les Mythes fondateurs de la politique israélienne*[7]. This essay, published in December 1995, probably came about as a moral necessity, as a compromise, since Garaudy was married to the Palestinian Salma Farouqui and had converted to Islam in 1982. Constrained by space constraints, we will nevertheless write a few paragraphs on his life trajectory. This will help us understand how Garaudy came to denounce the perversion of the Zionist state.

In the spring of 2013 we visited the Museum of the Three Cultures in the Calahorra Tower in Cordoba, a Muslim fortress whose use was ceded by the City Council to the Roger Garaudy Foundation in 1987. Ten years later, in September 1997, the Torre de la Calahorra, located opposite the mosque, on the other side of the Roman bridge over the Guadalquivir, was entered in the register of museums of the Autonomous Community. There we had the opportunity to acquire several of Garaudy's works translated into Spanish, including a memoir he began writing at the age of 75, *Mi vuelta al siglo en solitario*. We will therefore use his own voice to outline some moments in the intellectual, ethical and religious transformation of this synthetic and conciliatory thinker. His metamorphoses led him to move from militant communism to Islam, via Catholicism, and thus from supposed Marxist atheism to a profound faith in God.

Garaudy was born in Marseilles in 1913. His maternal grandmother was Spanish, a Menorcan exiled in Algiers in 1848. In the foreword to the memoirs he states: "The great quest of my life was precisely to find meaning in it. And also to history". In his twenties, he sought that meaning in Marxism and joined the French Communist Party in 1933. After having been a prisoner of Vichy France in Algeria, he lived through the liberation in Paris in 1945. He wrote some enlightening words on the situation in France: "In a country

---

[7] *Les Mythes fondateurs de la politique israélienne*, Omnia Veritas Limited, www.omnia-veritas.com.

where the vast majority has accepted both the occupation and the Vichy regime, the illusion of a unanimous and heroic resistance is now being created. In 1945 in France there were more resistance fighters than inhabitants". Since the Communist Party had been predominant in the internal resistance, its prestige was transformed into power. Garaudy was elected in 1945 as a deputy to the first Constituent Assembly. He then began his career as a PCF deputy, followed by "fourteen lost years in Parliament", in his own words. At the end of October 1956, after the nationalisation of the Suez Canal by Nasser, Garaudy witnessed as Vice-President of the Assembly the pre-war atmosphere and the preparations for the Anglo-French intervention in Egypt.

It was during these years that his doubts began and he formulated the significant dichotomy between "responsible communists and responsible communists", which was to lead to his expulsion from the party in 1970. Increasingly in favour of establishing a dialogue between Christians and Marxists, he claimed the figure of Father Teilhard de Chardin, paleontologist and philosopher, as a meeting point. During the 1960s, his views against atheism and his constant meetings with Christian theologians and philosophers often provoked adverse reactions from many comrades. No creator," he wrote, "can deny God. He is aware of his presence. Even if he does not say so..." It can be said that Garaudy was the great animator in Europe and America of the Christian-Marxist dialogues. In 1969, in answer to the question "Who is Christ for you?", he wrote beautiful words about Jesus and about Christians:

> "... A bonfire has been lit: it is the proof of the spark or the first flame that gave it birth. This bonfire was above all an uprising of the destitute, without which, from Nero to Diocletian, the 'establishment' would not have persecuted them so harshly. For these men (the Christians), love becomes militant, subversive; if it were not for that, He (Christ), the first, would not have been crucified. Up to this moment all wisdoms meditated on destiny and on foolishness confused with reason. He, the opposite of destiny, has pointed out its folly. He, the freedom, the creation, the life. He is the one who has defatalised history".

A year before he wrote these words, what he considered "the turning point of dreams" had already taken place in his life: after the fiasco of May 1968, Warsaw Pact troops led by the USSR invaded Czechoslovakia on 20 August and aborted the so-called "Prague

Spring". Garaudy condemned the intervention unreservedly, but the party denounced his "indiscipline". On 6 February 1970 he was expelled from the PCF.

Roger Garaudy's new phase was marked by his travels around the world. In his desire to delve deeper into the existence of God, he needed to see how God is conceived in the everyday life and artistic manifestations of other cultures and civilisations. To this end, he travelled to India, China and Japan. In 1979 he published *Appel aux vivants,* one of his best-received books, translated from French into seven languages, including Arabic, Spanish and Catalan, and translated into seven languages, including Arabic, Spanish and Catalan. The royalties brought him substantial profits and with them the opportunity to create the association "Appel aux vivants", which aimed to raise a movement of non-violent "resistance" against "the occupation of institutions and spirits by the ideology of growth and the anaesthesia of souls".

On 17 June 1982, a text by Garaudy appeared in *Le Monde* that was to mark a turning point in his life. As he denounces in *My Turn of the Century Alone*, the article was used "to throw me into the dungeons of oblivion". Jacques Fauvet, the editor of the newspaper with whom Garaudy had good relations, agreed to publish a paid page in which he and Father Michel Lelong and Pastor Mathiot harshly criticised Israel's massacres in Lebanon and explained their meaning: "We showed that this was not an oversight, but the internal logic of the political Zionism on which the State of Israel is founded". Garaudy explains in his memoirs the consequences of the text and denounces: "Through anonymous letters and by telephone I received up to nine death threats". LICRA (International League Against Racism and Anti-Semitism) filed a lawsuit in order to provoke a trial for "anti-Semitism and provocation to racial discrimination". Jacques Fauvet's lawyer insisted that the State of Israel could not be confused with the Jewish community; but the LICRA lawyer tried to prove that Garaudy was an anti-Semite.

Fortunately, it was all just a prologue to what years later would become the "Affaire Garaudy". On 24 March 1983, the Paris Court of Appeal ruled that it was a "lawful criticism of the policy of a state and the ideology that inspires it and not a racial provocation". Consequently, the lawsuit of the powerful Jewish lobby in France was rejected and LICRA had to pay the court costs. Instead of dropping the matter, they appealed; but again the judgment of the Upper Chamber of the Paris Court ruled in favour of Garaudy and the two clergymen who had co-signed the article. On 11 January 1984, a verdict was handed down confirming the previous court's judgement and once again ordering LICRA to pay the costs, and LICRA appealed again in cassation. It took almost four years. Finally, on 4 November 1987, the Zionists lost the legal battle. The Court rejected the cassation and ordered the plaintiffs to pay the costs. The defeat of the Jewish lobby was systematically ignored. Even *Le Monde*, whose former editor Fauvet was involved in the affair, was limited to a negligible review. Alongside the harassment in the courts, a much more pitiful one was launched for the philosopher:

> "But from that moment on, the media began to suffocate me: my access to television was blocked and all my articles were rejected. Up to that point, I had published forty books in all the major publishing houses, from Gallimard to Seuil, from Plon to Grasset and Laffont. They had been translated into twenty-seven languages. From that moment on, all doors were closed: one of my best publishers was told by the board of directors: 'If you publish a book by Garaudy, you will not have the right to translate any American work'. To accept me would have been to ruin the house. On the subject of another work, another 'big' (publisher) told his literary director, who, passionate about the book, had worked for three months to help me put the finishing touches to it: 'I don't want Garaudy in this house'. This is the story of the walling up of a man".

Garaudy refers to the period 1982-1988 as "my six years of wandering in the desert". The attempt to bury him literally reflects perfectly the plans outlined earlier by Adam Weishaupt and also in the *Protocols of the Learned Elders Zion*. The former, already at the end of the 18th century, wrote that they had to ruin writers who were hostile to them: "When by and by we shall have the whole book trade in our hands, we shall make them (hostile writers) have neither publishers nor readers." In the Twelfth Protocol, which deals with the control of public opinion through news agencies, the press and publications in general, we read: "We shall surely defeat our adversaries because, in consequence of our measures, they will have no newspapers at their disposal in which they can give vent to their opinion."

In 1982 Roger Garaudy married the Palestinian Salma Farouqui, and a fortnight after the publication in *Le Monde* of the paid page that unleashed the storm, on 2 July, "fully conscious and fully responsible", he made his profession of Muslim faith in Geneva before Imam Buzuzu: "God alone is God and Mohammed is his prophet". The news of his conversion was good news for the Muslim communities in the West, who sent him invitations one after the other. In a lecture in Belfort entitled "Jesus the Prophet of Islam", in which, as he admits in his memoirs, "the heart speaks more fervently of Jesus than of Mohammed", he quotes the suras of the Koran which recognise Mary's virginity and Jesus as God's prophet: "The Messiah, Jesus, son of Mary, is God's apostle. He is His Word deposited by God in Mary. He is the spirit that emanates from Him". Garaudy notes that while God said to Mohammed: "Repent of your sins, past and present", the Koran considers Jesus and his mother the Virgin Mary to be the only human beings who have never committed sin.

Almost inevitably, he saw in Spain the historical example of the dialogue of civilisations that he preached and, consequently, he ended up in Cordoba, where the largest mosque in the world is located. A city, the philosopher points out, "which during the Muslim period of Spanish history, was the largest city in Europe, when Paris and London were but small towns. It was established as a centre of cultural irradiation". In 1987, the city council of Cordoba granted him the Calahorra tower for a period of 49 years so that the evocation of Cordoba's heyday could be exhibited there: "That was the beginning for me," writes Garaudy, "of the marvellous adventure of realising a dream".

Unfortunately, dreams sometimes give rise to terrible nightmares, such as the one Garaudy experienced in 1996 following the publication in France of *Les mythes fondateurs de la politique israélienne* at the end of 1995. This work, which was published in Spain under the title *Los mitos fundacionales del Estado de Israel*[8], unleashed an unprecedented storm in France, since not even books by revisionists such as Paul Rassinier, Arthur R. Butz or Robert Faurisson provoked so much noise in the media and among the "intelligentsia". During the first half of 1996, the controversy did not

---

[8] *The Founding Myths of the State of Israel*, Omnia Veritas Limited, www.omnia-veritas.com.

cease and the affair was to go down in history as the "Affaire Garaudy". Previously, Garaudy had seen two of his books on the Palestinian question unofficially censored through the usual means used by Jewish pressure groups: intimidation and blackmail. Increasingly aware of the role of the Holocaust as an argument to silence criticism of Israel, Garaudy took up the offer of Pierre Guillaume, who in 1980 had relaunched the bookshop "La Vielle Taupe" as a publishing house specialising in revisionist books.

Robert Faurisson, who has been assaulted and threatened with death many times, and who knows first-hand the violence of these media storms, wrote a long article on 1 November 1996 entitled "Bilan de l'affaire Garaudy-abbé Pierre (janvier-octobre 1996)" ("The Garaudy-Father Pierre Affair (January-October 1996)"). Professor Faurisson explains that Pierre Guillaume, in order to avoid "the rays of the Fabius-Gayssot law", sold Garaudy's book outside the trade as "a confidential bulletin reserved for friends of the Vieille Taupe". Faurisson claims that, religious and political considerations aside, the pages that unleashed the wrath of Jewish organisations in France and much of the Western world were the revisionist-inspired pages at the heart of the book. In them, for the taste of a meticulous and precise revisionist like Faurisson, Nuremberg, the Final Solution, the alleged gas chambers and, finally, the Holocaust were hastily reviewed. In an excerpt from the article Faurisson said:

> "But as it was, with all its inadequacies, Garaudy's book could only worry the Jewish organisations, which already had an exaggerated tendency to see revisionists coming out of everywhere and which now discovered a man whose political views - he had been a Stalinist apparatchik of the most orthodox kind - could in no way be described as fascist. R. Garaudy had also been a Protestant, then a Catholic, before becoming a Muslim in the 1980s. In his various works, he had shown himself to be an opponent of any racism".

The first media to cry foul were *Le Canard enchaîné* and *Le Monde*. Then followed the anti-racist organisations, led by LICRA, which denounced it. On 11 March 1996, Pierre Guillaume tried to print a public edition as he had announced in the Vieille Taupe bulletin, but his usual printer refused, so Garaudy decided to clandestinely publish the remodelled work on his own. On 15 April, Henri Grouès, known as Father Pierre, wrote a long letter of support to his friend Garaudy. On 18 April, Garaudy, accompanied by his lawyer Jacques Vergès, gave a press conference at which he mentioned the names of some of the personalities who had shown their solidarity with him, including, in addition to Father Pierre, Father Michel Lelong and the Swiss essayist Jean Ziegler.

Faced with the virulence of the attacks, everyone, including Garaudy, soon tried to excuse themselves with arguments that sought to qualify their positions, a fact that Faurisson regrets: "It is regrettable that Roger Garaudy and Father Pierre did not show more courage. Since the media storm broke out in France, they have begun to beat a retreat". However, both Professor Faurisson and Henri Roques, accustomed to standing up, immediately publicly accepted a proposal from Chief Rabbi Joseph Sitruk, who on 27 April suggested a debate on the Shoah. The following day, the rabbi withdrew the proposal.

On 29 April, the newspaper *Liberation* headlined: "Father Pierre refuses to condemn Garaudy's denialist theses". It was the beginning of a general offensive: the Catholic hierarchy declared that it did not want to be dragged into the controversy. The Bishops' Conference deplored Father Pierre's attitude, reaffirmed that the extermination of the Jews was an indisputable fact and denounced the scandal of questioning the Shoah. The attacks grew louder and louder throughout the month of May. On 9 May, for example, Jean-Luc Allouche, one of *Liberation*'s star journalists, associated Garaudy and Father Pierre with Robert Faurisson, something both had tried to avoid, and accused the three of seeking only to delegitimise the State of Israel. In the United States, on the same day, 9 May, a certain Joseph Sobran accused Father Pierre of "having denied the divinity of Christ" in *The Wanderer*, a Catholic weekly in Ohio.

For his part, Roger Garaudy sought and found support. On 11 May *Tribune Juive* announced that Garaudy was planning to publish the book in the United States and that Rabbi Elmer Berger had written a text for him that he intended to use as a preface. On 23 May *Liberation* reported an editorial in *Al-Ahram*, a newspaper considered the unofficial voice of the Egyptian regime. The newspaper declared itself proud to have welcomed in its pages the author of a book persecuted in France and denounced the media campaign against him. The editorial reproached *Liberation* for being at the service of Zionist propaganda and reminded it that, on the other hand, it had defended Salman Rushdie's right to attack Islam. Finally, on 29 May, the press announced the withdrawal from the scene of Father Pierre, who had decided to go into seclusion in an Italian monastery, where he was visited by Garaudy. Father Pierre told the *Corriere della Sera* that the Church in France had intervened "to silence him under pressure from the press, inspired by an international Zionist lobby". These words provoked a worldwide scandal.

Back in June, Garaudy published a booklet entitled *Derecho de respuesta. Response to the media lynching of Father Pierre and Roger Garaudy*. In it he sought to clarify and qualify his views on revisionism. On the gas chambers, he insisted that no court had sought to examine the murder weapon and recalled the existence of the *Leuchter Report*. Acknowledging the persecution of the Jews, he denied the Zionists the right to monopolise Hitler's crimes and recalled that sixteen million Slavs had died during the Second World War.. Referring to the attacks in the press, he wrote: "Let the journalists know one thing: the vast majority of those deported to the Nazi camps were not Jews, even though all the media have credited the thesis that only Jews were deported and exterminated.

As for Father Pierre, in June he left Italy and settled in Switzerland, from where on 18 June he sent a twelve-page fax entitled "Long live the truth" to a journalist from *Le Monde*. Two days later, on 20 June, Monsignor Daniel Lustiger, the Jewish Cardinal Archbishop of Paris, declared in the weekly *Tribune Juive* that he had "experienced the controversy as an immense disaster". The archbishop issued a public reprimand to Father Pierre and exonerated the Church of any responsibility. Months later, on 26 September, on the occasion of a debate at the Sorbonne on the Holocaust (the Shoah), the Archbishop declared that "denialism was the same kind of lie as that of the man who kills his brother to escape the truth". His friend Elie Wiesel echoed the statement and declared: "Denialists may have no soul".

Finally, the offensive continued throughout the summer of 1996. On 16 July, the modest "Librairie du Savoir" in the Latin Quarter, owned by Georges Piscoci-Danesco, a Romanian political refugee who sold revisionist works, including Garaudy's, was attacked. He was wounded by members of Betar and the bookshop was razed to the ground, some two thousand volumes were damaged. The damage amounted to 250,000 francs. As usual, the Betar terrorists went unpunished, since, enjoying the prurient protection of the Ministry of the Interior, the police did not even bother to look for the criminals. In fact, more than fifty criminal acts perpetrated by Jewish organisations have gone unpunished in France. Also in July, Father Pierre finally retracted his statement in a text published on 23 July in *La Croix*: "I have decided to withdraw my words, relying once again entirely on the opinions of the Church's experts, and I apologise to all those whom I may have hurt. I want to leave God as the sole judge of the integrity of each one's intentions".

The witch-hunt waged by the media in general generated multiple victims, especially people suspected of having committed the sacrilege of being revisionists or denialists. About the two main victims. Robert Faurisson wrote the following:

> "Two octogenarians, who thought they knew life and men, have suddenly discovered, to their childish surprise, that in reality their past existence had been, in short, easy. The two of them, in the space of a few days, have had to face an exceptional ordeal: that which Jewish organisations are in the habit of inflicting on individuals who have the misfortune to provoke their anger. There is no plot or conspiracy on the part of these organisations, but a kind of ancestral reaction. The media, who work for them with devotion, because to go against them could be very costly, know how to mobilise against 'anti-Semites', i.e. against people who, with a few exceptions, do not hate Jews, but are hated by Jews. Old Testament hatred is one of the most formidable in existence: nervous, feverish, frenzied, boundless, it suffocates its victims through the suddenness and duration of its violence. It is an unquenchable hatred because those who suffer from it cannot afford to reveal the true motive and thus mitigate, at least in part, their fury. For example, for months Faurisson has been picked at for his 'minimising' estimate of the number of Jews killed during the world war. But this was only artifice, the real motive lay elsewhere; it lay in the sacrilege of casting doubt on the existence of the gas chambers. However, revealing this doubt was tantamount to running the risk of creating or increasing doubt among the general public. Hence the need to talk about something else...".

Complaints filed by LICRA and MRAP (Mouvement contre le Racisme et l'Amitié entre les Peuples) prompted the French state to prosecute Roger Garaudy for violation of the Gayssot law. The trial began in January 1998. It was followed with expectation in the Arab and Muslim world, no doubt due to the fact that a Muslim intellectual was on trial. From the Persian Gulf to the Nile, hundreds, if not thousands, of writers, journalists, lawyers and politicians publicly expressed their solidarity with and protests against the action of the French justice. Of course, Israeli Prime Minister Benjamin Netanyahu and the usual American Zionist groups were quick to point out that books like Garaudy's constituted "the main threat to Israel". The Paris court hearing the case handed down the verdict on 27 February and found the philosopher guilty of "denial of a crime against humanity" and "racial defamation". The judges specified that the writer's "anti-Semitism" and not his "anti-Zionism" had been judged, and the verdict argued that "although he takes refuge in a political criticism of Israel, he is in fact questioning the Jews as a whole". The court fined the defendant 240,000 francs and sentenced him to six months' imprisonment, which he did not serve. It should be noted that in 1998 Roger Garaudy was already 85 years old, so it would have been scandalous for a prestigious octogenarian intellectual to be sent to prison in France, as in Germany, for thought crimes. On 13 June 2012, Garaudy died at the age of 99 at his home on the outskirts of Paris.

Robert Faurisson, revisionism's essential alma mater

Robert Faurisson is one of the three main pillars of historical revisionism, the other two being Ernst Zündel and Germar Rudolf. The quantity and quality of Professor Faurisson's works place him at the head of revisionist writers. There is no subject on which he has not written, for he knows them all without exception. Moreover, his militant commitment to the intellectual and political challenge that revisionism demands has led him to intervene in one way or another in many legal proceedings in defence of other researchers harassed by "justice" in different countries: of particular relevance was his contribution to the two trials against Ernst Zündel in Canada. His complete work is compiled in four volumes totalling more than 2,200 pages entitled *Écrits révisionnistes*. In application of the Fabius-Gayssot law of 13 July 1990, this work cannot be disseminated and has been privately published outside the commercial circuits. Its content is therefore prohibited by law because the Holocaust (the Shoah) cannot be questioned in France. Interested readers who can read French can access it on the Internet. From the introduction to the first volume, we have translated Professor Faurisson's conception of historical revisionism:

"Revisionism is a question of method and not an ideology

It advocates, for any research, return to the starting point, examination followed by re-examination, re-reading and re-writing, evaluation followed by re-evaluation, reorientation examination followed by re-examination, re-reading and re-writing, evaluation followed by re-evaluation, re-orientation, revision, re-casting; it is, in spirit, the opposite of ideology. It does not deny, but aims to affirm more accurately. Revisionists are not 'deniers' or 'negationists'; they strive to seek and find where, it seems, there was nothing to seek and find.

Revisionism can be exercised in hundreds of activities of everyday life and in hundreds of fields of historical, scientific or literary research. It does not necessarily require the questioning of acquired ideas, but often leads to their nuance. It seeks to disentangle the true from the false. History is essentially revisionist; ideology is its enemy. Since ideology is never so strong as in times of war or conflict, and since it then manufactures falsehoods in abundance for the needs of its propaganda, the historian will, in this circumstance, have to redouble his vigilance: by passing through the sieve of analysis the examination of what has been foisted on him as 'truths'. He will undoubtedly realise that, wherever war has claimed tens of millions of victims, the first of the victims will have been the verifiable truth: a truth that he will try to seek out and re-establish.

The official history of the Second World War contains a little truth combined with a lot of falsehoods".

Methodological rigour and intellectual honesty characterise all of Faurisson's revisionist writings, and this is a consequence of his academic training and extraordinary work capacity. Born on 25 January 1929 in Shepperton (England) to a Scottish mother and a French father, after spending a few years in Singapore and Japan, he completed his youthful education in France, where in 1972 he received a doctorate in letters and humanities from the Sorbonne, where he taught from 1969 to 1974. From 1974 to 1990, Faurisson was Professor of French Literature at the University of Lyon. Author of four books on literature, he is also a recognised specialist in the analysis of texts and documents, a skill that allows him to access historical writings with unquestionable professional competence.

Professor Faurisson was the first to publish important revisionist documents on Auschwitz. In the archives of the Auschwitz State Museum he discovered the technical and architectural drawings of the morgues, crematoria and other facilities. Aware of the value of his discovery, he decided to exhibit it. By 1978 Faurisson had already written several articles expressing his critical view of the history of the extermination of the Jews. On 16 November 1978, the newspaper *Le Matin de Paris* published an article about an unknown professor at the University of Lyon named Robert Faurisson and his views on Auschwitz and the Holocaust. The fact that the press picked up on his revisionist views brought him into the limelight and thus began the "Affaire Faurisson", which was to continue indefinitely. From the beginning, he wrote years later, "I never had any illusions: I would be dragged into court, I would be convicted, there would be physical attacks, press campaigns and turbulence in my personal, family and professional life".

Everything he had imagined was soon to come true, for on 20 November 1978, four days after making the headlines in *Le Matin de Paris*, Faurisson suffered the first attack, praised by Bernard Schalscha, a Jewish journalist from *Liberation* de Lyon who had reported on the day, place and time Faurisson was giving the courses. Members of the Union of Jewish Students who had travelled to Lyon by train from Paris attacked the professor at the University in the presence of Dr Marc Aron, a cardiologist who was president of the Liaison Committee of Jewish Institutions and Organisations in Lyon. Faurisson not only refused to be intimidated, but stepped forward: in December 1978 and January 1979 *Le Monde* published two articles by him showing his scepticism about the gas chambers on Auschwitz. The response to such audacity was a new attack on the day he was trying to resume his courses. Marc Aron was again at the University that day.

In April 1979 he took part in an impressive debate on Swiss television, in the course of which he refuted the arguments of conspicuous advocates of exterminationist theories. The path had been mapped out and Robert Faurisson was determined to follow it without deviating from the marked route. It was also in these years that he had begun to contribute to *The Journal of Historical Review*, an organ of the Institute for Historical Review (IHR) in California, where in September 1983 he gave a lecture entitled "Revisionism on Trial: Events in France, 1979-1983", in which he explained the actions of Jewish organisations to silence revisionists through lawsuits and acts of intimidation.

Professor Faurisson faced a concerted campaign to silence him during those years and was forced to defend himself in French courts because of his statements and writings. His bank account was frozen and judicial officials repeatedly visited his home to threaten him and his wife with seizure of their assets to meet the financial burdens imposed by his comments. As a result of this campaign, his family life was disrupted and his health deteriorated. In December 1980, in an interview for the radio station "Europe 1", Robert Faurisson uttered the famous sentence summarising the result of his research in 60 words in French. Already quoted at the beginning of the chapter (Chapter XII *Proscribed History*), we now recall the 57 words of our English translation: "The alleged Hitlerian gas chambers and the alleged genocide of the Jews form a single historical lie, which has allowed a gigantic political-financial swindle, whose main beneficiaries are the State of Israel and Zionism and whose main victims are the German people - but not their leaders - and the Palestinian people in their entirety". Thirty-six years later, the professor considers that the phrase does not require the slightest change.

For these unbearable words, Faurisson was criminally prosecuted for racial defamation and incitement to hatred. Found guilty, he received a three-month prison sentence in July 1981, but his sentence was suspended. In addition to a fine of thousands of francs, he was ordered to pay 3.6 million francs in costs for the publication of the verdict on television and in print. On appeal, a court in June 1982 dropped the charge of incitement to racial hatred and eliminated the 3.6 million francs. From this point on, Faurisson was tied to a chain of legal proceedings with ruinous effects, as he himself found it necessary to take legal action against outrageously false defamatory attacks. He soon realised that if he persisted in defending himself in this way, he would end up destitute, for if he won, he would receive one franc in damages, while if he lost, he would have to pay the other side considerable sums.

On 25 April 1983, after having been sued by Jewish organisations, which had hoped for an exemplary sentence, he heard a relatively favourable verdict, as the judges of the Paris Court of Appeal said: "Faurisson is a serious researcher; we see no frivolity, negligence, deliberate omissions or lies in his writings on the gas chambers, but he is perhaps malicious and he is certainly dangerous. We condemn him for this probable malice and the danger it entails, but we do not condemn him for his work on the gas chambers, which is serious. On the contrary, since this work is serious, we guarantee every Frenchman the right to say, if he thinks so, that the gas chambers did not exist." Verdicts like this explain why the Zionist Laurent Fabius and the Jewish communist Jean-Claude Gayssot sponsored the Fabius-Gayssot law in 1990. The verdict, handed down on 26 April 1983, can therefore be considered a political achievement, but one that was achieved at the expense of Professor Faurisson, who was ordered to pay the costs of publishing the full verdict, estimated by the judges at a minimum of 60,000 francs.

LICRA published the verdict in the journal *History*, but the text was so badly falsified that Faurisson sued the Jewish lobby. The result of the lawsuit was that the professor was awarded one franc in damages, but had to pay 20,000 francs, despite which LICRA never published the correct text of the verdict. Another lawsuit brought by Professor Faurisson was against Jean Pierre Bloch, president of LICRA and author of a book in which he portrayed him as a Nazi and a falsifier convicted in court. A third lawsuit was against the communist newspaper *L'Humanité*. He lost the lawsuits and also the appeals. The judges acknowledged that he had been defamed, but added that his adversaries had done so in "good faith". Consequently, the defendants were acquitted and he had to pay all legal costs. In February 1985, *Droit de Vivre*, an LICRA publication, gloated with the following headline on one of its pages: "Treating Faurisson as a forger is defaming him, but 'in good faith'". This was an invitation to consider him a forger, which was henceforth the case, always "in good faith".

Robert Faurisson's role in the 1985 and 1988 trials of Ernst Zündel in Toronto was of the highest order. Apart from his testimony as a defence witness, his work as a shadow expert alongside the legendary Doug Christie, Zündel's lead lawyer, was extremely important. This has already been discussed in the pages on the "revisionist dynamo", but now it is time to expand on his contribution in those historic days to the international revival of revisionism. In June 1984 Professor Faurisson travelled to Canada to help what was to become one of his great friends. In January 1985, he returned to Toronto to spend the seven weeks of the trial with Zündel's team, whom he has since considered "an exceptional person". In his *Revisionist Writings* Faurisson has left much of his experience of those trials for posterity.

The court was presided over by Judge Hugh Locke; the prosecutor was Peter Griffiths. Attorney Douglas Christie was assisted by Keltie Zubko, the mother of his two children[9]. The jury was made up of twelve people. The costs were borne by the state, i.e. the taxpayers, and not by Sabina Citron of the Holocaust Remembrance Association, who had brought the case. Faurisson spent hundreds of hours, sometimes late into the night, with Douglas Christie, whom he briefed and advised on all matters, as there was no greater expert in the field at the time. Together they prepared the devastating interrogations of Raul Hilberg and Rudolf Vrba, the two main witnesses for the prosecution. We now give the floor to Professor Faurisson:

> "In Douglas Christie, Zündel was able to find a lawyer who, in addition to being courageous, was heroic. It was for this reason that I agreed to support Doug Christie, day in and day out, as he prepared and developed his work. I might add that without the help of his friend Keltie Zubko we would not have been able to succeed in the 1985 trial, a gruelling ordeal that in retrospect seems like a nightmare. The atmosphere prevailing in court was unbearable, especially because of the attitude of the judge, Hugh Locke. I have attended many trials in my life, including those in France during the time of the purge, the post-war purge of 'collaborators'. I have never encountered a judge as biased, autocratic and violent as Judge Hugh Locke. Anglo-Saxon law offers many more safeguards than French law, but it only takes one man to pervert the best of systems: Judge Locke was that man. I remember Locke shouting in my direction: 'Shut

---

[9] Douglas H. Christie, nicknamed "The Battling Barrister" by his friends, died at the age of 66 in 2013. The mainstream press took advantage of his death to recall that he had defended a number of "scoundrels", "neo-Nazis", etc. etc. etc.; however, there was a pleasant surprise: at least one newspaper in Canada, the *Times Colonist* of Victoria, in British Columbia, where Douglas had lived, reminded its readers that Douglas Christie was an extraordinary lawyer who had always defended freedom of expression. Lucien Larre, the priest who officiated at the funeral mass, gave an emotional farewell address and referred to him as a free speech warrior who fought for the truth. "He did not care," Larre said, "about the threats to his life or the number of times the windows of his office were broken. He stood tall." His wife Keltie Zubko preferred to define him in the words of his daughter, "I think my daughter said it best, that everyone talks about his legacy as a lawyer, as a public speaker, as an inspirational speaker - a person who helped a lot of people who were homeless and couldn't pay - but she said his real legacy was as a father."

up!' when, from a distance, without saying a word, he was pushing a document in Doug Christie's direction".

It would be interesting to devote a few pages to the interrogations of Hilberg and Vrba, as they were absolutely exposed and their credibility was in tatters. Since this is not feasible, as we must prioritise the pursuit of Faurisson, we will offer just a few sample paragraphs. Raul Hilberg, haloed with prestige, arrived in Toronto with no books, no notes, no documents, apparently sure of himself and confident of his experience in other trials in which he had testified against alleged war criminals. "He testified," writes Faurisson, "for several days probably at a rate of $150 an hour." To questions from the prosecutor, he answered the usual, viz: Hitler gave orders to exterminate the Jews, the Germans followed a plan, they used the gas chambers.... Hilberg defined himself in these terms: "I would describe myself as an empiricist who looks at materials".

Everything changed when the cross-examination began by Doug Christie, who, perfectly advised by Professor Faurisson, cornered the renowned Jewish historian, whose work is considered one of the bibles of the Holocaust. Faurisson himself tells the story:

> "For the first time in his life, he had to deal with a defendant who had decided to defend himself and was capable of doing so: Doug Christie, next to whom I was sitting, interrogated Hilberg harshly, mercilessly, for several days. His questions were incisive, precise, relentless. Until then I had had a certain respect for Hilberg because of the quantity, not the quality, of his work; in any case he stood head and shoulders above the Poliakovs, Wellers, Klarsfelds and the rest. As he testified, my regard was replaced by a feeling of irritation and pity: irritation because Hilberg was constantly engaged in evasive manoeuvres, and pity because Christie ended up scoring a goal almost every time. On every issue, if one had to conclude anything, it became clear that Hilberg was by no means 'an empirical who looks at materials.' He was exactly the opposite; he was a man lost in the clouds of his ideas, a kind of theologian who had constructed for himself a mental universe in which the physical aspects of facts had no place."

Doug Christie announced to the "empiricist who looks at the materials" that he was going to read him a list of concentration camps. When he had finished, he asked him which ones he had examined and how often he had done so. Hilberg admitted that he had not examined any of them, either before publishing the first edition of *The*

Destruction of the European Jews in 1961 or even for the publication of the definitive edition in 1985. In other words, the historian who had begun his research into the history of the Holocaust in 1948 and who was considered to be the leading authority on the subject had not examined a single camp and had only visited Auschwitz once and Treblinka once. When asked by lawyer Christie if he knew of any autopsy report of a prisoner's body which established that he had been killed by poison gas, Hilberg's reply was: "No". The transcript on pp. 828-858, Professor Faurisson explains, reflects Doug Christie's lengthy questioning of the two alleged orders that Hilberg claims Hitler issued for the extermination of the Jews. The Jewish historian was asked where they were, that is, where he had seen them. He had to admit that there was "no trace" of them. The lawyer then reminded him of a statement he had made in February 1983 at Avery Fisher Hall in New York, where Hilberg elaborated a thesis that had nothing to do with the existence of an extermination order. He said the following, verbatim:

> "What began in 1941 was a process of destruction not planned in advance, not centrally organised by any agency. There was no blueprint or budget for destructive measures. They were taken bit by bit, step by step. Thus what was carried out was not so much the execution of a plan as an incredible mental agreement, a consensus - telepathy of a vast bureaucracy."

This hallucinatory explanation would have more to do with parapsychology, as it claims that the extermination of six million Jews - a gigantic operation - was the result of no plan, no centralised orders, no project, no budget, but the mental consensus of a bureaucracy that communicated telepathically.

Faurisson explains that he prepared with lawyer Christie the interrogation of Rudolf Vrba, author of *I Cannot Forgive* and theoretical germ of the War Refugee Board (WRB) report on Auschwitz. Arthur R. Butz's book was a fundamental source that provided them with very useful elements to unmask the impostor. The lies about the gas chambers and about Himmler's visit to Auschwitz in January 1943 to inaugurate a crematorium and to witness the gassing of 3,000 people were exposed. It was shown that Vrba was a fake who had never set foot in either the crematoria or the "gas chambers". Documents proved that Himmler had been at Auschwitz in July 1942 and not in January 1943. The impossibility of his opening any crematoria was also proven, as the first of the new crematoria was not opened in January, but much later. In *I Cannot Forgive*, Vrba describes Himmler's visit in detail and even reports on his reflections and conversations. Vrba, a bundle of nerves, was portrayed for what he was, a lying charlatan who even outraged prosecutor Griffiths with his inane verbiage.

After making an essential contribution to Zündel's defence during the first trial, Faurisson returned to France, where the witch-hunt against revisionists was continuing. In 1985, Claude Lanzmann's *Shoah* had been released. Faurisson devoted a review to it, denouncing the film's propagandistic function. Pierre Guillaume, the revisionist book publisher, had published the professor's text and had chosen a May '68 slogan as the title: "Open your eyes, break your television set! Lanzmann turned to France-Presse (AFP) and managed to get the French state agency to publish a long statement in which he gave vent to his indignation at the revisionist criticism of the film. Naturally, freedom of expression, which is constantly claimed when merciless attacks are launched against everything and everyone, could not be exercised in this case. Consequently, on 1 July 1987, France-Presse called on the judicial authorities to act to "put an immediate stop to the machinations of the revisionists", in the name of "respect for freedom of enquiry and human rights". The Federation of Journalists denounced the *Shoah* analysis as unspeakable. Among other examples of its particular respect for freedom of expression, it said: "The Federation believes that individuals like Robert Faurisson should not be able to write with impunity.... To tarnish a film like *Shoah*, which can only be viewed with appalling awe and infinite compassion, is an attack on the Rights of Man".

In the absence of the Fabius-Gayssot law, the insults and threats led to two new attacks. The first was carried out by a certain Nicolas Ullmann on 12 June 1987. This individual violently beat Faurisson at the Sporting-Club in Vichy. Two months later, exactly on 12 September, a group of Jewish militants attacked the professor at the Sorbonne. It was not only he who was attacked, but also the people accompanying him, including the publisher Pierre Guillaume. All were injured to varying degrees, but it was Professor Henry Chauveau who was the most seriously injured. On this occasion, Sorbonne guards managed to arrest one of the attackers, but a plainclothes policeman ordered his release and also expelled Professor Faurisson from the Sorbonne, where he had taught.

In January 1988 Faurisson was back in Toronto to assist his friend Ernst Zündel. As we know, it was his idea to hire Fred Leuchter to travel to Poland to conduct research at Auschwitz. It was indeed a momentous contribution, for Leuchter's technical expertise became the *Leuchter Report*, which was to be a landmark in the history of the revisionist movement. Faurisson reasoned that the United States was the ideal place to look for an expert on gas chambers, since it was there that gas executions regularly took place. Zündel's lawyers contacted William M. Armontrout, warden of the Missouri State Penitentiary, who in a letter recommended Fred A. Leuchter as the most qualified expert. I suggest," he said in the letter, "that you contact Mr. Fred A. Leuchter.... Mr. Leuchter is an engineer specialising in gas chambers and executions. He is well versed in all areas and is the only consultant in the United States that I know of." The reader interested in learning more about Robert Faurisson's contribution to the second Zündel trial should refer to Barbara Kulaszka's book *Did Six Million Really Die: Report of the Evidence in the Canadian "False News" Trial of Ernst Zündel* (Toronto,1992).

Between 20 November 1978 and 31 May 1993, Robert Faurisson was the victim of ten violent attacks. The most serious of these occurred on 16 September 1989, when he was already in his sixties. While he was walking his dog in a park near his home in Vichy, three men set him up. After spraying his face with a stinging gas that momentarily blinded him, the assailants threw him to the ground and began punching him in the face and kicking him in the chest. It seems clear that the criminals, three Jewish thugs who are members of the group "fils de la mémoire juive" (children of Jewish memory), intended to kill him. Fortunately, a person who saw the scene intervened and was able to rescue the teacher, who was seriously injured. He was taken to a hospital and underwent a long surgical operation in the emergency room, as his jaw and a rib were broken, as well as severe head injuries. The Jewish group that claimed responsibility for the attack said in a statement: "Professor Faurisson is the first, but he will not be the last. We leave those who deny the Shoah warned." Faurisson later stated that on the eve of the attack he had noticed in surprise the presence in the park of Nicolas Ullmann, who two years earlier had already beaten him in a sports club in

Vichy. As usual, not a single arrest was made and the attackers went unpunished.

Robert Faurisson's merit is singular in that, as in the case of Ernst Zündel, we see a man alone who does not shrink back, an intellectual of great stature, almost unrepeatable, who has been and remains capable of enduring everything rather than renounce his convictions. In April 1991, following an interview that appeared in September 1990 in *Le Choc du Mois*, the 17th chamber of the Paris Correctional Court, presided over by Claude Grellier, imposed a fine of 250,000 francs on Faurisson and a further 180,000 on the editor of the publication. In the same year, the Jewish lobby succeeded in having him expelled from the university on the basis of the Fabius-Gayssot law. The professor appealed to the ICCPRHRC (International Covenant on Civil and Political Rights and Human Rights Committee) on the grounds that the Fabius-Gayssot Law violated international law; however the ICCPRHRC dismissed the appeal and said that the Fabius-Gayssot Law is necessary to counter "possible anti-Semitism". On 17 March 1992 Faurisson issued a challenge from Stockholm: he demanded a graphic display of the murder weapon and its operating technique. He demanded that someone show him or draw him a Nazi gas chamber. The response was a new aggression. A year later, on 22 May 1993, he was physically assaulted for the second time in Stockholm. On both occasions, the Swedish press reported the attacks on the French professor at some length.

Years later, when in April 1996 the 'Affaire Garaudy' was beginning to polarise attention in France, Robert Faurisson made a statement in which he expressed his solidarity with Roger Garaudy and confirmed 'the imposture of the gas chambers'. As a result of these words, Jewish organisations sued him for the umpteenth time on 25 September 1997. During the trial, Faurisson told the court: "We are only three years away from the year 2000 and millions of people are asked to believe in something they have never seen and do not even know how it worked". The prosecutor called for Faurisson to be jailed if he did not pay the appropriate fine, to which the professor replied, "I will neither buy nor pay for my freedom. No one has ever bought me and no one will ever buy me." Finally, on 23 October 1997, the court found him "guilty" and demanded that he pay 120,600 francs divided into three parts: 50,000 francs as a fine, 20,600 francs for the

Jewish accuser, and another 50,000 francs to pay for the publication of the sentence in two newspapers.

Only three months later, in December 1997, the Jews sued again. Faurisson was subpoenaed by a Paris court because of an article published on a website on 16 January 1997: "Les visions cornues de l'"Holocauste", in which he began by stating that "the Holocaust of the Jews was a fiction". The professor responded to the summons with a letter announcing his refusal to continue to collaborate with the French justice system and police in their repression of revisionism. The harassment continued: three months later, on 16 March 1998, he had to appear before a Paris court to be tried for a definition of "revisionism", which appeared in a newspaper incorrectly.

And so it goes on and on. On 8 April 1998 it was the Dutch Jews who went against Faurisson. Seven years earlier, in 1991, in collaboration with the Belgian revisionist Siegfried Verbeke, he had published in Dutch *Het "Dagboek" van Anne Frank. Een Kritische benadering* (*The "Diary" of Anne Frank. A critical evaluation*), a booklet which concluded that the "diary" was a forgery, since the handwriting of the original manuscript could not have been that of a child. The book was banned in the Netherlands, but both the Anne Frank Museum in Amsterdam and the Anne Frank Fonds in Basel were not satisfied with the censorship of the book and took joint legal action. The Museum complained that Faurisson's work had forced them to provide "special instruction" to the guides and that the professor's criticism could reduce the number of visitors to the museum and, consequently, its profits.

The cancellation of the congress "Historical Revisionism and Zionism", which was to be held in Beirut from 31 March to 3 April 2001, was a major setback for the revisionists from all over the world who had gathered in the Lebanese capital. The government of Lebanon, the victim of continuous Israeli attacks, gave in to pressure from the most important Zionist organisations, backed by the United States. Robert Faurisson then explained that Rafik Hariri, Lebanon's prime minister, was so trapped by his country's debt, which amounted to 24,000,000,000 dollars for four million inhabitants, that had no alternative but to give in to blackmail and ban the congress. Since then, the holding of an international revisionist conference had been in doubt. When Mahmoud Ahmadinejad became president of the

Islamic Republic of Iran in 2005, Tehran offered to host revisionists from all over the world. One hundred and thirty researchers from thirty countries converged on the Iranian capital, where the Tehran International Holocaust Review Conference finally took place on 11-12 December 2006, which was greeted in the West with all sorts of disqualifications and backlash.

On 11 December 2006, Professor Faurisson gave a speech based on a document entitled *The Victories of Revisionism*, which has since been translated into several languages, including Spanish, and published in many countries. In this text, dedicated to Professor Mahmoud Ahmadinejad and to Ernst Zündel, Germar Rudolf and Horst Mahler, whom Faurisson refers to as "our prisoners of conscience", up to twenty historical realities clarified by revisionist research are presented in detail, which have had to be explicitly or implicitly acknowledged by the exterminationists. 1. There were no gas chambers in the camps in Germany. 2. 2. There was no order from Hitler to exterminate the Jews. 3. At the Wannsee Conference, the extermination of the Jews was not decided upon, since the term "final solution" meant deportation to the East. 4. The formulation in which the German concentration camp system has been presented is doomed. 5. The Auschwitz gas chamber visited by millions of tourists is a fake. 6. No documents, traces or other material evidence of the existence of the gas chambers have been found. On 11 December 2006, Robert Faurisson gave a wide-ranging interview to Iranian television, during which he declared to millions of Iranian viewers that the Holocaust was a lie. This was bound to have consequences, as the usual people in France were waiting for him.

No sooner had the revisionist congress ended than the then President of the Republic Jacques Chirac condemned Faurisson's participation in the Tehran conference on 13 December 2006 and personally called for an investigation. Following the instructions of the highest authority of the state, the Minister of Justice instructed a Paris prosecutor to launch an investigation. On 16 April 2007, police lieutenant Séverine Besse and another colleague went to Vichy to question the professor. Obstinately, Faurisson refused to answer any of the questions and wrote the following in the official report: "I refuse to collaborate with the police and judicial system in the repression of historical revisionism".

Magistrate Marc Sommerer, assigned to the case, summoned Faurisson nine months later. At 9 a.m. on 24 January 2008, the professor presented himself at the local police station. As soon as he entered, three judicial police officers sent the day before from Paris, including Séverine Besse herself, notified him that he was in custody and that his home would be searched while he was being held. He, an old man who would have been 79 years old the following day, 25 January, had his body searched and his wallet, purse, pen, watch, belt, etc. were confiscated. Perhaps they were trying to intimidate the old professor, who said that his wife was ill at home, a fact known to the police, and that for serious medical reasons she needed his constant presence. Once again, Faurisson remained stubborn and did not answer any questions. He was then told that he was the subject of three criminal proceedings for which warrants had been issued by Judge Sommerer. The first two mentioned to him related to his participation in the Tehran Conference. In one, he was being prosecuted under the Fabius-Gayssot Law by the Public Prosecutor's Office and a host of "pious organisations" for "denying crimes against humanity". In another, the LICRA had sued him for "defamation". The third lawsuit had been brought by the daily *Libération* for tortuous reasons that we will spare you the explanation. Faurisson was then taken to his home, where the search continued for six hours. Finally, on 25 July 2012, a judge in Paris notified him of the trial of the three criminal complaints.

The persecution of Robert Faurisson for thought crimes has been ongoing for forty years. On the night of 19 November 2014, two policemen from the neighbouring town of Clermond-Ferrand, one of whom was a major, turned up at his home in Vichy with a search warrant: they wanted to seize a computer and certain documents. They found neither. Once again, the LICRA had asked the public prosecutor to take action against the appearance of an unofficial "Blog" by the professor. There is no doubt that Faurisson possessed an inner strength of a superior nature. Faced with the scale of the attacks and the sheer scale of the fight against such powerful enemies, any normal person would have given up; however, Faurisson, who in 2014 had a heart attack, neither flinched nor broke down. On 29 January 2016, his 87th birthday, he was still holding on with his 83-year-old wife, who has been able to stay with the professor despite the fact that she too has a heart condition. Faurisson had recently complained that he was constantly receiving threats, both by telephone and in writing, and had unsuccessfully asked the police to protect them, as his wife was being harassed more and more each day, and was suffering more and more from her illness.

Robert Faurisson, the alma mater of revisionism whose legacy is essential for future generations, bravely persisted in the battle until the very last moment. He died at around 7pm on 21 October 2018. He was 89 years old. As he was crossing the threshold of his home in Vichy, the professor suffered a massive heart attack. He was returning from Shepperton, his home town in England, where the day before, at the invitation of Lady Renouf, he had given a final lecture in English. Jean Faurisson, announcing his brother Robert's death, explained that in Shepperton he had met with friends and reported that on two occasions he had been violently harassed by a group of "anti-hate" bigots. Attacks and aggression were a constant feature of Professor Faurisson's life, and he was never intimidated. Jean Faurisson alluded to the possible traumatic effect that the harassment could have had on the already fragile health of his brother, who would have turned 90 in January 2019.

Vincent Reynouard, "Hearts go up!"

The case of the young revisionist Vincent Reynouard is another example of the will to resist: in the face of endless adversity, he has shown commendable courage and courage worthy of respect. Born in 1969, he married in 1991 and is now the father of eight children. A Catholic traditionalist, a convinced National Socialist and a revisionist, Reynouard has put everything at risk rather than give an inch in his denunciation of the falsity of official history. At the age of twenty-three, he had his first setback with the Fabius-Gayssot law. On 8 October 1992, a court in Caen sentenced him to a month's imprisonment, suspended, and a fine of 5,000 francs for having anonymously given twenty-four of his students texts questioning the gas chamber murders. Graduated as a chemical engineer with a diploma from ISMRA (Institute of Materials and Radiation), he worked as a high school teacher of mathematics and as a freelance historian specialising in the Second World War. In 1997, after revisionist texts were found on the hard drive of the computer he used at school, he was dismissed from the secondary school teaching profession by Education Minister François Bayrou. Since then, he has had to survive on his writings, his videos and his work as a researcher.

Author of a dozen essays and pamphlets on historical topics. Reynouard worked with Siegfried Verbeke on *Vrij Historisch Onderzook, VHO (Free Historical Research)*, a website that became the largest revisionist publishing site in Europe. He himself edited the publication *Sans Concession*. His most famous book was the result of an investigation into the Oradour-sur-Glane massacre. At 14:00 on 10 June 1944, shortly after the landing of Normandy, the Waffen SS entered this small, quiet village in the Limousin, where resistance fighters were sheltering. Six hours later, at 20:00, the Waffen SS left the village. Behind them lay a ruined place littered with corpses, five hundred of them charred women and children. Academic historiography attributed the massacre to the Germans. Officially, they retreated through the village and set fire to the church where women and children had taken refuge. This is exactly what Reynouard questioned in his 450-page book, published in Belgium in 1997. In France the book appeared in June 1997, after he had been expelled from teaching for his revisionist views. Three months later, in September, Interior Minister Jean-Pierre Chevènement ordered the book to be seized and banned its distribution and circulation throughout France.

Between 1998 and 1999, a team of Reynouard's collaborators produced a video cassette summarising the book and encouraging people to buy it. The film was released in 2000 and distribution began in January 2001. On 8 February 2001, the prefect of Haute-Vienne, a department in central France, issued a decree banning the cassette in the whole department. On 27 September 2001, four years after the banning of the book, the Ministry of the Interior banned the video throughout France. The proceedings against Vincent Reynouard led to a trial which took place in first instance on 18 November 2003. Reynouard was sentenced for "apology of a war crime" to one year in prison, a fine of 10,000 euros, and the confiscation of all his seized files. The appeal proceedings were held on 14 April 2004. Reynouard was sentenced to two years, of which six months was actual imprisonment and the rest was probation, but the fine of 10,000 euros was changed to 3,000 euros. In addition, he had to compensate the three civil parties that had appeared in the case, including the inescapable LICRA.

Nevertheless, Reynouard continued to pursue revisionist ideas and in 2005 wrote a sixteen-page pamphlet entitled *Holocaust? Here is what they hide from us*, in which he openly questioned the official history and presented a completely opposite view. The French judiciary was quick to pounce on him. The retrial took place on 8 November 2007 in Saverne, where a court sentenced him to one year in prison and a fine of 10,000 euros for "questioning crimes against humanity" through the aforementioned pamphlet. He was also ordered to pay 3,000 euros to LICRA. The judgment was appealed, but on 25 June 2008, the Colmar Court of Appeal upheld it and also imposed a new fine of 60,000 euros. Simultaneously, on 19 June 2008, six days earlier, the Brussels Court of Appeal had sentenced Reynouard and Siegfried Verbeke to one year in prison and a fine of 25,000 euros for having written and published texts denying the Holocaust and questioning crimes against humanity.

Moreover, as Reynouard resided in Belgium, the French authorities issued a European arrest warrant in order for the Belgians to extradite him, since, according to the ratification of the sentence by the court of appeal of Colmar, Reynouard should also serve one year of imprisonment in France. On 9 July 2010, he was incarcerated in Forest Prison (Brussels). On 23 July 2010, Judge Chambers in Brussels declared that the arrest warrant for Reynouard issued by France was valid, so on 19 August 2010 he was extradited and imprisoned in Valenciennes prison. While awaiting extradition he declared: "When you have no other argument than prison to free yourself from a dialectical opponent, it is because you lack arguments".

Paul-Éric Blanrue, founding historian of the research group Cercle Zététique and author of the book *Sarkozy, Israël, et les juifs,* issued a press release denouncing the Gayssot law, calling for solidarity with Vincent Reynouard and launching a campaign to collect signatures in defence of freedom of expression and demanding Reynouard's release. Blanrue, in addition to denouncing the suspicious silence of the French and international media, noted the abnormality of the fact that not a single NGO had said a word in defence of Reynouard's freedom of expression and freedom of thought,.

Early in the morning of Tuesday, 5 April 2011, the 42-year-old revisionist left Valenciennes prison. His wife Marina, his son Pierre and a group of friends, including Siegfried Verbeke, his wife Edna and a group of Belgian and German revisionists, were waiting for him outside the gate. Reynouard's seven other children were waiting in a café near the prison, making drawings to give to their father. After eating together in a joyful atmosphere, the Reynouard family had to separate again, as Marina and the children had to return to Brussels. Vincent could not go with them, as he was under judicial supervision and forbidden to leave France. In fact, the next day, 6 April, he was summoned by an examining magistrate in Amiens on another matter: he was suspected of having sent revisionist CDs to 120 high schools in France in 2009.

On the day of his release, Reynouard gave an interview to a journalist from *Rivarol* magazine. His first words were for his wife, whom he thanked for her attitude and congratulated for her heroism. Secondly, he thanked Paul-Éric Blanrue for his courage and all those who had assisted him financially and written to him. He expressed his intention to write a book of testimony and to resume the publication of the review *San Concessions*, which had been interrupted since his arrest, since all his collaborators had remained faithful to their posts. The last words of the interview were words of encouragement: "In spite of all the vicissitudes and all the traps, the fight goes on. Let your hearts soar!

In February 2015, a court of first instance in Coutances, Lower Normandy, again sentenced Vincent Reynouard to two years in prison for publishing a video in which he denounced the political manipulation and brainwashing inflicted on the youth of his country and refuted the theory of the systematic extermination of European Jews during the Second World War. He was also fined 35,000 euros. Faced with the severity of the sentence, as the Gayssot Law provides for a maximum of one year in prison for "Holocaust denial", the prosecutor himself appealed to the court of appeal in Caen, the regional capital. In a video posted on the internet, Reynouard had announced that he did not intend to pay a single cent. On 17 June 2015, in view of the evidence that the sentence imposed by the Coutances court was "illegal", the Caen court reduced it to one year and revoked the financial penalty. Reynouard did not appear before the Caen court, two months earlier, on 25 April 2015, he had announced in a video that he was going underground to flee the political persecution he was suffering in France: "So," he said in the video, "you can say that I am on the run. This time I have lost everything, or almost everything. Here I am without a home, with my rucksack. I have only been able to save a few fragments of files to try to make the promised videos". At the time of writing, we do not know what has become of Reynouard, as we have not been able to find out anything new about him.

3. Main victims of persecution in Austria

Gerd Honsik, victim of PSOE's surrender to Zionism

Hans Strobl, president of the Burgenland Cultural Federation, wrote in 1988 in the epilogue of *A Solution for Hitler?* that the Austrian state police had threatened Gerd Honsik in 1978 with committal to a psychiatric clinic. He does not, however, explain why Honsik was so seriously intimidated, and instead of being sent to an insane asylum he ended up in prison. In prison he wrote two books of poems. The first, *Lüge, wo ist dein Sieg?* (*Lie, where is your Victory?*), was published in 1981; the second, *Fürchtet euch nicht!* (*Don't be afraid!*), in 1983. Both manuscripts were smuggled out of prison with the help of prison guards sympathetic to the poet, who had been forbidden to write. The first book, composed in classical verse, was eventually confiscated and cost Honsik a fine of 41,000 shillings (then Austrian currency). The president of the Supreme Court, apparently an expert in literary criticism, ruled that it was "not art". As for the latter, it was also prosecuted and banned.

In 1986, for political reasons, Honsik was dismissed from his job, where he had been employed for fifteen years. The persecution affected his school-age children, who were subjected to pressure, including from some teachers. Between 1987 and 1988, Honsik had to go to court eighteen times: he had to spend 140,000 shillings in court fees and legal costs. The worst came in 1988 with the publication of *Freispruch für Hitler?* (*Solution for Hitler?*), a book purporting to be a book of reconciliation. Gerd Honsik consulted a Catholic parish priest, Robert Viktor Knirsch, to find out whether the priest understood that there were any moral impediments. The parish priest wrote him a letter in which, as a Roman Catholic priest, he encouraged him to continue with the book:

> "...Truth is part of the retinue of good. Everyone who seeks the truth has the right to be able to doubt, to investigate and to weigh up. And where people are required to believe blindly, there is a haughtiness, with so much blasphemy, that it gives us pause for thought. While now those whose thesis you question have reason on their side, they will accept all questions calmly, they will give their answers with all patience. And they

will no longer conceal their evidence and records. But if they lie, they will cry out to the judge. Thus they will be known. The truth is always calm; but a lie is always in a struggle for an earthly trial!

With my compliments, I send you my best regards.

Priest Robert Viktor Knirsch

Kahlenbergerdorf, 2/6/1988".

After writing these words to Honsik, which the poet reproduced in his work, the parish priest was admitted to a psychiatric clinic, where he soon fell ill. He died on Monday 26 June 1989. Before his death, he expressed the wish that the German anthem should be played at his burial. At 9.30 a.m. on 30 June, a funeral mass was held in Kahlenbergerdorf, after which Knirsch's body was buried in the parish cemetery. About seven hundred people attended the funeral, including Archbishop Krätztl and Provost Koberger, but also numerous secret agents and a police dog unit. When, at the end of the ceremony, Honsik asked for the priest's last wishes to be carried out, the police intervened and began asking the attendees to identify themselves. Gerd Honsik was momentarily detained and reproached for requesting the playing of the German anthem in circumstances where it was forbidden.

As for the consequences of the book's publication, the process dragged on for years and even led to the creation of a law that applied exclusively to the case. In January 1992, Honsik left the country after being publicly defamed on television, where Dr. Neugebauer, director of the Austrian Resistance Documentary Archives, accused him in the presence of the Minister of the Interior of planning a coup d'état. When it was proved to be slander and falsehoods, Honsik returned to Austria to attend the trial, which lasted several weeks. Gerd Honsik was sentenced on 5 May 1992 to eighteen months imprisonment for "revitalisation of National Socialist activities". The Austrian Supreme Court rejected the appeal. To avoid further imprisonment, he fled to Spain, where he had already lived for a year as an eight-year-old boy. In 1949 he crossed the Pyrenees in a special train with a thousand severely malnourished Austrian children fleeing the ethnic cleansing perpetrated in Europe against the German people between 1945 and 1948, the perfectly documented genocide that has been concealed.

In 1993, Honsik published another book for which he would also later be prosecuted, *Schelm und Scheusal* (*Rogue and Monster*), in which he denounced Simon Wisenthal, who had expressed his satisfaction with the letter bomb sent from Austria to former SS Alois Brunner, who lost an eye and eight fingers. A close associate of Adolf Eichmann, Brunner lived in Damascus, where Zionist assassins had tried to kill him on several occasions. Wiesenthal was well aware of the details of the bombing and referred to the victim as his "most wanted murderer of Jews". However, in August 1988 Gerd Honsik had visited him in the Syrian capital and to the question "When did you learn about the gas chambers?", Brunner replied, "After the war, through the newspapers."

On 7 October 1993, the Spanish Prime Minister, Felipe González, travelled to Vienna. There, the Chancellor of the Republic of Austria, Franz Vranitzky, took advantage of the occasion to ask him to extradite Honsik. This clearly reveals the extent of the power of Jewish lobbies, which are capable of getting a high-ranking European leader to ask another to hand over a political refugee because of the publication of a book. Having learned of this circumstance, Gerd Honsik addressed an open letter to the Spanish Parliament requesting political refuge in Spain. In the text he recalled that Spain had taken him in as a child in the post-war period and that he had already learned Spanish. The letter ended with these words: "I am addressing the Spanish parliamentarians, both on the right and on the left, and the Spanish people, begging them to remain firm in the face of the international pressures that are calling for my extradition. In Spain then I found refuge from hunger. In Spain today I seek refuge from prison". The Austrian authorities requested the Spanish Government to extradite him, but on 7 November 1995 the Audiencia Nacional refused. The Public Prosecutor's Office objected and considered, as the defence pointed out, that it was "a political crime and, therefore, excluded from extradition". The reasoning of the Audiencia Nacional considered that "it was not feasible to frame such conduct as provocation to the crime of genocide, as this requires the purpose of destroying, totally or partially, a religious group", a purpose that could not be affirmed "from the facts (writing and publishing *A solution for Hitler?*) for which the defendant has been convicted...". Both the judge and the Audiencia prosecutor agreed that Honsik's book did not violate Spanish law. Therefore, without any harassment by the Spanish authorities, Gerd Honsik lived in Malaga for nearly fifteen years.

Finally, a European arrest warrant issued by the Vienna court was served by the Spanish authorities: on 23 August 2007, police arrested Honsik in Malaga. In September 2007, the president of the Jewish Religious Community of Austria, tycoon Ariel Muzicant, a Haifa-born Israeli, told the newspaper *Die Gemeinde* (*The Community*) that the Jewish community was working for uniform European legislation against neo-Nazis and Holocaust revisionists. Commenting on Honsik's arrest in Spain, he said:

> "Gerd Honsik was arrested after spending fifteen years in Spain and will be extradited to Austria. Personally, I am delighted about this because it shows once again that my talks with the Spanish Prime Minister, the Foreign Minister and the Minister of Justice in January this year have helped to get the Spanish government to adopt a corresponding stance

Without a hint of dissimulation, on the contrary, Muzicant boasted shamelessly about his power and took credit for getting the Spanish socialist government to do the right thing, i.e. what Zionism wanted. In January 2007, Spain had a PSOE government headed by José Luis Rodríguez Zapatero. The foreign minister was the ineffable Miguel Ángel Moratinos and the justice minister was Juan Fernando López Aguilar. The judge who allowed the extradition was Baltasar Garzón, who four years later would be sentenced to eleven years of disqualification and expelled from the judiciary by a unanimous decision of the members of the Criminal Chamber of the Supreme Court. This unscrupulous judge, unfortunately defended by many sectarians of the Spanish left, put himself at the service of the Zionists without considering that Spain had twice refused extradition and that the Audiencia Nacional had ruled in a 1995 decision that Honsik's was "a political crime and therefore excluded from extradition". Gerd Honsik's surrender to Austria took place on 4 October 2007. The Austrian Minister of Justice, the Socialist Maria Berger, publicly expressed her special thanks to Judge Baltasar Garzón in a press release issued by the Ministry of Justice on 5 October.

Four years later, on 26 January 2012, Göran Holming, a retired Swedish army commander and member of European Action, a movement for a free Europe, filed criminal charges against Baltasar

Garzón, Prime Minister Rodríguez Zapatero and the aforementioned ministers with the Audiencia Nacional. The letter denounced the meeting with Ariel Muzicant and the political agreements reached at the meeting in January 2007. It argued at length about the false pretexts invoked to grant the extradition and specifically accused Judge Garzón of prevarication and violation of the law and the Spanish Constitution, which prohibits extradition for political crimes unless there are "terrorist acts". Here is the text of the request:

> "I would like to ask the public prosecutor to verify whether the former Prime Minister José Luis Rodríguez Zapatero and his former Ministers of Justice and Foreign Affairs, in collaboration with Judge Baltasar Garzón, have to answer for the extradition of the Austrian poet and writer Gerd Honsik, promoted through a conspiracy with the foreigner Ariel Muzicant and Ms. Maria Berger, and carried out with the purpose of carrying out an inhumane and unjust political persecution in Austria, and whether the aforementioned persons have cumulatively committed Maria Berger and carried out for the purpose of inhumane and unjust political persecution in Austria, and whether the aforementioned persons have cumulatively committed:
>
> I) A crime against humanity,
>
> II) the offence of abuse of power,
>
> III) for falsification of the EU Arrest Warrant,
>
> IV) of conspiracy in an agreement against the Spanish Constitution.
>
> I hereby request that the above-mentioned persons be brought to trial before the competent court for the above-mentioned offences.
>
> Sincerely
>
> Göran Holming, retired commander of the Swedish Army".

Let us now return to the case of G. Honsik. On 3 December 2007, the appeal hearing, which had been cancelled in 1992 due to "failure of the person concerned to appear", was held in Vienna. The appeal was dismissed and the sentence of eighteen months unconditional imprisonment was confirmed. In May 2008, the Vienna Public Prosecutor's Office brought new charges against Honsik for "revitalisation of National Socialist activities". On 20 April 2009, the trial before the Vienna Regional Court began and on 27 April Honsik was sentenced to five years imprisonment because of his views on the existence of the gas chambers in the National Socialist labour camps.

The verdict was upheld by the Supreme Court, but on 1 March 2010 the sentence was reduced to four years by the Vienna Court of Appeal.

Still on 20 July 2010, a new trial was held against Honsik for the publication of two books, one of which was *Schelm und Scheusal* and the other *Rassismus Legal?* This was a "3g trial", i.e. a trial under Section 3g of the Austrian Prohibition Act (Verbotgesetz) of 1947, which severely represses the "revival of National Socialist sentiments". Judge Andreas Böhm, who sentenced Honsik to five years in the April 2009 trial, had instructed public prosecutor Stefan Apostol to exclude the incriminating books in order to subsequently open a new trial that would allow for an additional sentence. At the trial, the books were considered separately. Honsik, despite serving time in prison, or perhaps because of it, was not deterred and lashed out at Simon Wiesenthal. What information we have about the trial sessions comes from the Austrian press, servile as all of them are to the controlling Jewish lobbies, so we will spare you the quotes. In short, Honsik reiterated that it was an admitted fact that there was not a single gas chamber on German or Austrian soil and that the liar was not he, but Wiesenthal. The judge tried to get Honsik's lawyer, Dr. Herbert Schaller, to deny the existence of the gas chambers. He repeatedly asked him if he, too, claimed that there were no gas chambers; but the lawyer always avoided answering questions that in Germany were asked to incriminate the defendants' lawyers.

Theoretically, Honsik was not due to be released until 2013, but an appeal to the Vienna Court finally achieved the goal of a favourable sentence, which reduced the length of his sentence by eighteen months. His advanced age (70 years) and his "successful social integration" in Spain, where he returned after his release at the end of 2011 to settle again in Malaga, where he had been arrested in 2007, were reportedly taken into account. Throughout his life, Gerd Honsik has been imprisoned for nearly six years for expressing ideas considered thought crimes.

David Irving, sentenced to three years in prison in Vienna.

The second Ernst Zündel trial in Toronto was a milestone in the evolution of the revisionist thinking of David Irving, who, along with Robert Faurisson, acted as counsel to lawyer Doug Christie and testified at the trial as a defence witness. It appears that it was Irving who contacted Bill Armontrout, and when he recommended Fred Leuchter, he flew to Boston in the company of Faurisson to meet with the gas chamber expert to convince him to provide the technical expertise. The *Leuchter Report* dispelled all of Irving's doubts about the alleged extermination of European Jewry, if he still had any. Upon his return to London after the trial, Irving published the American engineer's report in the UK under the title *Auschwitz the End of the Line: The Leuchter Report* and wrote the foreword. Neither pleased the political establishment, and so on 20 June 1989 Irving and Leuchter were convicted in a proposition tabled in the House of Commons. It described David Irving as "a Nazi propagandist and apologist for Hitler". As for the text released, it was deemed a "fascist publication". Irving issued a scathing press release in response to the Commons motion. On 23 June 1989, Irving published a text in which he stated unequivocally that the Auschwitz gas chambers were a "fable".

On 6 November 1989, David Irving gave a lecture at the Park Hotel in Vienna that sixteen years later would cost him a three-year prison sentence. Jewish organisations and various communist and extreme left-wing groups brought five thousand demonstrators onto the streets in an attempt to prevent the event. About five hundred riot police had to form a protective cordon to prevent the most exalted protesters from storming the building. As a result of the content of the two lectures given in Austria, the government issued an arrest warrant for Irving and banned him from entering the country.

In January 1990 David Irving gave a lecture in Moers, Germany, where he alluded to Allied air terror and claimed that as many people died in Auschwitz between 1940 and 1945 as died in any of the criminal bombing raids on German cities. On 21 April 1990 Irving repeated the same speech in Munich, prompting a court in the Bavarian capital to sentence him on 11 July 1991 to a fine of DM 7,000 for Holocaust denial. Irving appealed, and during the hearing on 5 May 1992, he on those present in the Munich courtroom to fight for the German people to "put an end to the bloody lie of the Holocaust that had been woven against the country for fifty years". Irving referred to Auschwitz as "a tourist attraction". In addition to a fine of 10,000 marks, he was henceforth banned from entering Germany.

Other countries followed suit and the veto against Irving began to become widespread. In Canada he was arrested in November 1992 and deported to the UK. He was also refused entry to Italy and Australia. On 27 April 1993 he was summoned before a French court on charges related to the Gayssot Law. As this law does not provide for extradition, the historian refused to travel to France and did not appear. In 1994, he was sentenced in the UK to three months in prison for contempt of court during a legal dispute over publishing rights. He was finally locked up for ten days in London's Pentonville Prison.

The legal confrontation between David Irving and the Jewish historian Deborah Lipstadt, well known in revisionist circles, was a turning point that marked the British historian. It was a lengthy trial in the United Kingdom, of which we will only note the essential facts, since Irving appears in these pages as a victim of persecution in Austria, and we must not deviate from our objective. For readers unfamiliar with the issue, the controversy between Deborah Lipstadt, Professor of Modern Judaism and Holocaust Studies at Emory University (USA), and David Irving began in 1993, when Lipstadt disqualified Irving in *Denying the Holocaust: The Growing Assault on Truth and Memory*. In the book, Lipstadt referred to the British historian as "an anti-Semite who falsifies documents for ideological reasons" and concluded that he was "a dangerous Holocaust denialist spokesman". In 1996 Irving decided to sue Lipstadt and his British publisher Penguin Books Ltd. for libel, claiming that his reputation as a historian had been damaged. The trial began on 11 January 2000 and ended on 11 April with Judge Charles Gray ruling in favour of Lipstadt and Penguin Books. Gray found that Irving "for his own ideological reasons had persistently and deliberately misrepresented and manipulated the historical evidence". Despite the fact that, as Germar Rudolf revealed, David Irving has Jewish origins, Judge Gray argued in the verdict that Irving was an "active Holocaust denier"; that he was "anti-Semitic and racist"; and that he had "associated with far-right radicals to promote neo-Nazism". The trial and verdict went around the world.

On 11 November 2005 David Irving became the most high-profile victim of the persecution of revisionists in Austria. He himself later recounted the whole story in an article published in the *American Free Press*. According to his account, he had travelled to the country to speak to a student association, the student fraternity "Olympia".

The subject of the lecture, discussed earlier in this work (*Proscribed History*), was Joel Brand's negotiation in Hungary with Adolf Eichmann to free Hungarian Jews in exchange for trucks. Irving planned to explain that the British secret services had cracked the communication codes and were aware of what was being discussed between the Zionists and the Nazis. Since there had been a warrant for his arrest issued by the Vienna Regional Court for Holocaust denial since November 1989, Irving did not want to risk entering Austria by direct flight and opted to travel by car from Zurich. After driving through the night, he arrived in Vienna at 8:00 a.m. after having driven 900 kilometres.

Once he had rested, he called the student who had invited him, Christopher V., from a train station: "Rendezvous A," Irving said without identifying himself, "in one hour. Security was necessary and everything had been arranged six months in advance. Christopher, a young man in his twenties, picked him up in the station foyer and drove him to where over two hundred students were supposedly waiting for him. The event was scheduled to start at 18:00. Once the car was parked, they approached the building on foot. Leaning against the wall, they saw "three burly bouncers". As soon as he realised that they were from the "Stapo" (State Police), the young man handed the car keys to Irving and they parted ways. As he walked back to the Ford Focus, Irving recounts, "one of the bouncers was following me about eighty yards behind; the other two were chasing Christopher." Out of habit, he entered the car from the right, as if it were an English vehicle; but the steering wheel was on the other side. The man started to run. When he finally started, the policeman was only about ten yards away. In the rear-view mirror, he saw him writing down the car's details on a notepad. The plan was to try to get to Basel, where he was to catch a plane the next day. About 250 kilometres outside Vienna, two police cars forced him to stop: "Eight uniformed policemen suddenly jumped out and came running towards me, shouting hysterically". This is the tight summary of how Irving experienced his arrest.

A spokesman for the Austrian Interior Ministry, Rudolf Gollia, reported that the British historian had been arrested on 11 November by motorway police officers near the town of Johann in der Heide in the state of Styria. The international press reported that he had been arrested for denying the Holocaust 16 years earlier in a lecture given in 1989. A spokesman for the public prosecutor's office was quoted in the media as saying that if he was tried and found guilty, he could be sentenced to between one and ten years in prison.

After three months in custody, he was sentenced to three years in prison by the Vienna Regional Court on 20 February 2006. In the indictment, the prosecutor specified that in the two public speeches in 1989 Irving had said that "Hitler actually maintained his protective hand over the Jews" and had denied the existence of the gas chambers. According to the prosecutor, Irving had also maintained in 1989 that "Kristallnacht" was not perpetrated by the Nazis, but by individuals disguised as Nazis.

In all fairness, it must be said that Irving's concessions before the Viennese court deeply disappointed some revisionists, who would have wished for a more dignified, more stoic attitude. Irving declared that he had changed his mind about the Holocaust because on a trip to Argentina he had found new materials on Adolf Eichmann. He agreed to retract some of his claims and even admitted to the existence of gas chambers, thereby admitting his guilt of falsifying history. It seems that with this strategy he was hoping for an acquittal. So confident was he that he had even bought a plane ticket back to London in advance. However, the eight members of the jury were unanimous, and in the verdict the judge Peter Liebetreu said: "The previous confession did not seem to us to be an act of repentance and was therefore not taken into account in the weight of the sentence". The judge asked him if he had understood the sentence. "I am not sure about that," he replied dumbfounded. As he was led out of the courtroom he declared that he was shocked by the severity of the sentence.

The Court of Appeal, presided over by Judge Ernest Maurer, accepted an appeal. On 20 December 2006, Judge Maurer agreed to reduce the initial sentence to one year's imprisonment and two years' probation. Since Irving had already been in prison for thirteen months, he could be released. However, he was still banned from re-entering Austria. The verdict sparked the anger of Vienna's Jewish community and the Historical Documentation Centre of the Resistance. Brigitte Bailer, director of the centre, expressed her indignation. The verdict, she said, "is worrying because it is a sign that there are sectors in the Austrian justice system that minimise the crime of Holocaust denial."

Bailer accused Judge Maurer of being a sympathiser of the far-right FPÖ party. As soon as Irving was in England, he reaffirmed his revisionist positions and stated that "there was no longer any need to show remorse".

Thus, David Irving resumed his activities and gave revisionist lectures in Europe and America. In December 2007, the Catalan government tried to ban one of the planned events in Spain. The Mossos d'Esquadra (Catalan regional police), in addition to searching and filming the attendees in order to intimidate them, proceeded to seize some books. The speaker was warned that he would be arrested if there was any indication of a crime of opinion. In view of the situation, it was decided to suspend the conference and David Irving held a press conference with his freedom of expression alibied.

We continue in Spain. On the occasion of the seventieth anniversary of the outbreak of World War II, the newspaper *El Mundo* prepared a special edition in 2009 with interviews with specialists of different tendencies, including Irving. Israel's ambassador to Spain, Raphael Schutz, sent a letter of protest to the newspaper demanding censorship of Irving's contributions. Schutz, with his usual victimhood, claimed that it was not enough to invoke the right to "freedom of expression". The newspaper called the ambassador "intransigent" and replied that the newspaper *El Mundo* did not deny the Holocaust, quite the contrary.

Let's finish with an anecdote. In March 2013, David Irving's ban on entering Germany, which was to last until 2022, was lifted. In July of the same year he tried to book a room in Berlin because a conference was scheduled to take place in the German capital on 10 September at which attendees had to pay 119 dollars to get in. Volker Beck of the Green Party contacted the German hoteliers' association to boycott Irving. In this way he managed to get Berlin's leading hotels to refuse to accommodate the British revisionist, who was supposed to have found other accommodation.

Wolfgang Fröhlich, the "canary" still singing in the cage

Wolfgang Fröhlich is on track to break all records, having already spent nine years of his life in prison and currently serving another five, which amounts to fourteen years in prison for thought crimes. In an article published in *Smith's Report* in October 2015, Roberto Hernández equated Fröhlich with that canary to which Professor Faurisson alluded in his well-known phrase: "Putting a canary in a cage can't stop it from singing its songs." Wolfgang Fröhlich is an Austrian chemical engineer who is convinced that the thesis of the extermination of deportees in gas chambers is scientifically absurd. Fröhlich, our caged canary, is a specialist in disinfection processes and the construction of gas chambers for pest control and the elimination of microbes.

It has already been said that freedom of expression and freedom as a whole is prevented in Austria by a 1947 law, the "Verbotsgesetz" (Prohibition Law), which was originally intended to prevent the existence of anything that might be related to National Socialism. In 1992 this law was amended in order to punish Holocaust denial and any attempt to minimise Nazi atrocities. Despite the new implementation of the Prohibition Law, during the 1990s Fröhlich sent hundreds of texts to lawyers, judges, parliamentarians, journalists, etc., denouncing the alleged Nazi gas chambers as a lie. In 1998 he participated as an expert for the defence in the trial in Switzerland against Jürgen Graf and his publisher Gerhard Förster, to whom we will return later. Now it must be said that the court was not at all pleased with his testimony on the technical impossibility of mass gassings, so that the prosecutor Dominik Aufdenblatten threatened to charge him. The passage from the interrogation is as follows:

"Aufdenblatten: In your opinion, were mass gassings with Zyklon B technically possible?

Fröhlich: No.

Aufdenblatten: Why not?

Fröhlich: The pesticide Zyklon B is hydrocyanic acid in granular form. It is released on contact with air. The boiling point of hydrocyanic acid is 25.7 degrees (Celsius). The higher the temperature, the faster the evaporation rate. The delousing chambers in which Zyklon B was used in the camps and elsewhere were heated to thirty degrees and even higher, so that the hydrocyanic acid was quickly released from its granules. However, in the semi-underground morgues of the crematoria at Auschwitz-Birkenau, where, according to witnesses, mass exterminations with Zyklon B were carried out, the temperatures were much lower. If one admits that the rooms were heated by the bodies of the prisoners, the temperature would not have exceeded 15 degrees Celsius, even in summer. Consequently, it would have taken many hours for the hydrocyanic acid to evaporate. According to witness reports, the victims died quickly. Witnesses mention time periods from 'instantaneous' to '15 minutes'. In order to kill the prisoners in such a short time, the Germans would have had to use enormous quantities of Zyklon B - I estimate between 40 and 50 kilos in each gassing. This would have made any work in the gas chamber totally impossible. The special detachment (Sonderkomando), which according to witnesses emptied the chambers of bodies, would have collapsed immediately on entering, even while wearing gas masks. Huge quantities of hydrocyanic acid would have flooded out and the whole camp would have been poisoned".

Fröhlich's statement was greeted with applause; but prosecutor Aufdenblatten reacted indignantly and said: "For this statement I ask the court to charge you with racial discrimination according to Article 261 or else I will do it myself. Upon hearing these words, Förster's lawyer, Jürg Stehrenberger, stood up and informed the court that in view of the intolerable intimidation of the witness, he was withdrawing from the case. In the company of Graf's counsel, he left the courtroom for several minutes. When they returned, they both expressed their vehement objection to the prosecutor's behaviour, but announced that despite everything, they would continue with their duties as defence counsel.

In 2001 Wolfgang Fröhlich published *Die Gaskammer Lüge (The Gas Chamber Lie)*, a book of almost 400 pages that earned him an arrest warrant and forced him to go into hiding somewhere in Austria to avoid capture. In hiding, he conceived the project of sending out CDs entitled *Gaskammerschwiendel (The Gas Chamber Fraud)*, in which he detailed his research findings and referred to the fraud as "psychological terrorism". On 30 May 2003, he wrote in a letter that he was well and that he was eagerly continuing his project of sending CDs to people across the whole spectrum of Austrian society. To date, he had sent out some 800 CDs in the hope that his action would hasten the end of the "Holocaust story that millions of Jews had been gassed". Fröhlich saw this as an unprecedented historical deception of an entire people ("Volksbetrug"). Finally, on Saturday, 21 June 2003, Fröhlich was arrested and imprisoned in Vienna. In early 2004 he was tried and sentenced to three years in prison for violating the Prohibition Act ("Verbotsgesetz"), of which he spent two years on probation. When he was released from prison on 9 June 2004, he found himself unemployed and without resources.

While on parole, in June 2005, a new indictment was brought against him for issuing the 800 CDs proving the absolute impossibility of the gassings. He had to return to prison, where he awaited his retrial. On 29 August 2005, Judge Claudia Bandion-Ortner sentenced Frölich to two years in prison and annulled the suspension of the previous sentence, which meant that Frölich had been imprisoned for a total of four years. Fortunately, his appeal to the Supreme Court was successful, so that his sentence was reduced by 29 months and he was again granted provisional release. In December 2006, just out of prison, Wolfgang Fröhlich attended the International Holocaust Conference in Tehran, but did not speak, so that, despite allegations and pressure on the Austrian authorities, he was not charged for having travelled to Iran.

While on parole, the indefatigable Wolfgang Fröhlich asked a member of parliament and the provincial governors to abolish the Prohibition Act. For this reason he was re-arrested at the end of July/beginning of August 2007 and returned to prison, where he remained until a new trial was held. Judge Martina Spreitzer-Kropiunik of the Vienna Regional Court on 14 January 2008 returned a guilty verdict and sentenced him to four years' imprisonment, to be added to the 29 months that had been revoked by the Supreme Court. He was thus sentenced to a total of six years and four months imprisonment for simple offences of opinion.

Imprisoned as a political prisoner, Fröhlich, the "canary" who cannot stop singing, wrote to Barbara Prammer of the National Council of the SPÖ (Social Democratic Party of Austria), Cardinal Christoph Schönborn and others to explain his thesis that the extermination of millions of Jews in the gas chambers is technically impossible and that the death of six million Jews is "the most atrocious lie in the history of mankind". Wolfgang Fröhlich's irrepressible chant resulted in a new indictment against him: on 4 October 2010 he was sentenced to an additional two years in prison. And so it goes on and on. Half a year before he was due to be released, on 9 July 2015, the Krems District Court, presided over by Judge Dr. Gerhard Wittmann, sentenced him to a further three years' imprisonment. This time, prosecutor Elisabeth Sebek had brought charges against him for sending letters to Austrian Chancellor Werner Faymann, a Catholic Social Democrat, the news magazine *Profil* and other influential people. In these letters, he once again expressed his views on the Holocaust.

The latest we have heard from Wolfgang Fröhlich is that on 25 November 2015 he sent a letter of formal notice to the United Nations Human Rights Committee and to the European Convention on Human Rights. Since both Robert Faurisson and Ernst Zündel unsuccessfully went to international bodies, the former to denounce the Gayssot Law and the latter to denounce the violation of his rights, it is unlikely that Fröhlich will obtain any protection. The hidden tyranny of global power does not allow the slightest concession when it comes to revisionists seeking to unmask the imposture. In any case, we shall record the text as a tribute to this honest Austrian engineer who has tried everything and lost everything:

> "Ladies, gentlemen,
>
> I hereby formulate a REQUIREMENT
>
> in order that my human rights complaint no. 56264/09 against the Austrian Republic, which, by criminalising my opinions, is an attack on my fundamental rights, in particular those relating to the freedom of scientific research, be re-examined and that justice be done!
>
> I had already turned to the ECHR as a complainant against several convictions handed down by the Vienna criminal court solely because I had used my freedom of expression. By letter of 15 May 2012 (GZ ECHR LGer11.2R), this complaint was rejected as inadmissible!
>
> Through the press, I have recently learned that the ECHR had in the meantime modified its legal view concerning the human rights guarantees for freedom of expression. In October 2015, a Turkish politician who had been convicted in Switzerland for having expressed his opinion in public was ultimately cleared of all charges by the ECHR and Switzerland convicted of human rights violations. I refer to this matter in my letter of 13 July 2015 to the Council of Ministers of the Austrian Republic, which you will find in attachment no. 1.
>
> To sum up my question: I have been imprisoned in Austria for one and the same 'crime' for more than ten years now! On 9 July 2015 I was sentenced by the Krems court to an additional three years in prison, because I persist in defending the fundamental right to express myself freely! I refer to this matter in a letter addressed on 13 July 2015 to the Austrian Minister of Justice, Mr Wolfgang Brandstetter, which you will find in the attached document no. 2

Since the Austrian Republic is bound by the same legal standards (UN CCPR and ECHR) as Switzerland with regard to human rights, I therefore request that my application no. 56264/09 be investigated.

With my warmest regards,

Wolfgang Fröhlich".

4. Main victims of persecution in Switzerland

Jürgen Graf and Gerhard Förster sentenced for writing and publishing books

Born in 1951, Jürgen Graf, who initially sympathised with the Palestinian cause and consequently rejected Zionism for its crimes, had no doubt until 1991 that the Nazis had exterminated the Jews by means of gas chambers. He then met Arthur Vogt (1917-2003), considered the first Swiss revisionist, who provided him with a series of books that opened his eyes and cleared his mind. From then on, "I decided to dedicate my life," Graf confesses, "to the fight against the most monstrous fraud ever devised by human minds. So profound was the impact of reading the revisionist texts that in March 1992 he visited Professor Robert Faurisson in Vichy, who corrected his book *Der Holocaust auf dem Prüfstand*, published in early 1993.

Jürgen Graf, who studied French, English and Scandinavian philology, speaks more than ten languages. As a result of his first revisionist publication, he was dismissed in March 1993 as a teacher of Latin and French, the languages he taught at a secondary school in Therwill, a town near Basel. A month later he met publisher Gerhard Förster, whose father, a native of Silesia, had died during the brutal ethnic cleansing of millions of East European Germans. Unable to stop himself, Graf visited Carlo Mattogno, living near Rome, in September 1993, who provided him with valuable materials written in Polish, which he had been studying and researching for a decade. From this first visit, the two began a close collaboration and a deep friendship, as Graf became the translator of many of the Italian revisionist's writings. Subsequently, they made half a dozen research trips together (Poland, Russia, Lithuania, Belgium, Holland), from which they produced several books that they eventually co-wrote. In September 1994, Graf flew to California to attend a revisionist conference organised by the Institute for Historical Review. There he met Mark Weber, director of the IHR, Ernst Zündel, Bradley Smith and other revisionists. In October 1994 he got a new job as a German teacher in Basel; but he was dismissed in 1998, after the trial in Baden, which, after this hasty introduction, will be dealt with in the following lines.

Since we have been citing Jürgen Graf as a source throughout this work (*Proscribed History*), his name should be familiar to us by now. The collaboration with the Italian revisionist Carlo Mattogno resulted, as mentioned above, in important works on the transit camps in eastern Poland, which were turned into extermination camps by propaganda. *Treblinka: Extermination Camp or Transit Camp?* has been one of our main sources when studying the camps of the so-called "Aktion Reinhard". However, when Graf was convicted in 1998, it was for his early works, from which we have used *El Holocausto bajo la Lupa*, an English edition of *Der Holocaust auf dem Prüfstand*, one of the four books that led to his conviction. The five-member court was presided over by Judge Andrea Staubli, who, in justifying the verdict, rejected the defendants' arguments about the academic content of the books, which the court considered "cynical and inhuman".

In terms of the importance of his work and research and the number of books he has published, Jürgen Graf is the most important revisionist convicted in Switzerland. He and his publisher Gerhard Förster were sentenced on 21 July 1998 to fifteen and twelve months in prison respectively for writing one and publishing the other allegedly anti-Jewish books inciting "racial discrimination". The "Anti-Racism Law" which permitted the prosecution had been enacted on 1 January 1995 at the request of the Jewish community in Switzerland. It prohibited unspecified crimes such as "denial or trivialisation of genocide or other crimes against humanity". Gerhard Förster was found guilty of having published the writings of Graf and two other authors. Jürgen Graf was also convicted of sending "racist" CDs to Sweden for Ahmed Rami and to Canada for Ernst Zündel, who distributed them via the internet. In addition to imprisonment, the court in the northern Swiss town of Baden fined each of them CHF 8,000 and ordered them to return the CHF 55,000 they had made from the sale of the books, of which CHF 45,000 went to Förster and CHF 10,000 to Graf.

The Journal of Hisorical Review published in its July/August 1998 issue an extensive summary of the trial, which began on 16 July. According to this source, all sixty seats in the courtroom were filled with Graf and Förster sympathisers. At the outset, the court refused to allow Robert Faurisson, whose erudition was already feared everywhere, to testify. Instead, it accepted the testimony of the lesser-known Wolfgang Fröhlich, an excerpt of which has been reproduced above. Jürgen Graf's testimony lasted about two hours and was characterised by a vigorous defence of the views and arguments in his books. It is of interest to quote some of the questions and answers from the cross-examination. In response to Judge Staubli's question as to whether or not there had been a Holocaust, Graf replied:

> "It is a question of definition. If by Holocaust we mean a brutal persecution of Jews, mass deportations to camps, and the death of many Jews from disease, exhaustion and malnutrition, then it is of course a historical fact. But the Greek term 'holocaust' means 'utterly burned' or 'sacrifice by fire', and is used by orthodox historians for the alleged mass gassing of Jews in 'extermination camps'. That is a myth."

The judge then tried to question Graf on the fact that he was not a qualified historian. She then reproached him for not caring about offending Jews with his books. In his rejoinder, Graf cited examples of offences against the Swiss without anyone bothering about it. "Why," he asked Staubli, "is it only that the feelings of Jews are taken into account and never the feelings of non-Jews? The judge reminded him that the Anti-Racism Law was passed through a democratic referendum. "Shouldn't you respect that?". Response:

> "At the time, people were led to believe that the law served to protect foreigners against racist violence. In reality it serves exclusively to protect Jews against any criticism. This is irrefutably proven in the booklet 'Abschied von Rechtsstaat' (Farewell to the Rule of Law), to which I contributed two short essays. So far, not a single Swiss citizen has been charged for having criticised a black, an Arab or a Turk. Only people who have criticised Jews have been charged and convicted".

The public prosecution, represented by prosecutor Aufdenblatten, was very harsh in its conclusions and used expressions such as "pseudo-scientific", "anti-Semitic incitement" and "racist propaganda" to refer to the "criminal books". He concluded that Graf's writings fanned the flames of anti-Semitism, of hatred, and did not seek the truth, but distorted it. The prosecutor stressed that Graf showed no remorse, that he reaffirmed his revisionist views and was unlikely to amend them. He therefore asked the court not to consider a suspended sentence for either Graf or Förster, whom he said was as unreasonable as his colleague. As for the publicist's poor health, he said it was no excuse for leniency, as it was not for the court to consider whether he was too ill to go to prison, but for the doctors. Gerhard Förster died in September 1998, nine weeks after the trial.

After the final interventions by Jürg Stehrenberger and Urs Oswald, the lawyers for Förster and Graf, Judge Staubli gave Graf ten minutes to make a final statement, provided that it was limited to relevant issues related to the trial. After thanking her for the gesture, Jürgen Graf insisted that the revisionists were seeking the truth: "We try to get as close as possible to the historical truth. To have our mistakes pointed out to us is what we want. There are indeed errors in my books, but do you know who has shown them to me? Other revisionists! On the other side, the only reaction has been insults, slander, threats, legal action and lawsuits." As for his possible conviction, he informed the court that since the beginning of the 19th century no one had been imprisoned in Switzerland for the non-violent expression of his opinion.

> Do you, ladies and gentlemen of the court," he appealed to the judges, "want to break this tradition on the threshold of the 21st century? And if you insist on imprisoning one of us, then please look to me and not to Mr. Förster, who is mortally ill! By putting me in prison, you will not humiliate me. If you do so, you will humiliate the whole country, Switzerland. A Switzerland in which freedom of speech has been abolished. A Switzerland in which a minority of 0.6 percent of the population is allowed to decide what can be written, read, said or thought is a dead Switzerland."

The fact that some of the books for which Graf and Förster were charged had been published before the enactment of the 1995 law was not considered relevant as a mitigating factor. The verdict, of course, was appealed by Dr. Urs Oswald, Graf's lawyer. On 23 June 1999, the court of the canton of Aargau upheld the verdict, whereupon an appeal was made to a higher instance, the Federal Court in Lausanne. The Swiss organisation "Verité et Justice", which is led by René-Louis Berclaz, Philippe Brennenstuhl and Graf himself and works for the restoration of intellectual freedom in Switzerland, published the documentation of the trial under the title *A Political Trial to Escaner. The Case of Jürgen Graf*, a report that was translated into several languages. In April 2000, Graf learned that his appeal had been rejected and that he was to be sent to prison on 2 October.

In those days he was already engaged to Olga Stepanova, a Belarusian historian from Minsk. The two decided that they did not want to be separated for so long, and Graf opted for exile. On 15 August 2000, his 49th birthday, he emigrated to Iran, where he lived until April 2001. For a polyglot like him, studying Farsi during the months that spent in Tehran was a diversion. From there he eventually moved to Russia, where he settled after marrying Olga. Since 2002 Graf and his wife have lived in Russia, where he earns his living by translating texts written in English, Russian and other European languages into German. In addition, of course, to his efforts to denounce the Holocaust religion, the lie that has been poisoning the world, he continues to publish books: *Sobibor. Holocaust Propaganda and Reality*, published by Castle Hill Publisher, Germar Rudolf's publishing house, and *White World Awake!* are perhaps the last two.

Gaston-Armand Amaudruz, one year in prison for an octogenarian

Born in Lausanne, Gaston-Armand Amaudruz founded and published the *Courrier du Continent*, a newsletter written in French, in 1946. Amaudruz was only 28 years old when he challenged in his book *Ubu Justicier au Premier Procés de Nuremberg* (1949) the assertions about the homicidal gas chambers. He can therefore be said to be one of the first revisionists. Amaudruz wrote that "the Nuremberg trial had made him realise that the victory of the Allies was the victory of decadence". Amaudruz, who in 1951 set up the "New European Order", a nationalist, anti-capitalist and anti-communist organisation in Switzerland, was sympathetic to such prominent Swiss as the Lausanne-born François Genoud, the Swiss financier who had been a convinced National Socialist all his life. A devoted advocate of the Palestinian cause and a great patron of the PLO, Genoud founded the Arab Commercial Bank in Geneva in 1958. It was not for nothing that he was known as "Sheik François" among

Arabs[10]. Genoud described Gaston-Armand Amaudruz as "a man of integrity, racist, disinterested, a man of the past".

It was precisely because of two articles published in 1995 in the *Courrier du Continent* that Gaston-Armand Amaudruz was denounced. In one of them he had written: "For my part, I maintain my position. I do not believe in gas chambers. Let the exterminationists present the proof and I will believe in them. But as I have been waiting for this proof for decades, I don't think I will see it any time soon." The trial against him followed that of Jürgen Graf, who had a personal friendship with Amaudruz and used the ten minutes given to him by Judge Staubli to vindicate at the end of his speech the figure of his friend before the court in Baden:

> "I would like to close my remarks by quoting a friend from Western Switzerland, Gaston-Armand Amaudruz, against whom a trial similar to the one here is being prepared in Lausanne against Förster and me. In issue 371 of his bulletin *Courrier du Continent*, Amaudruz writes: "As in the old historical times, trying to impose dogma by force is a sign of weakness. The exterminationists may win trials through laws that muzzle freedom of expression. But they will lose the final judgement in the court of future generations".

Shortly before the start of his trial, in April 2000, Amaudruz wrote an intentionally provocative article in issue 418 of his bulletin, entitled "Long Live Revisionism! In it, he again denounced the untouchable dogma of the Holocaust imposed on humanity, claimed

---

[10] There are few people as extraordinary and as little recognised as François Genoud. The biographies that have been written about him fail to present him adequately because their authors show little courage and/or too much concern for political correctness. Genoud, besides being a banker and publicist, was an eminent international strategist who opposed the New World Order with all his might. After the war, he played an essential role in rescuing anti-communist and nationalist refugees fleeing the vengeance of the Judeo-communists who had taken over half of Europe. As early as 1936, François Genoud formed a lifelong friendship with the Grand Mufti of Jerusalem, the spiritual leader of the Muslims in Palestine. With the founding of the Arab Commercial Bank, he put himself at the financial service of Arab nationalist causes, which were trying to gain independence from the Rothschilds' financial empire. This exceptional man of privileged intelligence fought to the end against international Zionism and the global empire.

that he was prepared to face impeachment and announced: "I prefer to obey my conscience rather than an immoral and criminal law. I stand by my convictions. Long live revisionism!" After the long investigation was over, the trial began on 8 April 2000, and the verdict was delivered on 10 April 2000. The court sentenced the defendant to one year in prison for "denying" the existence of homicidal gas chambers in German concentration camps during World War II. The 79-year-old retired publicist and professor was found guilty of violating the Anti-Racism Act, which makes it a crime to "deny, grossly minimise or attempt to justify genocide or other crimes against humanity." In addition to the year's imprisonment, the Lausanne court ordered Amaudruz to pay 1,000 Swiss francs to each of the parties to the case: the Swiss Federation of Jewish Communities; the Paris-based LICRA; the Association of Sons and Daughters of Jewish Deportees in France; and a Jewish concentration camp survivor. The costs of the trial and the publication of the verdict in three newspapers and an official gazette were also borne by the convicted defendant.

After the trial, Gaston-Armand Amaudruz narrated his judicial experience in a book including the inculpatory reports. In September 2000, "Verité et Justice" published the text in the third issue of its bulletin under the title *The Amaudruz Trial. A judicial farce*. In this way, the organisation helped to publicise the cruelties of the trial against a 79-year-old dissident. The authorities considered it a new violation of the Anti-Racism Law and sued Amaudruz and René-Louis Berclaz and Philippe Georges Brennenstuhl, co-founders with Jürgen Graf of "Verité et Justice". In March 2002, "Verité et Justice" was dissolved by court order. On 22 May 2002, the criminal court of Veveyse in the canton of Fribourg sentenced Amaudruz and Brennenstuhl to three months' imprisonment and Berclaz to eight months' imprisonment.

In the meantime, an appeal court had reduced the April 2000 sentence against Gaston-Armand Amaudruz to three months. In January 2003, at the age of 82 and already in very poor health, he entered the Plaine de l'Orbe prison in Vaud, in the canton of Waadt, to serve the sentence imposed by the Swiss justice system.

5. Main victims of persecution in Belgium and the Netherlands

Siegfried Verbeke, stubborn fighter for freedom of expression

A Belgian of Flemish origin, Siegfried Verbeke is one of Europe's most prominent revisionists. He and his brother Herbert founded in 1983 the aforementioned *Vrij Historisch Onderzook* (*Free Historical Research*), known by the acronym *VHO*, which over the years became Europe's leading centre for the publication of texts critical of official historiography and Holocaust dogma. A whole range of books, pamphlets, leaflets and articles in English, Dutch, French and German have been published by *VHO*, which for a time also published a newsletter. Since 1991, when Verbeke and Faurisson published a 125-page booklet on the fraudulent diary of Anne Frank, a persecution has been unleashed that has increased over time. Government institutions, with the usual support of the usual Zionist organisations, have relentlessly harassed Verbecke, who has time and again been sentenced to prison and fined for his political dissent and his consistently peaceful views. The Belgian authorities have, moreover, for years confiscated tons of books and other texts produced by Verbeke, which have been systematically destroyed.

The first sentence imposed by a Belgian court on Siegfried Verbeke came in 1992: for distributing writings questioning the Holocaust, he was sentenced to one year in prison. Fortunately, his imprisonment was suspended, but he lost his civil rights and his right to vote for ten years. Nevertheless, Jewish lobbies continued the harassment and in 1992 the Masonic lodge B'nai B'rith, the Israel Information and Documentation Centre and the Anne Frank Foundation joined the National Department for Combating Racism and brought a civil suit against Verbeke for publishing materials including the *Leuchter Report*. At the end of the year, a Dutch court ordered Verbeke to pay 10,000 guilders for each of the texts. In 1993, the Anne Frank Foundation in the Netherlands and the Anne Frank Fund in Switzerland sued Verbeke, Faurisson and a colleague of theirs at *VHO* for the publication of the booklet on Anne Frank's diary. In the indictment, it was pointed out that "Anne Frank had for years been a symbol of the Jewish victims of the Holocaust, and her name and diary had therefore acquired additional value".

While Switzerland passed the Anti-Racism Law in 1995, in Belgium the same year the parliament gave the green light to a new anti-revisionist law that made it a crime to question the official version of the Holocaust. According to the new law, denying, minimising or trying to justify the genocide of the National Socialist regime was punishable by up to one year's imprisonment and a fine. This was an anti-free speech legislation very similar to that which already existed in France and Austria. This showed that the offensive against revisionism was being pushed behind the scenes by the hidden forces that have subdued the puppet "democracies" born after the world war. In fact, well before that, on 23 April 1982, the *Jewish Chronicle* (London) had already reported that the Institute of Jewish Affairs in London, a branch of the World Jewish Congress, was announcing a campaign to pressure and persuade governments to outlaw "Holocaust denial". The anti-revisionist thought crime laws introduced in several European countries reflect the success of this initiative.

In 1996, Siegfried Verbeke started co-operating with a German revisionist publicist to create a German-language division of *VHO* supervised by Germar Rudolf. In September 1997 Germar Rudolf launched the website vho.org on the internet, which became the largest revisionist website in the world. On 6 November 1997, in the course of a discussion following a round table in Antwerp (Belgium), Verbeke distributed hundreds of copies of a revisionist booklet written by himself, *Goldhagen and Spielberg Lies*, which was being very well received[11]. This activity, which followed the launch of *VHO* on the internet, was the straw that broke the camel's back. In a 2004 article, Germar Rudolf himself pointed to "the well-known Belgian witch hunter Johan Leman", who was allegedly in the audience in

---

[11] Daniel Goldhagen, whose father was one of the countless "Holocaust" survivors, had published *Hitler's Willing Executioners* in 1996, a work in which he criminalises all Germans who, according to this American Jew, not only knew about the extermination but supported it. About Steven Spielberg and his *Schindler's List*, we think that no comment is necessary.

Antwerp, as the person who put pressure on the Belgian government to act against Verbeke. A series of raids on four of his premises took place on 21 and 29 November 1997 and 7 January 1998. Large quantities of books and documents were seized and the warehouses were sealed. On the basis of this experience, the German division of *VHO* became independent at the beginning of 1998. In order to escape prosecution, Castle Hill Publishers, Germar Rudolf's publishing house in England, took over the publication of the German texts. In 1998, the Frankfurt public prosecutor's office filed a criminal complaint against Siegfried Verbeke. The initiative had come from Ignatz Bubis, head of the Central Council of Jews in Germany. The motive was the distribution of tens of thousands of copies of the German version of *Goldhagen and Spielberg's Lies* to German households. The booklet was confiscated and destroyed by order of a Munich court. The court proceedings lasted two years.

In the end, a ruling by the Amsterdam Court of Appeal on 27 April 2000 prohibited *VHO* from continuing to publish and distribute Verbeke and Faurisson's booklet, which questioned the authenticity of Anne Frank's alleged diary. In May 2001, the Belgian Ministry of Culture ordered all bookshops in Belgium to remove Verbeke's works from their shelves. Consequently, all revisionist texts were taken out of the shops and discreetly destroyed. With this unspeakable outrage against freedom of expression, the epic of this unspeakable publicist was reaching its climax.

During 2002, Verbeke's house was repeatedly raided by the Belgian police. On 12 February 2002, the Belgian authorities officially banned *Vrij Historisch Onderzook* and its post office box was temporarily confiscated. The publisher's premises were again searched and he was subjected to intense interrogation during the twenty-four hours he was under arrest. In the following months, the warehouses where Verbeke kept his materials were constantly visited by the police. As a result, Siegfried Verbeke decided to reorganise. After taking over new post office boxes, he renamed his foundation *Vogelvrij Historisch Onderzook (Proscribed Historical Research)*. The French section or division became independent and became *Vision Historique Objective*. Months later, the confiscation of its former post office box was lifted and Siegfried Verbeke's organisation regained its original name and addresses.

On 9 September 2003, a court in Antwerp sentenced the two Verbeke brothers to one year's imprisonment and the payment of 2,500 euros. Both were released on probation and for the second time Siegfried Verbeke was deprived of his civil rights for a period of ten years. The reason for the conviction had been the distribution of materials that "minimised the Nazi genocide against the Jews". Only three weeks later, at the end of the same month of September, the Belgian police raided the premises of the publishing house for the umpteenth time, looking for evidence that revisionist materials bearing Verbeke's name and address were being distributed by him.

One year later, on 27 November 2004, following an arrest warrant issued by the German authorities, Verbeke was arrested at his residence in Kortrijk in Flanders. The European Arrest Warrant, allegedly introduced under the pretext of combating terrorism, is a legal decision issued by a Member State of the Union and has been applied in most countries since 1 January 2004. Such orders are usually executed discreetly and without any legal impediment. Germany immediately requested extradition to Belgium, but surprisingly a judge rejected the request on the grounds that Verbeke had already been convicted of the same crimes in Belgium in September 2003. Under Belgian law, a person cannot be charged or prosecuted twice for the same acts.[12]

In any case, the harassment of Siegfried Verbeke did not stop. On 4 April 2005, a Belgian court again sentenced him to one year in prison and a fine of 2,500 euros for denying the genocide of the Jews during World War II. Since he appealed the verdict, his imprisonment was once again postponed. Taking advantage of her freedom, Verbeke tried to travel with her Filipino girlfriend to Manila. When he was about to board the plane at Schiphol airport near Amsterdam on 4 August 2005, he was arrested by the Dutch police, as the European Arrest Warrant was still valid in the Netherlands. It is clear that, as his

---

[12] Scandalously, in July 2005 the German Constitutional Court, in response to a Spanish request for the extradition of a German of Syrian origin suspected of involvement in the brutal 11 March 2004 Madrid bombing, ruled that the European Arrest Warrant was invalid in Germany. The German Constitutional Court argued that a German citizen is entitled to a verdict in German courts. Therefore, the German authorities released the alleged terrorist.

lawyer regretted, Verbeke made a serious mistake, since if he had wanted to travel from Brussels he would probably not have been arrested because the extradition request had been rejected by a Belgian magistrate.

After three months in detention in the Netherlands, he was finally extradited to Germany. The Dutch authorities ignored the fact that Verbeke had Belgian nationality and that a Belgian judge had perfectly justified his refusal to extradite him to Germany. Naturally, Verbeke was fighting against the impostors of history and was far more dangerous than any terrorist wanted by the Spanish police for alleged involvement in the murder of some 200 people. In Germany, where the German suspect of Syrian origin had just been refused extradition to Spain, Verbeke was held for half a year in solitary confinement in Heildelberg prison. Suddenly, we don't know why, he was allowed out on bail. In total, without having been convicted either in the Netherlands or in Germany, Siegfried Verbeke was imprisoned for nine months as a dangerous revisionist.

Back in Flanders, he was arrested again in November 2006 at his home in Kortrijk. The reason for the new arrest seems to have been the execution of a previous sentence of a Belgian court. This time he was imprisoned in Belgium. Verbeke told friends that he hoped to regain his freedom in July 2007. Verbeke's last known conviction was on 19 June 2008. We have already seen in the pages on Vincent Reynouard that the Brussels Court of Appeal sentenced them both to one year in prison and a fine of 25,000 euros for the publication of denialist texts questioning crimes against humanity. Since neither of them appeared, the Belgian authorities issued a national arrest warrant and prepared to prepare the European arrest warrant.

As we are about to conclude these pages on Siegfried Verbeke, we have learned that the Flemish-language newspaper *De Morgen* published an extensive three-page interview with the Belgian revisionist in its *Zeno* supplement on Saturday 9 January 2016. In it, unmoved, Verbeke insisted that the only gas chambers in Auschwitz were those used to disinfect the detainees' clothes. The Antwerp-based monthly *Joods Actueel* (*Jewish News*), which takes a belligerent stance against anything that moves against Israel, has taken *De Morgen* to task for welcoming a "stinker" like Verbeke into its pages. According to reports the Belgian press, these Zionists are ready to sue the Flemish newspaper. Michael Freilich, editor and owner of the Jewish newspaper, informed the *Jewish Telegraphic Agency* that he had filed a complaint against *De Morgen* and Verbeke with the ICKG (Interfederal Centre for Equal Opportunities and the Fight against Racism). Freilich stated that "*De Morgen* is to all intents and purposes an accomplice to this offence and should be held accountable for his actions". According to Freilich, officials from the state agency had assured him that they were considering legal action. The mayor of Antwerp, Bart de Wever, was quick to support the initiative.

6. Main victims of persecution in Spain

In Spain, the most blatant cases of political persecution of revisionists and submission to Zionism in the courts of justice are to be found in Catalonia. There, for example, Pilar Rahola, defined as "Zionist scum" by Antonio Baños, a member of the CUP in the Catalan Parliament after the 2015 autonomous elections, exhibits herself shamelessly, with absolute shamelessness, in the numerous media outlets that offer her their sets and microphones day in and day out. For years a leader of Equerra Republicana de Catalunya, a party with a deep Masonic tradition throughout its history, Rahola admitted in an interview to a pro-independence digital media her contacts with Israel. When the journalist asked her if she worked as a liaison between the president of the Generalitat, Artur Mas, and the Zionist government, her reply was: "The best answer I can give you is that I don't give it. Allow me to keep these things confidential. We will not show all the cards. When the journalist replied, "I understand that we do work", Rahola confirmed, "There is information that is too sensitive to give out.... We work a lot and talk little". It is therefore unquestionable that Zionism has in Catalonia a well-fertilised terrain in which it moves with arrogance thanks to the acquiescence and shameful servility of the media and the complicity of certain pro-independence politicians.

In Spain, the most blatant case, the most bleeding injustice, has been committed against a bookseller and publisher from Barcelona, Pedro Varela, whose dignified and honest struggle is known in all international revisionist circles. His case, however, is not the only one; other booksellers and publishers based in Catalonia have also been victims of harassment. Ramón Bau, Óscar Panadero, Carlos García and Juan Antonio Llopart are other names that should appear in this section, since they have been persecuted for publishing revisionist books or for expressing their opinions on political issues that have to do with revisionism. We shall therefore devote the first section on persecution in Spain to Pedro Varela and then present the other cases.

Pedro Varela, an honest bookseller victim of hatred and sectarian intolerance

We will write about Pedro Varela adequately. Since our work was born in Spain, we know its hardships perfectly well, we have had access to sufficient information and we can explain the case as it deserves. His name is associated with CEDADE (Círculo Español de Amigos de Europa), an organisation of National Socialist ideology created in Barcelona in 1966. The first congress of this group was held in 1969 and Jorge Mota was its first president and at the same time director of the magazine *CEDADE*. During these early years, militancy grew and the organisation spread to all regions of Spain, with fifty branches. The groups in Catalonia even displayed the Catalan "senyera" during the Franco years. Pedro Varela became president of CEDADE and editor of the publication in 1978.

Little by little, revisionist ideas became the fundamental basis of Varela's ideas and of the organisation he presided over. He contacted Robert Faurisson and brought about the publication of an extract from Arthur R. Butz's essential book. Likewise, other authors close to the Institute for Historical Review, as well as IHR publications and texts, were translated and introduced in Spain thanks to CEDADE. In 1989, for example, CEDADE published in Spain the explosive *Leuchter Report* with a foreword by David Irving. One of CEDADE's last events took place in Madrid in 1992, where a number of revisionist personalities gathered to demand the inalienable right to freedom of expression. The meeting was attended by Gerd Honsik, Thies Christophersen and others who were persecuted in their countries for speaking out freely. It should be noted that by this time the two trials against Ernst Zündel in Toronto had already taken place and that things were going from bad to worse in Germany. Finally, also in Spain, a new legal framework similar to the one being forged in Europe was being created, so Pedro Varela announced his resignation as president of CEDADE and in October 1993 the organisation finally disappeared.

During the 1980s, Pedro Varela had become increasingly committed to historical revisionism, and in 1988 he travelled to Canada to attend the second Zündel trial in Toronto. There he met Faurisson, Irving, Zündel and other revisionists, and had the opportunity to meet Fred Leuchter in person. Around the same time, together with David Irving, he also staged a protest rally in Berlin in front of the German television headquarters. Holding placards reading "German historians, liars and cowards", Varela and Irving led a small group of demonstrators in calling for an end to the falsification of history. These were the years when revisionism had achieved the decisive success of engineer Leuchter's expertise at Auschwitz. At the same time, the enemies of the revisionists and of historical truth were becoming more radical: as we know, in 1989 Robert Faurisson was the victim of a cowardly attack by Jewish terrorists, who beat him to death.

In March 1991 Pedro Varela spoke in German at the "Leuchter Kongress", an open-air meeting in Munich organised by Ernst Zündel. On 25 September 1992, thirty-five years old, with ideals, firm convictions and a lot of hope in his backpack, he was arrested in Austria, a country he was visiting as part of a tour of Europe. The reason for the arrest was that on a previous visit he had made a speech praising Hitler's policies. He was brought before the police and imprisoned in Steyr prison, a former Cistercian monastery, for the crime of propagating National Socialism. His correspondence was monitored. Before the letters were handed over to him, they were translated into German to be attached to the trial dossier in case they could be used as incriminating evidence. He spent three months behind bars before being arraigned on Wednesday 16 December 1992 before a court of three judges and a jury of eight. In the end, he was surprisingly acquitted, as it was concluded that the defendant did not know Austrian law, which is why he could not have known he was committing a crime when he expressed his opinion on a historical figure.

Compared to Austria or Germany, Spain remained an oasis of free speech in a Europe that was increasingly condescending to Jewish lobbies. In 1995, the year in which Switzerland and Belgium enacted anti-racist laws intended to combat 'hatred' and 'Holocaust denial', Spain finally embarked on the same path. On 11 May 1995, Parliament approved a revision of the Penal Code in order to bring Spanish legislation into line with that of certain European nations. In the preamble, the law justified itself as follows: "The proliferation in several European countries of incidents of racist and anti-Semitic violence, carried out under flags and symbols of Nazi ideology, obliges democratic states to take decisive action to combat...". We have already noted that the laws against "hatred" and "Holocaust denial" in Europe were not a consequence of spontaneous expression or justified indignation on the part of the people, but the result of a prefabricated and well-organised campaign in the service of Zionism. Three years later, in June 1998, the International Association of Jewish Lawyers and Jurists again called for new and tougher laws against Holocaust revisionism.

In 1991, four years before Spain submitted to outside pressure to change its legislation, Pedro Varela had opened the doors of the Librería Europa at number 12, Calle Séneca. From there he tried to work honestly selling books; but the fanaticism and intolerance of the champions of "freedom of expression" were not going to allow it: insulting graffiti on the walls and windows of the establishment have been a constant since then and the shop has been attacked on several occasions. It all started when in May 1995, the same month in which the Spanish Parliament approved the modification of the Penal Code, a self-styled "Civic Platform Anne Frank" tried to change the name of Seneca Street to that of the unfortunate Jewish girl who died in Bergen-Belsen. Interestingly, the Bergen City Council had previously refused to name a school after Anne Frank and later also opposed the naming of the street leading to the camp memorial after her.

Between 12 May 1995 and autumn 1996, this misnamed civic platform collected signatures and lobbied the two hundred and thirty families living in Seneca Street to support the renaming of the street. The promoters made no secret of the fact that the aim of the campaign was to "boycott the activities of the Europa bookshop". Quite an example of respect for freedom of expression (theirs, of course). The civic and, of course, democratic groups that were part of the platform were the usual left and extreme left. Seneca Street lost its tranquillity and the neighbourhood had to endure demonstrations of democratic violence and intolerance, i.e. insulting graffiti, stones, Molotov cocktails, etc. Pedro Varela, in order to offer the neighbours and public opinion in general information that could be contrasted with that provided by the promoters of the change of name of the street, published in the form of a circular letter a text he had written while studying Contemporary History at the University. It was a text that offered a rigorously accurate overview or synthesis of the work of Faurisson, Verbeke, Felderer and Irving on the most fruitful and profitable literary forgery of the twentieth century. In this text, the only one written by Varela among all those presented against him by the Mossos d'Esquadra and the Public Prosecutor's Office, no evidence of hatred against anyone can be found.

On 12 December 1996, the Catalan police raided the Librería Europa. Pedro Varela's sister was working in the shop and his daughter was playing in the backyard. The Mossos seized some 20,000 books, as well as periodicals, magazines, posters, videos... Varela was subsequently arrested at his family home. The operation, which, according to *El País*, had been three months in the making, was ordered at the behest of José María Mena, who in 1996 was appointed chief prosecutor of the Public Prosecutor's Office of the High Court of Justice of Catalonia. This "progressive" jurist, who had been a militant of the PSUC (Catalan communists) in the 1970s, was of the opinion that Varela "was pursuing hatred and not an ideology".

The information that appeared on 13 December 1996 in *El País*, a newspaper close to the Spanish socialists, was an example of a lack of objectivity: after praising the Mossos d'Esquadra for having had the honour of being "the first police force in Spain to arrest a person for genocide apologia", the newspaper said that the Librería Europa was a "centre for the sale and distribution of Nazi books published in South American countries". It went on to state that the residents of the Gracia neighbourhood welcomed the arrest and that the City Council was considering appearing in the case as a private prosecutor. He concluded by confirming that the Anne Frank Civic Platform, the Gay-Lesbian Coordinating Committee, the Mauthausen Friends Association and SOS Racism were all very satisfied because they had dismantled "a neo-Nazi plot that used the bookshop as a cover".

The proceedings were delayed for almost two years because many of the books seized were in English, German and French, so the Prosecutor's Office insisted on translating them to find out what part of their contents violated the law. Finally, the head of Barcelona Criminal Court No. 3, Santiago Vidal, set Friday 16 October 1998 for the start of the first trial in Spain for advocacy of genocide and incitement to racial hatred. As soon as the date became known, the Anne Frank supporters, now a Civic Platform against the Spread of Hatred, called a rally against Pedro Varela in front of the court building. Supporting the demonstration were the B'nai B'rith lodge, the Comunidad Israelita de Barcelona, the Baruch Spinoza Foundation, the Anti-Defamation League, Maccabi Barcelona, Asociación Judía Atid de Cataluña, Asociación de Relaciones Culturales Cataluña-Israel, Amical Mauthausen, Coordinadora Gai-Lesbiana, Sos Racismo and Unión Romaní. The participants carried cardboard coffins and candles in memory of the victims. Evidently, the purpose of staging a street spectacle was to exert social and political pressure.

The two trial sessions were held on 16 and 17 October. Shimon Samuel, President of the Wiesenthal Centre Europe, attended as an observer, escorted by police officers and accompanied by Israeli television cameras. "This trial," he said, "is a historic opportunity for Spain to join European jurisprudence and condemn the Spanish godfather of neo-Nazism." The prosecutor cited some thirty works sold in the Europa bookshop that praised the Third Reich and its policies or presented revisionist arguments on the subject of the Holocaust. In the case against Varela, the Comunitat Jueva Atid (future) de Catalunya, SOS Racismo and the Comunidad Israelí de Barcelona (Israeli Community of Barcelona) had filed a popular action. Varela's two lawyers made it clear from the outset that the law under which their client was being tried was unconstitutional, and therefore requested the suspension and annulment of the proceedings. The bookseller was questioned for more than four hours and rejected the charges: "I have never provoked racial hatred", he told the court, adding that as a historian he "had a moral obligation to tell the truth". As for revisionism, he said: "In my opinion, revision of history is necessary because it is an open subject and everything is subject to revision. Historians must be sceptical about everything and they must also revise what has been said so far". In relation to the books in his bookshop, he explained that he could not know the contents of the 232 titles he had in his shop and that he was not obliged to do so. He pointed out that in his shop he sold books of different ideologies and among the authors he mentioned the Basque nationalist Sabino Arana, Francisco de Quevedo and also cited Marx's *Das Kapital*. As for the text on Anne Frank, he acknowledged his authorship. In his final statement he said: "It has fallen to me to play the role of the bad guy in this film as the scapegoat for a deliberately created 'social alarm' (expression used by the prosecutor). I condemn, condemn and attack any form of genocide. I am not a genocidal person, nor have I murdered anyone. I have never desired the genocide of anyone or the murder of any ethnic or religious minority".

The public prosecution, which recalled that the facts of the case were a crime in the European Union, requested two years' imprisonment for advocacy of genocide and two years' imprisonment for incitement to racial hatred. This, despite the fact that the second paragraph of article 607 of the new Penal Code stipulated that the crimes contemplated in this article would be punishable "with a prison sentence of one or two years". For his part, Jordi Galdeano, the lawyer for SOS Racismo and the Comunitat Jueva Atid de Catalunya, called for an exemplary sentence of eight years in prison. "What is a crime and constitutes a risk to democracy," he said, "is the dissemination of an ideology that despises certain groups." On 16 November 1998, the court found Varela guilty of incitement to racial hatred and guilty also of having denied or justified genocide. Consequently, Judge Santiago Vidal,[13] who in his sentence referred to Varela as "a university

---

[13] Judge Santiago Vidal, who belonged to the "progressive" association Judges for Democracy, is now a famous figure in Spain. His relations with SOS Racismo were revealed when in September 2013 the General Council of the Judiciary banned him from collaborating with this NGO, as it was incompatible with his duties as a judge. In April 2014, it emerged that Vidal, who is deeply committed to Catalan separatist nationalism, was drafting a Constitution for Catalonia, in violation of the Spanish Constitution, as Catalonia is a community with a Statute of Autonomy. Once again, the General Council of the Judiciary summoned him to remind him of the limitations of his jurisdictional work. Vidal issued a statement in which he assured that his work was "on his own altruistic initiative, without any official commission from any public or private institution". He denied "political intentionality" and proclaimed his independence and impartiality. In October 2014, the judiciary opened a disciplinary case against him and pointed to a precautionary suspension, "given the extreme relevance of the facts and the evident public and social projection". In January 2015, after having said that he acted with independence, impartiality and without "political intentionality", this delusional judge presented the draft of the Catalan Constitution and declared textually: "I have a dream: to see the birth of the Catalan republic as a judge". In February 2015, the General Council of the Judiciary suspended him for three years, a sanction that entailed the loss of his seat in the Barcelona Court. Having become a martyr for the secessionists, in March 2015 the news came out that President Artur Mas had incorporated him into the Government of the Generalitat to "plan" and "design" the state structures linked to the judicial sphere. Vidal, without any political intentions, of course, then set about recruiting the 250 judges who would begin to practice in an independent Catalonia, which prompted the High Court of Justice of Catalonia to

graduate with a brilliant academic record, expert in matters of historical revisionism", sentenced him to five years' imprisonment and a fine of 720,000 pesetas. It also ordered Varela to surrender his passport and to appear in court every month. As for the 20,000 books, they were ordered to be burned, despite the fact that only thirty of the nearly two hundred works seized were in violation of the law. The very severe sentence exceeded the provisions of article 607.2 of the Penal Code, which led Galdeano to express his "intimate satisfaction". Pedro Varela, for his part, declared that it was "a political sentence and a tremendous injustice" and recalled that for two years, from the police search of his bookshop to the trial, terrible pressure had been created. On 10 December 1998, Pedro Varela's lawyers appealed the verdict and the sentence, so that he was able to avoid imprisonment pending the decision of the court of appeal.

As if the bookshop and its commercial activity had not been damaged enough for two years, a demonstration was called for Saturday, 16 January 1999 under the slogans: "Let's close the bookshop Europe, young people and workers in the struggle against fascism". "Against fascism: Let's close the Nazi bookshop". Two days earlier, on Thursday 14 January, Maite Varela, Pedro's sister who worked in the establishment, warned the National Police about what was being prepared and about the risk of an attack. On the same day, around 13:15 hours, a call was made to the regional police and the situation was explained to the Complaints Department. At 20:00 on Saturday 16, friends or acquaintances of the Librería Europa reported to 091 that the demonstration was heading towards Séneca Street. At 20:30 the bookshop was attacked. In order to enter and smash up the shop, the shutters at had to be smashed. Some of the

---

demand that the Generalitat take action against Vidal, as it understood that it was "undermining collective confidence in the judiciary". It then emerged that the Generalitat's Justice Department had signed a three-year contract with Vidal as temporary staff. Eventually, Vidal resigned from the contract to run for the Senate as head of the Esquerra Republicana de Catalunya list. As a senator, in January 2017 he revealed that the Generalitat had illegally obtained the tax data of Catalans, that the separatist authorities already had a selection of sympathetic judges in order to purge opponents, and that a non-European country (Israel) was training a unit of the Mossos in counter-espionage tactics. ERC forced him to resign.

demonstrators hooded themselves, entered the shop and began the destruction: windows, showcases, displays, doors, shelves, photocopiers, telephone, fire extinguisher, stairs, even some tiles. Everything was razed to the ground. Once the furniture was overturned, they piled the books on the floor with the intention of burning them inside. In the end, they chose to throw some 300 volumes into the street and set fire to them on the asphalt. Naturally, some neighbours, who were frightened by the scenes of violence, made further calls for help, but no police force turned up. As for the Guardia Urbana escorting the demonstrators, they withdrew when the assault on the bookshop began.

El País, which from the outset supported the public lynching of a man who defended himself alone against almost everyone, reported the news with this headline: "Demonstration by 1,600 young people to demand the closure of the Europa bookshop". In the body of the news item it said: "The protest was peaceful, but on arriving at the bookshop a group of demonstrators burned some books they had taken out of the shop, which was slightly damaged". Naturally, the news item was not illustrated with photographs, as only one would have sufficed to see how the bookshop was left after suffering "minor damage". In a well-known expression, Lenin described as "useful fools" those who are used as instruments for a certain cause or policy. It seems clear that the individuals who hooded themselves and razed the bookshop to the ground were political terrorists, probably paid, who were among the "useful fools" disguised as "peaceful demonstrators" in the service of the real power.

To complete the disgraceful action of the forces of law and order, the court dismissed the complaint on the grounds that the culprits were not known. However, television cameras filmed the aggressors and the City Council had the names of the two dozen groups that participated in the demonstration: Assemblea d'Okupes de Terrassa, Assamblea Llibertària del Vallés Oriental, Associació d'Estudiants Progressistes, Departament de Joves de CC.OO., Esquerra Unida i Alternativa, Federació d'Associacions d'Associacions de Veïns de Barcelona, Joves Comunistes, Joves Socialistes de Catalunya, Maulets, Partido Obrero Revolucionario, Partits dels Comunistes de Catalunya, PSUC viu, Amical de Mauthausen... As many as 23 associations were listed in the complaint filed by Pedro Varela in an ordinary court on 10 February 1999. The complaint included a list of the damages assessed and their estimated value, which amounted to 2,815,682 pesetas in "small damages".

Finally, on 30 April 1999, Pedro Varela received some wonderful news: by a unanimous decision, the three judges of the Third Section of the Barcelona Provincial Court, presided over by Judge Ana Ingelmo, upheld the appeal lodged by the lawyer José María Ruiz Puerta and challenged the sentence handed down by Judge Santiago Vidal. Considering that it violated the right to freedom of expression, they considered referring the matter to the Constitutional Court in Madrid. The three judges considered that doubting the Holocaust could not be considered a crime under the Spanish Constitution. Instead of ruling on the conviction, they reflected in their ruling brief all doubts about the constitutionality of article 607.2 of the new Penal Code. The Provincial Court judges argued that the article for which Varela had been convicted conflicted with Article 20 of the Constitution, which upholds the right to freely express and disseminate thoughts, ideas and opinions by word, writing or any other means of reproduction. As was to be expected, the accusers reacted angrily. The intrepid Jordi Galdeano decided not to be outdone and ruled that the court's decision was "an attack on the democratic system". That is to say, when instead of sympathetic judges and prosecutors they were faced with truly independent magistrates, they were accused of endangering freedoms. The lawyer for Amical Mauthausen, Mateu Seguí Parpal, described the court that doubted Pedro Varela's criminality as "unpresentable".

The Constitutional Court, however, before admitting the consideration of the constitutionality raised by the judges of the Third Section of the High Court, demanded as a formal prerequisite that the Barcelona High Court should first hear the appeal against the conviction, so that the Third Section Chamber then set the date of 9 March 2000 for the hearing of the appeal. A week earlier, the judge, Ana Ingelmo, had been challenged by SOS Racismo, which denounced her to the Public Prosecutor's Office for prevarication and requested that she abstain in the case. The Chamber upheld the challenge and agreed to a change of rapporteur, and therefore ordered the suspension of the oral hearing and processed the challenge in a separate piece. On 19 June 2000, an order of the Seventh Section of the Barcelona Provincial Court dismissed the challenge.

The hearing was finally scheduled for 13 July. Varela did not attend because he was in Austria. His lawyer described the five-year prison sentence as "scandalous". On the other hand, the prosecutor Ana Crespo and the private prosecutors asked the Audiencia to confirm the sentence imposed on the owner of Librería Europa. In the end, by Order of 14 September 2000, the Third Section of the Provincial Court again raised the question of unconstitutionality. Pedro Varela remained on probation and the case was pending the ruling of the Constitutional Court. Defenders of freedom of expression and revisionists all over the world considered that a victory had been achieved in Spain, at least temporarily, and awaited the decision of the high court, which was to take seven years to issue the long-awaited ruling.

During this temporary period, Pedro Varela continued his activities as a bookseller and publisher with the Asociación Cultural Editorial Ojeda, which he had founded at the beginning of 1998. The Librería Europa also began to organise conferences on its premises, often given by revisionist authors who came from abroad. Suddenly, on Monday 10 April 2006, the Catalan autonomous police unexpectedly burst into the premises of the Librería Europa. At 9:30 in the morning, about fifteen masked police officers began a search that lasted until five o'clock in the afternoon. Some six thousand books valued at more than 120,000 euros were seized. In addition, the officers of the political police of the Generalitat removed from the premises eight large boxes full of documentation, hundreds of folders and thousands of photos and slides, catalogues ready to be sent out and thirteen thousand conference programmes. The six computers containing dozens of books that had been corrected, typeset and prepared for publication were confiscated. These computers also contained all the information on clients and friends of the publishing company and the bookshop. Hard disks, back-up copies, savings books, bank accounts, the bookshop's chequebooks, personal and business contracts were also confiscated. As if that were not enough, the "mossos" took away framed photographs that recalled events from the CEDADE era and even the flags of the autonomous communities that, together with the Catalan flag, adorned the conference room.

Pedro Varela was arrested. Once at the police station, he was forced to strip naked to pass the search and then locked in a cell. He then went on to "play the piano", which in prison jargon means inking his fingers to take fingerprints, and was photographed face and profile with his offender number. He was told that on this occasion the reason for his arrest was that Editorial Ojeda was publishing books "contrary to the international community", books that were "against public freedoms and fundamental rights". In other words, in a "democracy" where freedom of expression, dissemination and communication are sacrosanct signs of identity, the publishing and sale of books became a criminal activity because the ideas contained in the texts were "contrary to the international community". If it were not so serious and pathetic, it would be laughable.

Two days after his arrest, Varela was released with charges. He was charged with crimes against an entelechy called the international community, against the exercise of fundamental rights and against public freedoms for the defence of genocide. Juan Carlos Molinero, deputy chief of the General Criminal Investigation Office, explained to the media that the operation had not been directed against the bookshop, which had already been investigated in the 1990s, but against the publishing house Ojeda, which is why neither the shop nor its website was closed down. In reality it was a "legal" ruse to be able to act again against Varela.

Given that we are historicising the events of Pedro Varela, victim of the greatest attack on freedom of expression and publication perpetrated in "democratic" Spain, it is pertinent to note that power in Catalonia in April 2006 was in the hands of a government known as the tripartite, which emerged after the signing of the so-called Pact of Tinell. Chaired by the Socialist Pasqual Maragall, the parties that formed part of it were the Partit dels Socialistes de Catalunya (PSC), Iniciativa per Catalunya Verds-Esquerra Unida i Alternativa (offshoots of the PSUC communists) and Esquerra Republicana de Catalunya (whose emblem, according to its leaders, is a Masonic triangle). This government was thus politically responsible for the persecution in Spain of a businessman for publishing books "contrary to the international community", most of which were published almost everywhere in Europe without any problem.

As is well known, when the aim is to criminalise a leader who somewhere in the world opposes the designs of the co-opted puppets at the head of the powerful countries that unleash wars, the latter claim to represent the "international community". The state or nation that does not submit is then accused of "defying the international community". In the unprecedented case we have just described, we understand that there would be an index of banned books whose contents threaten an inconceivable abstraction called the international community.

On 7 November 2007, the Constitutional Court finally issued STC 235/2007, the ruling on the question of unconstitutionality raised by the Third Section of the Provincial Court with respect to Article 607, second paragraph, of the Criminal Code. The rapporteur was Judge Eugeni Gay Montalvo. The ruling, after setting out the legal grounds at length, read as follows:

> "In view of the foregoing, the Constitutional Court, by the authority conferred upon it by the Constitution of the Spanish nation, has decided to partially uphold the present question of unconstitutionality, and as a consequence:
>
> 1° Declare unconstitutional and null and void the inclusion of the expression 'deny or' in the first paragraph of Article 607.2 of the Criminal Code.
>
> 2. To declare that the first clause of Article 607.2 of the Criminal Code, which punishes the dissemination of ideas or doctrines tending to justify the crime of genocide, interpreted in the terms of legal ground 9 of this Judgment, is not unconstitutional.
>
> 3. Dismisses the remainder of the constitutional challenge.
>
> This judgment shall be published in the Boletín Oficial del Estado.
>
> Given in Madrid, this seventh day of November two thousand and seven.

In other words, since STC 235/2007, the dogma of faith of the Holocaust can be denied in Spain, just as, for example, the dogma of the Immaculate Conception, the existence of God or any other dogma of the Church can be denied. The Constitutional Court considered that such denial "remains at a stage prior to that which justifies the intervention of criminal law, insofar as it does not even constitute a potential danger to the legal interests protected by the rule in question, so that its inclusion in the precept entails the infringement of the right to freedom of expression". The judgement stated that "the mere denial of the offence is in principle inane". The Court, on the other hand, did consider the dissemination "by any means" of ideas justifying genocide to be a crime. But this is not the case with the revisionists who have been appearing in these pages: none of them justifies or has ever justified genocide. Pedro Varela stated time and again that he disapproved of it in his statement to the judge who sentenced him to five years.

Two months after the Constitutional Court's ruling, the Provincial Court, nine years after Pedro Varela was sentenced to five years, held the hearing of the appeal against the sentence on 10 January 2008. Pedro Varela's defence had requested more time to prepare, as the Constitutional Court's ruling was sufficiently important to study its legal implications thoroughly; but the Chamber rejected the request. Both the prosecution and the defence reiterated their demands. Finally, on 6 March, the judges of the Provincial Court issued the sentence partially upholding the appeal and reducing the sentence to seven months' imprisonment. It was considered that Varela had made an apology for genocide through his work of disseminating genocidal doctrines through the sale of books, but that he had not directly discriminated in a personal way, and was therefore acquitted of the crime of incitement to racial hatred. Pedro Varela did not have to go to prison and announced that he would consider filing an appeal for amparo.

In any case, the harassment of Varela was at its peak, since after his arrest in April 2006 he was still at liberty with charges and was awaiting a new trial. It was on 29 January 2010 when the hearing took place in the 11th Criminal Court of Barcelona. Faced with the obligation to comply with the doctrine of the Constitutional Court, according to which denying the Holocaust is not a crime, but justifying it is; the bookseller and publisher was accused of disseminating ideas that justified genocide and incited racial hatred, despite the fact that he had always said actively and passively that he condemned all forms of violence against any ethnic minority and, of course, all genocide. Prosecutor Miguel Ángel Aguilar assured that they were not judging ideas, "but the dissemination of the doctrine of hatred". From among the books selected, the prosecutor quoted fragments to support his ramshackle thesis. Pedro Varela's lawyer denounced that the paragraphs extracted by the prosecutor from more than a dozen books sold in the Europa bookshop were "taken out of context" and recalled that some of the books chosen, such as Hitler's *My Struggle*[14], could also be bought in department stores.

On 5 March 2010, Estela María Pérez Franco, an unopposed substitute judge, who was appointed on a discretionary basis to Criminal Court no. 11, handed down her sentence, which became known on 8 March. In the section on proven facts, this magistrate-judge dedicated fifteen pages to commenting on texts of the seventeen books that she ordered to be destroyed. Here are a few samples. From *Mi lucha* (36 copies seized), she insisted on quoting fragments that allude to race. It seems clear that this judge was unaware that the racial question has always been the raison d'être of the Jewish people. Suffice it to quote an embarrassing statement by Golda Meir, the revered Zionist leader and former prime minister of Israel, that "intermarriage is worse than the Holocaust". This racist, alluding to the Palestinians, once said: "There is no such thing as a Palestinian people. They do not exist. Would the magistrate-judge consider that Golda Meir hated the Palestinians? From Joaquín Bochaca's *Los crímenes de los buenos*[15] (2 copies tapped), the judge quoted as condemnable the sentence "It was not the Arabs, but the good ones, the Jews, who implanted terrorism in Palestine". If this assertion is considered false, one wonders whether at the time of Pedro Varela's conviction the judge had the slightest idea of how the Zionist state came into being. The inclusion of *Yusuf's Green Rain* (222 copies seized), a work by the Jewish author Israel Adam Shamir, among the books to be destroyed is striking. In the sentence, the judge quotes, among others, the following statement by Shamir: "P. 35, lines 3-6, 'The world press, from New York to Moscow, via Paris and London, is perfectly controlled by the Jewish supremacists; not a gnashing of teeth can be heard without their prior authorisation'". Does Estela Maria Perez Franco think that Shamir is a liar and an anti-Semite? Zionists could explain to her that they consider Jews who dare to criticise them to be "Jews who hate themselves because they are Jews" rather than anti-Semites. Israel Shamir, famous for his commitment to the Palestinian cause, is the author of a trilogy, which in addition to

---

[14] *My Struggle-Mein Kampf*, Omnia Veritas Limited, www.omnia-veritas.com.

[15] *Los crimines de los buenos*, Omnia Veritas Limited, www.omnia-veritas.com.

the above-mentioned work includes *The Spirit of James* and *Pardes. A Study of the Kabbalah*, both of which were sold at Libreria Europa. Two months before the trial, at the invitation of Pedro Varela, Shamir had participated in the Librería Europa lecture series: on Sunday 8 November 2009, in Madrid, and on Monday 9 November 2009, in San Sebastián. The title of his lecture was *The Battle of Discourse: The Yoke of Zion*.

If we analyse the selection of quotes from the sentence, we could write at least fifteen pages, the same as those written by Estela María Pérez; but it is now time to look at the ruling, in which the judge sentenced Pedro Varela Geiss to one year and three months in prison "as criminally responsible as the perpetrator of a crime of spreading genocidal ideas", and to one year and six months in prison for "a crime committed against fundamental rights and public freedoms guaranteed by the Constitution". It is an unbearable sarcasm, a manifest injustice, that Varela was sentenced for a crime against fundamental rights and constitutional freedoms, when he was precisely the victim of the violation of these rights and freedoms in his person. It was also agreed "to confiscate all the books described in the proven facts... and to proceed to their destruction once the sentence is final".

The judgment did not become final until the end of October 2010. Prior to that, in May 2010, the Provincial Court heard the appeal. This court of the Audiencia at least kept the decorum it owed itself as a court of justice and acquitted Pedro Varela of the second offence, for which he had been sentenced to one year and six months in prison; but upheld the first: "dissemination of genocidal ideas", for which he had been sentenced to one year and three months. Finally, another judge in Barcelona, the head of Criminal Court no. 15, did not agree to grant Pedro Varela the suspended sentence he had requested. The judge stated in her ruling that in ordering the bookseller's imprisonment she had taken into account the fact that he had another seven-month prison sentence from 2008, a fact that from a criminal point of view showed "a criminal record that demonstrates his dangerousness".

Pedro Varela entered prison on Sunday 12 December 2010. It was a bright winter morning, clear of clouds, just as Pedro was clear of crime. He arrived in a small caravan of cars, accompanied by a large group of friends and supporters who surrounded him and cheered him on until the last moment. A large banner carried by several people read: "For the right to inform. No more editors in jail". Another companion carried an individual banner with the phrase "Books are banned and publishers are locked up". With admirable fortitude and dignity, aware of the need to set an example of fortitude, Varela urged his friends not to lose heart. He evoked Quevedo's imprisonment in the dungeons of San Marcos de León and assumed that the time had come to face imprisonment. He asked everyone to remind the world that books were being hunted down and publishers sent to prison. We can make sure," he told them, "that no one else is imprisoned for this reason". With hugs and kisses, he said goodbye after thanking them and crossed the gate. He walked away towards the access control offices to a backdrop of applause and excited shouts of "Come on Pedro!" "Bravo!" and "We won't forget you Pedro!". Fortunately, he was not forbidden to write, which allowed him to write a series of letters in cell 88 of the Can Brians 1 penitentiary centre, where he served his sentence. These texts were later published under the title *Cartas desde prisión. Thoughts and reflections of a dissident*.

On 8 March 2011, Isabel Gallardo Hernández, another substitute judge assigned to the 15th Criminal Court of Barcelona, issued an order in which she ordered the execution of the destruction of the books, as ordered in the sentence of 5 March 2010. We will quote a fragment of the operative part of the order so that there is a record of the index of banned books in Spain, a country where theoretically there is freedom of expression and, consequently, there are no banned books.

> "I DECIDE: to order the destruction of all copies of the books with the following titles:
>
> 1st My struggle. 2nd Self-portrait of Leon Degrelle, a fascist. 3rd Hitler and his philosophers. 4th Hitler, speeches of the years 1933/1934/1935. Complete works (volume 1). 5th The crimes of the 'good guys'. 6th Foundations of biopolitics: forgetting and exaggerating the racial factor. 7. Race, intelligence and education. 8. Nobilitas. 9. The new man. 10th Revolutionary ethics. 11th Iron Guard. Romanian fascism. 12th The Protocols of the Elders of Zion. 13° Ecumenism on three sides: Jews, Christians and Muslims. 14° The green rain of Yusuf. 15° Wagnerian thought. 16° The history of the vanquished (the suicide of the West). Volume II. 17th The chief's handbook. Of the Iron Guard.

The bust of Hitler, the iron swastika, military helmets, as well as the photographs and posters with National Socialist themes that have been removed should also be destroyed.

Return the flags and stationery to the prisoner".

To note that everything is done in the name of democracy, freedom and fundamental rights is deplorable in the extreme. The question arises as to why busts of historical figures, swastikas, military helmets, photos or posters should be destroyed. If we are told that Hitler represents absolute evil, we have to argue that communism has produced the worst criminals in history. As far as we know, there are no rulings requiring the destruction of busts of Lenin, Trotsky, Kaganóvich, Beria or Stalin in private homes. It is a different matter that statues in public places have been removed in some countries, if not torn down by outraged populations after years of communist totalitarianism.

As for books, what can be said about the destruction of works that are read all over the world and can be freely consulted in Spanish libraries. How can one accept the banning of texts in Spain just because a court in Barcelona has considered it a proven fact that "the content of the occupied books reflects contempt for the Jewish people and other minorities". It is insulting sarcasm that works critical of Jews have to be destroyed, while in Israel racial hatred is at the basis of education. The Talmudists, who hate viscerally Christians, teach in "Abhodah Zarah" that "even the best of the goyim (gentiles or non-Jews) must be killed". Does this teaching not exude racial hatred and bigotry of the worst kind? Maurice Samuel (1895-1972), a Zionist intellectual, in Chapter XIV of his work *You Gentiles*, entitled "We, the Destroyers", writes these words to the gentiles: "We Jews are the destroyers and will remain so. Nothing you can do will meet our demands and needs. We will destroy eternally because we want the world to be ours." Is this not criminal racism?

It is to be assumed that Judge Pérez Franco did not prevaricate and that if she had been sufficiently erudite on the subjects she was judging she would not have ordered the burning of, for example, *Wagnerian Thought (*12 copies of which were seized), a work by the British thinker Houston Stewart Chamberlain, because on page 83 the author dared to write that "the influence of Judaism accelerates and favours the progress of degeneration by pushing man into an unbridled whirlwind which leaves him no time either to recognise himself or to become aware of this lamentable decadence..."..." The quote comes from the "proven facts" section, in the distressing judgment of 5 March 2010.

"From the school of the war of life. - What doesn't kill me, makes me stronger". This phrase from Nietzsche's *Twilight of the Idols* is ideal to explain the state of mind in which Pedro Varela left Can Brians prison on 8 March 2012. "From now on, I will redouble my efforts", he declared after showing his determination to resume activities in his bookshop and to continue fighting against repression. A year later, on 5 March 2013, the European Court of Human Rights in Strasbourg ordered Spain to pay Varela 13,000 euros, as it found that the Barcelona Provincial Court should have allowed him to prepare and exercise his defence more effectively and with more time after the Constitutional Court's ruling in 2007. It was a moral victory, as the bookseller had requested 125,000 euros in compensation. The judges of the Strasbourg Court unanimously considered that "was only belatedly allowed to know about the change of qualification" of the offence for which he was sentenced to seven months in prison.

The fact that Librería Europa and its owner had been able to continue with the lecture series and to reorganise its commercial and cultural activities again did not please its enemies. A dozen hooded henchmen were sent on 11 March 2014 to Seneca Street. These brave men showed up at the bookshop at around half past ten in the morning and in broad daylight, with the insolence of those who know they are unpunished, began the attack: from the street they smashed the windows of the shop windows with blunt objects and then threw paint cans at books and furniture. Fortunately, the staff of the bookshop were not attacked. According to eyewitnesses, the group consisted of about twenty people, but only the hooded men acted violently. Pedro Varela filed a complaint with the Mossos d'Esquadra, although with little hope, if any, that anyone would be arrested, as there had never been any arrests before.

Germany, the state that persecutes its own shadow, could not remain on the sidelines without participating in the harassment of the Spanish bookseller and publisher. His appearance in the persecution took place in February 2009, when the German Consulate General in Barcelona filed a complaint against Pedro Varela for marketing *Mein*

Kampf (*My Struggle*) without authorisation from the State of Bavaria. The publication of the work in Germany was an offence until 30 April 2015, when, seventy years after Hitler's death, the book fell into the public domain. Under this pretext, the indefatigable Miguel Ángel Aguilar, a "progressive" jurist of the ilk of Baltasar Garzón, Santiago Vidal, José María Mena and the like, known as the prosecutor of hate, since he heads the Service against Hate Crimes and Discrimination of the Barcelona Public Prosecutor's Office, charged Pedro Varela in September 2015 with a crime against intellectual property, a crime which, incidentally, has nothing to do with hate and discrimination. The hate prosecutor submissively asked for two years in prison for Varela, his disqualification for three years as a publisher and trader and a fine of 10,800 euros for publishing the book without authorisation or licence, despite knowing that the rights to the work belonged to the German state of Bavaria by virtue of a ruling by the Munich Chamber of Justice. In addition, he claimed a further fine of 216,000 euros and compensation of 67,637 euros from the State of Bavaria.

Regarding the rights to Hitler's works, we know that Paula Hitler, the "Führer's" sister, had entrusted François Genoud, "Sheik François" (see note 9), with the editorial management of numerous texts by her brother, including *Mein Kampf*. The Swiss banker was working on a global agreement with her to acquire the rights to all of Adolf Hitler's works, but Paula died in 1960. Even then, the Bavarian authorities, who had seized the contract between Hitler and the NSDAP publishing house (Franz Eher Verlag), anxiously claimed the rights for the State of Bavaria.

Be that as it may, the hatred of Pedro Varela should be among the proven facts, since *Mein Kampf* has been and is being sold all over the world. In India, for example, Hitler is a cult author. His famous work has become a classic and has long been a bestseller. It can be bought in street stalls and from time to time it makes the top ten bestseller list. Pedro Varela's lawyer, Fernando Oriente, rejected in his defence that the State of Bavaria and the Federal Republic of Germany had or had had the rights and argued that the German consul "lacked any legitimacy". The lawyer recalled that the first edition of the book in Spain dates back to 1935 and that the copyright of a person who died before 7 December 1987 is free, as established in a 1996 royal decree on the Law on Intellectual Property. Varela's lawyer regretted that Bavaria's intention was to "act as a censor of thought, preventing the free dissemination of ideas enshrined in the Constitution".

We were about to conclude, but we read in the 28 January 2016 edition of *El País* in Catalonia the following headline: "The prosecutor studies the act of a neo-Nazi in the Europa bookshop". At the news reads: "the historic ultra-right-wing leader Ernesto Milá will present there (in the Europa bookshop) his new book *El tiempo del despertar*, which praises the rise of Nazism". In other words, the prosecutor of hate understands that the presentation of a book can be a criminal act. After having buried more than a hundred million victims of communism all over the world, after the oppression of this totalitarian ideology in half of Europe for fifty years, a lecture on the communist champions is still "progressive"; but if the lecturer is "a neo-Nazi", we are faced with absolute evil, with the apology of national socialism, racial hatred, anti-Semitism.

Unfortunately, revanchism, resentment and hatred are the order of the day in Spain today, but they nestle in the chests of the ever so democratic "anti-fascists". Eighty years after the civil war, protected by a Law of Historical Memory that is used sectarianistically to remember only the crimes of one of the sides in the fratricidal conflict, the parties of the so-called "progressive left", which have gained power in the big town halls thanks to pacts of all against one, are dedicated to destroying monuments, removing plaques in memory of religious people who were shot, changing the names of streets... Armed with reason and moral superiority, as usual, they display an intolerance and fanaticism that threaten harmony and reconciliation among Spaniards, which seemed to be assured thanks to the 1978 Constitution. For this reason, given the atmosphere that prevails, one can suspect that the persecution of Pedro Varela will not cease.

Post Scriptum

Unfortunately, months after writing the last sentence, our suspicion has come true: having already concluded *Proscribed History*, we have learned that on 7 July 2016 a new complaint filed by the Public Prosecutor's Office against the Asociación Cultural Editorial Ojeda as a legal entity and against its vice-president Pedro Varela entered the Juzgado de Guardia (Juzgado de Instrucción number 18 of Barcelona). The complaint was also directed against Carlos Sanagustín García, Antonio de Zuloaga Canet, Viorica Minzararu and Nicoleta Aurelia Damian, persons linked to the association and the Europa bookshop. Judge Carmen García Martínez immediately ordered "urgent precautionary" measures, which included: the cessation of the activities of Editorial Ojeda, the closure of Librería Europa and the blocking of the bookshop's two websites. Absurdly, the Barcelona Hate Prosecutor's Office invoked article 510.1 a, of the Spanish Constitution, which refers to Fundamental Rights and Public Freedoms, to continue its ruthless harassment of Varela.

On Friday 8 July, the Mossos d'Esquadra arrested the two shop assistants of the Europa bookshop, both of Romanian origin, and the two members of the Editorial Ojeda Cultural Association at their homes. Pedro Varela was not in town, as he had travelled with his youngest daughter and was camping in the mountains somewhere in Spain. During the search of the bookshop, fifteen thousand books and computer equipment were seized. The Europa bookshop was sealed. At 7:00 the same morning, the Catalan police also raided the home of Pedro Varela. In addition to the computers, the officers seized all the cash he kept in his house.

After learning that an arrest warrant had been issued, Pedro Varela issued a statement announcing that he would appear in court, which he did on 15 July. Accompanied by his lawyers, the bookseller and publisher arrived at the ninth examining magistrate's court, which had issued the arrest warrant. He refused to testify. The prosecutor, Miguel Ángel Aguilar, requested that he be remanded in prison on the grounds that he was a flight risk and that his crimes were repeated. The judge ordered his release on bail of 30,000 euros, which Varela was unable to pay. Luis Gómez and Javier Berzosa, the lawyers, tried to get a reduction. They argued that their client was not a rich man and that he could not use the money seized by the Mossos d'Esquadra at his home to pay the bail. What he has," said Berzosa, "was taken in the search of his house. Varela was thus admitted to the Modelo prison at Barcelona. Fortunately, a friend paid the judicial deposit the same day and Pedro was able to regain his freedom in the evening.

As for the other persons, after 24 hours in detention, they were released with charges of promoting hatred and discrimination for participating in the "organisation of conferences in the bookshop where the Nazi genocide is glorified and justified and the Jewish Holocaust is denied". The prosecution intended to imprison the two men, the president and treasurer of the Asociación Cultural Editorial Ojeda, but the judge released them. A few days after the sealing of the Librería Europa, a splendid wreath appeared in front of the zippered door, laid on a wooden easel with the following inscription: "From culture and freedom to Librería Europa".

On 18 July, Esteban Ibarra, a supposed champion of tolerance who presides over the Movement Against Intolerance, an NGO that has received nearly seven million euros in public subsidies since 1995, filed a lawsuit against Pedro Varela and the other managers of the bookshop and the publishing house. Ibarra announced that he was going to bring a popular action and that he was counting on the participation of the Federation of Jewish Communities of Spain, the International League Against Racism (LICRA), the Jewish Community Bet Shalom of Barcelona, etc., etc... To finish off the public lynching of a single man, the Barcelona City Council announced through the mouth of the deputy mayor Jaume Asens, head of state human rights in Podemos, that the City Council would appear as a prosecutor in the case "for the offence to the whole city". Jaume Asens, an "anti-system" turned separatist, declared that "Librería Europa was a headquarters of the extreme right in the city".

During Franco's regime there was censorship, which served to protect booksellers, as they knew which works they could not sell. Now there is no censorship in Spain and in theory no bookseller should fear anything. However, a businessman, a man capable of "offending a whole city" by selling books, is being viciously persecuted. We fear that this time the enemies of Pedro Varela are determined to lock him up forever in a prison of silence. After more than twenty years of persecution, Varela has become a legendary dissident in Spain and one of the most tenacious in Europe. His convictions and his dignity as a person are exemplified by his exemplary attitude of peaceful resistance. His struggle for freedom of expression and thought deserves the recognition not only of those of us who share his revisionist views, but of all those who truly believe in freedom

At the time of reviewing these lines for the edition of *Criminales de pensamiento*, more than three years after having written the above, the trial is still pending and both the Librería Europa and the Ojeda publishing house are still closed.

Other booksellers and publishers persecuted in Catalonia

The following case confirms the injustice done to Pedro Varela. Known as the Librería Kalki case, it involved four booksellers and publishers who were acquitted by the Supreme Court while Varela, also a bookseller and publisher, was serving a prison sentence for identical acts. Many and varied conclusions could be drawn from this, which we will leave for the end. We will now limit ourselves to a succinct account of the facts after outlining the characters: Óscar Panadero, Ramón Bau, Juan Antonio Llopart and Carlos García, convicted by the Provincial Court of Barcelona for disseminating genocidal ideas in a judgment of 28 September 2009.

The first, Óscar Panadero, son of a PSUC leader, nephew of anarchists and grandson of Falangists, was educated as a child in the discussions of the three ideological creeds and ended up choosing National Socialism. Born in Barcelona in 1977, he dropped out of school with excellent marks and opted for a self-taught education. Neither the teachers nor his parents managed to convince the young teenager, who confirmed that he had no intention of giving in to a school that taught falsehoods. After going through associations such as Alternativa Europea and the Movimiento Social Republicano, he ended up in the Círculo de Estudios Indoeuropeos (CEI), whose president was Ramón Bau. In January 2003, after selling his farm and giving up a good job, he opened the Kalki Bookshop, which he owned and managed. Only half a year later, his political persecution process began: on 8 July 2003 and 25 May 2004, the regional police raided the establishment and, as in the case of the Europa bookshop, seized thousands of books and magazines, as well as catalogues, leaflets, etc.

The second, Ramón Bau, also from Barcelona, participated at the age of seventeen in the founding of the Círculo Español de Amigos de Europa and worked with Pedro Varela in its publishing activities. Bau worked closely with Varela and became secretary general of CEDADE. In 1984 he set up Ediciones Bau, Bausp y Wotton and published more than a hundred magazines. In June 1998 he founded the Círculo de Estudios Indoeuropeos. Bau, an intellectual with a wealth of knowledge, is a convinced National Socialist and a self-proclaimed Wagnerian.

Juan Antonio Llopart, the third of the persecuted Catalans, was born in Molins de Rei into a Falangist family. Founder of Ediciones Nueva República, he was also the promoter of the magazine *Nihil Obstat*. Llopart, from Ediciones Nueva República, sponsored and organised the Jornades de Disidència, which for several years was attended by international personalities, fighters against the current in the field of culture. He is the author of several works and has contributed to various publications.

The fourth, Carlos García, a member of the CEI and also of Falangist tradition, claims to be a student of National Socialism. Secretary to Óscar Panadero, he told a significant anecdote about his arrest: when ten policemen burst into his home at night in 2004, the one who was calling the shots was in civilian clothes and wore a red communist star on his lapel. García believes that this was a way of letting him know who was after him.

Well, after being arrested in a humiliating manner and being held for several days in the dungeons, proceedings were opened against them in the Juzgado de Instrucción n° 4 de Sant Feliu de Llobregat (Sant Feliu de Llobregat Court of Instruction n° 4). Once the opening of oral proceedings had been decreed, the case was referred to the Provincial Court of Barcelona, which handed down its sentence on 28 September 2009. The four were sentenced to prison terms of up to three and a half years for crimes of dissemination of genocidal ideas, crimes against fundamental rights and freedoms, and unlawful association. Ramón Bau, president of CEI, and Óscar Panadero, owner of Librería Kalki, received three and a half years; Carlos García, three years; Juan Antonio Llopart, administrator of Ediciones Nueva República, was not convicted of illicit association, and was therefore sentenced to two and a half years in prison.

The lawyers lodged an appeal in cassation before the Supreme Court for infringement of the law and of constitutional precepts, as well as for breach of form. On 12 April 2011, the Supreme Court handed down Ruling 259/2011, whose rapporteur was Judge Miguel Colmenero Menéndez de Luarca. The ruling considered that the cassation appeals were admissible for infringement of the Law and Constitutional precept, as well as for breach of form. As a result, the defendants were acquitted of the crimes for which they had been convicted and all the rulings of the High Court judgement were rendered null and void. The sentence consisted of 218 pages. In the section on "Fundamentos de Derecho" (legal grounds), the same arguments were given which, when put forward by Pedro Varela's defence, had been rejected by the Catalan courts which had tried and convicted him. An excerpt is quoted below:

> "Therefore, in the case of publishers or booksellers, the possession of some copies of such works, in greater or lesser numbers, with the aim of selling or distributing them, as would be the case with many other possible works with similar themes, or even contrary ones in their deepest but equally discriminatory and exclusionary sense, does not in itself constitute an act of dissemination of ideas beyond the mere fact of making their documentary supports available to potential users, and therefore, nothing different from what is to be expected from their professional dedication, even if they contain some form of justification of genocide, they do not constitute direct incitement to hatred, discrimination or violence against these groups, or indirect incitement to the commission of acts constituting genocide, and even if these works contain concepts, ideas or doctrines that are discriminatory or offensive to groups of people, it cannot be considered that these acts of dissemination alone create a climate of hostility that entails a certain danger of materialising in specific acts of violence against them.
>
> There is no description in the proven facts, as would be necessary to apply the offence, of any act of promotion, publicity, public defence, recommendation, praise or incitement or similar acts attributed to the accused which referred to the goodness of the ideas or doctrines contained in the books which they edited, distributed or sold because of their philhonazi content, discriminatory or genocide-prone or genocide-justifying content, or the desirability of acquiring them for the knowledge and development of those ideas or doctrines, or in any way advocating their implementation, which could be considered as dissemination activities, which had a wider scope and were different from the fact of publishing certain works or making copies available to potential customers.
>
> Nor can the acts alleged in the factual account be seen to glorify Nazi leaders on account of their discriminatory or genocidal activities, and therefore, without prejudice to the opinion that such persons may deserve, in relation to what has been said so far, they cannot be considered as an indirect incitement to genocide or as an activity aimed at creating a hostile climate from which specific acts against the offended persons or against the groups of which they form part could be inferred".

To put it in plain English ("in which the people usually talk to their neighbours"), the fact that booksellers or publishers, in the exercise of their professional activity, sell or publish certain books does not mean that they justify genocide, hatred or violence against anyone. The Supreme Court, and this would be applicable to the case of Pedro Varela, did not consider that in the "proven facts" there was anything related to acts of promotion or justification of the practice of the ideas contained in the books published or distributed. Nor did consider that any incitement to genocide could be attributed to those convicted on the basis of the acts alleged in the account of the facts. As for the claim that the defendants formed part of an unlawful association, the Supreme Court explained in the ruling that "it is not enough to prove the ideology of the group or its members" and considered that the available data did not show that the group was "a structured organisation with the means to transform ideological orientation into the promotion of discrimination".

STC 235 of 7 November 2007 and Ruling no. 259 of 12 April 2011 of the Criminal Division of the Supreme Court protect the rights to ideological freedom and freedom of expression, so that any idea can be defended and disseminated. However, instead of congratulating themselves on two rulings that protect the freedoms of all, some "progressive" media, always servile to the voice of their masters, tore their garments and considered the rulings to be a step backwards. In other words, when judges and prosecutors act in accordance with certain interests, even if they restrict fundamental rights, they are exemplary rulings; but otherwise the magistrates are conservative and carcas. In their sectarianism, these media and the groups behind them ignore the fact that the Constitution does not prohibit ideologies, whether they are at one end of the political spectrum or the other. According to the Supreme Court judges, the Constitution "does not prohibit ideologies", so "ideas as such should not be criminally prosecuted". The Supreme Court insisted that tolerance of all kinds of ideas allows for the acceptance of even those that question the Constitution itself, "however reprehensible they may be considered". In short, the Supreme Court relied on the jurisprudence of the Constitutional Court, according to which "in the protection of freedom of opinion there is room for any opinion, however mistaken or dangerous it may seem to the reader, even those that attack the democratic system itself. The Constitution also protects those who deny it".

The Supreme Court's ruling was a setback, a setback, for the Barcelona High Court. At the time, Pedro Varela was still in Can Brians prison. In June 2011, half a year after being voluntarily admitted, the prison's treatment board denied him permission to see his wife and young daughter, whom he had not seen since. Since the powers of prison enforcement have been transferred to the Generalitat de Catalunya, it is clear that the prison officials were obeying political instructions from the Catalan government. Pedro Varela had applied for the third degree and had been denied. On 3 March 2011, he lodged an appeal against the refusal. If justice had been served, as soon as the Supreme Court judgement acquitting the four booksellers and publishers convicted of the same offences became known, the corresponding Prison Supervision Court should have resolved the appeal against the denial of the third degree and automatically ordered the conditional release of the prisoner. Despite the fact that the case law of the Supreme Court does not consider the facts for which he was in prison to be a crime, Varela served his sentence in full. Thus, it was demonstrated once again that his case was political and had nothing to do with fairness and justice.

7. Main victims of persecution in Sweden

Ditlieb Felderer, the mocking Jew using corrosive satire

This revisionist, who has been accused, prosecuted, convicted and imprisoned in Sweden, currently maintains an irreverent website, *Ditliebradio*, where he has opted for sardonic humour to denounce impostures. In a sarcastic, macabre way, he uses all kinds of ironic photographs, including pornographic ones, to mock the lies about the Holocaust, the crimes of Zionism, the Catholic Church's adherence to dogma, Jehovah's Witnesses and whatever else is needed. Sometimes he uses bold and ingenious photomontages to better illustrate his denunciations. For all this, Felderer is known as the eccentric revisionist. His bizarre sense of humour has been used by exterminationists and propagandists to discredit him. He seems to care little for it, believing that the "sensibilities" of history falsifiers and compulsive liars should not be respected at all.

According to Elliot Y. Neaman, Ph.D. in history at the University of California at Berkeley and professor at the University of San Francisco, Ditlieb Felderer is Jewish, as was his mother, who was descended from a family of Jehovah's Witnesses. Born in Innsbruck in 1942, he fled the Nazis with his family: they went to Italy and from there emigrated to Sweden, where he was educated. He therefore has Swedish nationality. In 1976, working for a Jehovah's Witness publication, he began to travel to the camps. Years later, between 1978 and 1980, he made a second round of visits to what were supposedly extermination camps. He was one of the first researchers to look for evidence at Auschwitz. On these trips, he took nearly 30,000 photos, recording even the most trivial details of the facilities. Many of them are used in his photomontages. At Auschwitz, Felderer photographed the swimming pool, the modern hospital and its gynaecology section, the theatre, the library, the classrooms where sculpture classes were held, the kitchen, which was one of the largest facilities in the camp. He had access to archives that required special permission and discovered in them the musical score of a piece entitled "Auschwitz Waltz", which was supposedly performed by the camp orchestra.

Among his main contributions as a revisionist was the discovery of the role played in the camps by Jehovah's Witnesses, who cooperated with the SS administration. We have already mentioned above that, as a prominent Jehovah's Witness, he was expelled from the sect when he denounced that it was false that the Germans had exterminated 60,000 members, since according to his investigations he established that only 203 of them had died (see note 3). It was at the same time as this dispute with the sect's leadership that Richard Verrall's (Richard Harwood) book *Did Six Million Realy Die?* fell into his hands, of which he published a Swedish edition in 1977 and distributed some 10,000 copies. Since then his commitment to historical revisionism has been permanent. After founding the magazine *Bible Researcher* in 1978, in 1979, the year he met Ernst Zündel, he published the book *Auschwitz Exit* under the pseudonym Abraham Cohen. As a result of his research, in the same year his *Diary of Anne Frank - A Hoax?*

Felderer was already fond of certain eccentricities, some of which disturbed Zündel, as he considered them counterproductive. One of them ended up costing him imprisonment. Since the Auschwitz Museum exhibits hair from alleged victims murdered in the gas chambers, Felderer came up with the idea of making fun of it in a widely circulated pamphlet entitled: 'Please accept this hair from a gassed victim'. The leaflet was sent to the officials of the Auschwitz Museum. Interspersed in the text of the leaflet were drawings and jokes mocking the museum officials and of the exterminationists. In the first drawing, a smiling woman held a wrapped gift with the inscription: "Please send us all your junk. We need it for our authentic exhibits and documentation". The second joke was a clown saying: "I am an expert exterminationist. Generously send us your documents to all our addresses. You will be remembered for it. The third illustration was a man crying crocodile tears, the text below read: "I was gassed six times! No! Ten times, No!... and there are 5,999,999 others like me in Neu Jork! The six million gassed Jews are a hoax!". During Zündel's first trial he was questioned and explained that in his opinion satire was necessary to denounce an imposture supported by powerful states and the power of money.

In 1980, the Swedish police arrested Ditlieb Felderer for publishing the pamphlet. On this first occasion he spent three weeks in prison. In 1982 he was arrested a second time because of the controversial pamphlet. This time he was charged with agitation against an ethnic group, and a Stockholm court sentenced him to six months in prison. Felderer stated that during this imprisonment he was treated inhumanely. Not knowing whether it was day or night, he said, he spent most of the time staring at the wall of a two-by-three metre concrete bunker, as he was hardly allowed to go outside to breathe fresh air. The cell had no toilet and he was escorted and locked in a washroom when he needed to relieve himself. In protest at his situation and because he was prevented from writing, he went on three hunger strikes, until he was finally allowed to do some exercise and was provided with paper and pencil. Felderer reported that he was beaten several times and had to endure insults.

In 1988, at Zündel's second trial, he showed 300 leaflets taken during his visits to the camps and demanded protection for revisionism and freedom of speech instead of persecution. The Crown presented him with several of his pamphlets. It asked him to read one entitled "Three Jewish Contributions to Western Civilisation". The contributions referred to the atomic bomb, developed by Robert Oppenheimer; the hydrogen bomb, whose father was Edward Teller; and the neutron bomb, by Samuel Cohen. All three were Jewish. Felderer testified that his flyer spoke volumes about certain people who had created these terrible weapons of destruction. Another of the leaflets he was shown alluded to his admission to a psychiatric hospital while on trial: he complained that in Sweden detractors were interned and compared this practice to that used in the Soviet Union. The Crown Prosecution replied to Felderer that it could not accept that the Swedish authorities thought he was ill and needed help; but he insisted that the tests he had undergone showed that he was perfectly sane.

It seems that after his testimony at the Toronto trial, he thought he had done all he could and his research had stopped. Ernst Zündel always acknowledged Felderer's excellent work on the camps and on Anne Frank's diary, but considered that satire was not an effective genre for a historian because it can call into question the seriousness of the rest of the work. Zündel came to regret that Feldererer had gone too far in his mockery through pamphlets and drawings. Despite his disappearance from the scene, Feldererer has reported repeated harassment and insults. Not for nothing is he considered one of the pioneering researchers of revisionism.

As we noted in footnote 3, the latest we have heard from Ditlieb Felderer is that in November 2013 he blamed Jewish judge Johan Hirschfeldt for being behind "terrorist actions" against him and his Filipino wife. On his website *Ditliebradio*, Feldererer referred to secret documents from the Swedish Foreign Ministry to make very serious accusations against Hirschfeldt, whom he accused of having instigated attacks against them by thugs on behalf of the ADL (Anti-Defamation League). It seems that in one of these acts, which Feldererer describes as state terrorism, his wife almost lost her life. According to Felderer, Carl Bildt, then foreign minister, could be held responsible for his inaction. Felderer also accused Judge Hirschfeldt of harassing Ahmed Rami, a Moroccan revisionist who has been attacked several times and has been running the website *Radio Islam* for many years, with false accusations.

Ahmed Rahmi, the architect of *Radio Islam* and leading Muslim revisionist

This Moroccan of Berber origin was an officer in the Royal Moroccan Army when, on 16 August 1972, he took part in a failed coup d'état against King Hassan II, whom he considered a puppet of Jewish power. After going underground, Ahmed Rami went to Paris and from there to Sweden, where he applied for and was granted political asylum in 1973. Since then he has lived in Stockholm, where he has published five books in Swedish. His appearance in these pages is due to the revisionist activities that ended up costing him imprisonment in the country that had taken him in.

In 1987 he founded and ran a radio station called *Radio Islam*, which enabled him to communicate with Swedes and the eighty thousand or so Muslims living in the country. His slogan was "Radio Islam - The Freedom Fighter - Join the fight against Jewish domination and racism! In its radio broadcasts it began to launch revisionist content, in particular the works of Robert Faurisson. In 1988, the station reported on the Ernst Zündel trial in Toronto. A staunch supporter of the Palestinian cause, Rami linked the Holocaust to the Zionist usurpation of Palestine from the outset, and consequently linked the liberation of the Palestinian people to the uncovering of the lies imposed by Zionism. This frankness led to the radio station being branded as anti-Semitic, and in 1989 the Minister of Justice, under pressure from the Jewish lobby, brought a charge of incitement to racial hatred.

A trial against Ahmed Rami began in September 1989 and lasted until November. The trial began at the Stockholm District Court on 15 September. From the outset, Rami's defence rejected the accusations of ethnic slurs and defamation, and made the argument that freedom of expression could not be restricted because someone feels insulted. In addition, lawyer Ingemar Folke insisted that Rami had merely quoted passages from the Bible in which Jews were depicted as blackmailers, greedy, sadistic, exploitative and criminal. The fact that the texts came from the Pentateuch led the Swedish press to believe that the court should ultimately interpret whether they contained expressions of racism or contempt for other ethnic groups. Prosecutor Hakan Bondestam called Rabbi Morton Narrowe and former Stockholm Lutheran bishop Krister Stendahl, an honorary professor at Harvard University, who flew in from the United States to testify against the Moroccan revisionist. Stendahl declared that Luther's *The Jews and Their Lies* was not Christian and that Luther was an anti-Semite. For his part, Rami presented as witnesses Jan Hjärpe, a renowned professor of Islam at Lund University, and Jan Bergman, a professor of religion at Uppsala University. Both testified that in their opinion freedom of expression in Sweden was under attack when it was intended to silence criticism of Israel and silence the Palestinian issue. Lawyer Folke insisted that a distinction had to be made between anti-Semitism and anti-Zionism and stressed that his client was seeking to defend the rights of the Palestinian people and that criticism of a state's policies could not be considered racial hatred. The daily *Expressen*, in a display of insidious bad faith, considered in its 23 October 1989 edition that it was "practically impossible to separate anti-Semitism from anti-Zionism".

On the other issues, Rami was accused of Holocaust denial. He maintained impassively that the alleged genocide of six million Jews "was a huge propaganda hoax". Some newspapers indignantly picked up on Rami's quotes from *The Protocols of the Elders of Zion* and his claim that Jews had not been exterminated in the gas chambers. The main defender of Rami and Professors Hjärpe and Bergman in the Swedish press was Jan Myrdal, son of Nobel laureate Gunner Myrdal. As the trial progressed, prosecutor Bondestam realised that the prolongation of the trial was counterproductive, because Rami was using it to "continue with his anti-Semitic propaganda while on trial". On 14 November, the verdict was pronounced and Ahmed Rami was found guilty. When sentenced, he was sentenced to six months in prison for "incitement against an ethnic group", and in February 1990 he was imprisoned. *Radio Islam's* licence was cancelled for a year. Robert Faurisson subsequently reported on the activities of his revisionist colleague in prison. According to the professor, Rami successfully explained his views not only to the prisoners, but also to the guards, which is why the authorities transferred him to another, smaller facility, where the result was the same.

As for the cancellation of the radio permit, the Stockholm Community Radio Council allowed the station to continue broadcasting until 28 November 1990. When the station resumed its activities in 1991, it did so under the leadership of David Janzon, a Swedish nationalist member of the "Sveriges Nationella Förbund" (Swedish National Alliance), who was subsequently convicted of the same offence in 1993. The radio station thus remained inactive between 1993 and 1995. Programming was re-established under the leadership of Ahmed Rami in 1996, when he also launched his famous website, which kept the same name of *Radio Islam*. Initially, this website was very active in its criticism of Jewish racism and Zionist world domination. In addition, very interesting revisionist texts appeared in up to 23 languages. Today, and for some years now, the site, maintained by a group of self-styled "freedom fighters" from different countries who support Ahmed Rami, is rarely renewed. We do not know what the reason for this lack of activity is, although it is likely to be due to the harassment of Rami.

In this regard, in his *Écrits révisionnistes*[16] Robert Faurisson recounts that between 17 and 21 March 1992, he travelled to Stockholm at the invitation of his Moroccan friend. On the afternoon/evening of the same day of his arrival, Rami, two young Swedes and Professor Faurisson were attacked and nearly lynched by individuals armed with sticks, knives and tear gas bombs. The leaders of the group of attackers were the heads of a Jewish student club.

---

[16] *Écrits révisionnistes*, 4 volumes, Omnia Veritas Limited, www.omnia-veritas.com.

Thanks to these threats, the Jewish community in Stockholm succeeded in cancelling all the lectures that Ahmed Rami had organised for Professor Faurisson to speak; but he could not be prevented from expressing himself freely and extensively on *Radio Islam*'s airwaves. The professor's second stay in Stockholm took place between 3 and 6 December of the same year. At the airport, the "Nazi prophet", as some media described him, was met by Rami, some Arab friends and a Somali. Paradoxically, two Jewish demonstrators were holding a banner with the inscription "Down with racism! Faurisson stayed at his host's house and recounts in the *Écrits* that there were two night-time attacks on Rami's home.

In October 2000 Rami was again convicted of "incitement to racial hatred". The Swedish court that tried him in absentia fined him about $25,000. In both France and Sweden he was investigated for "hate crimes" because of his role in maintaining *Radio Islam*. In Sweden, the investigation ended in 2004 and the prosecutor was unable to provide evidence that Ahmed Rami was responsible for the content displayed on the site. The *Radio Islam* affair reached the Swedish Parliament in November 2005. The debate took place due to the large number of lawsuits that Jewish organisations filed in court, demanding that Ahmed Rami be prosecuted in Sweden or brought before an international court. This idea had been proposed in Morocco by Robert Assaraf, the leader of the Moroccan Jewish community, who in March 2000, in a statement to the magazine *Jeune Afrique*, asked rhetorically: "Shouldn't Moroccan Jews, who are scattered all over the world, mobilise in order to bring Ahmed Rami to trial?"

The debate in the Swedish Parliament took place on 10 November 2005. Jewish members of the chamber criticised the government for having abdicated to Ahmed Rami and his anti-Jewish activities in Sweden. Justice and Home Affairs Minister Thomas Bodström defended himself with these words: 'In a state under the rule of law, it is not up to me or the members of parliament to charge or judge Ahmed Rami. This is a matter for the public prosecutor's office. But the prosecution has not been able to find any evidence to prove that Ahmed Rami has violated Swedish law". To the discomfort of some MPs, the minister reminded: "Swedish law does not prohibit questioning or denying the Holocaust". Minister Bodström recalled that it had been agreed in Sweden that citizens could not be forced to believe in the Holocaust and that it was not possible to prohibit questioning its historical veracity. However, he suggested "the possibility of exerting some influence in Parliament by proposing a law and, of course, contributing to the work done in the European Union".

The latest we know about Ahmed Rami and *Radio Islam* is that in December 2015 the Italian police opened an investigation. The reason was the publication in Italian on the website of a list of influential Jews operating in the country. The names of journalists, businessmen, actors, and various personalities were listed, who were described as "Judeo-Nazi mafia". Representatives of the Jewish community considered this an incitement to sectarian violence and used adjectives such as "unacceptable" or "despicable" to refer to the issue. The leader of Rome's Jewish community told *Corriere della Sera* that "it was an unbearable representation of anti-Semitic hatred". Some lawyers called for the website to be shut down immediately. Meanwhile, Giuseppe Giulietti and Raffaele Lorusso, president and secretary general of the Italian National Press Federation, called the publication of the list "a miserable, racist and intolerable act". In a press release they wrote: "It offends first of all Muslims who have chosen the path of dialogue and respect. This list evokes the dark times and the walls that we should all tear down together".

These two hypocrites were, of course, referring to all the walls except the eight-metre high wall erected by the Zionists in Palestine. As for "dialogue and respect", it does not include, of course, the Palestinian people, let alone the 1.5 million Gazans living in subhuman conditions in their open-air prison. As is well known, in July/August 2014 some two thousand people, a quarter of them children, were killed and nine thousand were badly injured, if not severely mutilated. Of course, this was not "a miserable, racist and intolerable act". Two years after the "tolerable" bombardment of Palestinian civilians, Gaza, thanks to "dialogue and respect", is still in ruins and its inhabitants remain destitute.

8. Main victims of persecution in Australia

Frederick Töben, imprisoned in Germany, England and Australia

Dr. Fredrick Töben is one of the most illustrious and courageous victims of the revisionist movement. This German-born Australian could have been listed among the victims in Germany, as the "Bundesrepublik" is the country that has been most vicious in its persecution. However, we have chosen to dedicate an exclusive space to him and place him in Australia because it is there that he founded the Adelaide Institute in 1994, an institution dedicated to historical research that would be the equivalent in Australia of the Institute for Historical Review in California.

The Jewish lobbies in Australia have been relentless in their efforts to shut down the Adelaide Institute's website. In 1996 the powerful Jewish lobby "Executive Council of Australian Jewry" (ECAJ) took the first legal action to shut down the Institute's website. Dr. Töben, author of numerous works on history, education and political issues, has researched most of the concentration camps in existence today: Buchenwald, Dachau, Oranienburg, Sachsenhausen, Auschwitz-Birkenau, among others. In the latter, he inspected the alleged gas chamber in April 1997 and shot a highly recommendable video which is part of the documentary *Judea Declares War on Germany*, released by the IHR in Los Angeles.

In 1999 he travelled to Europe to conduct research in several countries, including Poland, Ukraine, Hungary, the Czech Republic and Germany. While in the office of a German prosecutor famous for his work against deniers, Hans-Heiko Klein, with whom he allegedly discussed the German law prohibiting dissent from the official version of World War II, he was arrested on 9 April 1999 for having published or forwarded to Germany revisionist texts of the Adelaide Institute. The arrest warrant stated: "since April 1996 and most recently between January and April 1999, he has mailed from Adelaide (Australia) to recipients in the Federal Republic of Germany, inter alia, a monthly newsletter of the Adelaide Institute, of which he is the responsible editor". A criminal offence, no doubt, which justified, as the arrest warrant stated, his being remanded in custody pending trial.

This pre-trial detention was ignominiously prolonged for seven months. On 3 May, the prosecutor's office of the Mannheim district court confirmed it in a new arrest warrant. The charges, in addition to the sending of the newsletter, specified that she was "one of the leading revisionists" and specified some of the inadmissible contents of the newsletter, such as the statement that "the extermination was a legend invented by the Jews for the purpose of subjugating the German people". This second arrest warrant accused him of incitement to hatred, attacks on the dignity of others and denigrating the memory of dead Jews, all of which disturbed the public peace.

As soon as news broke in Australia of the Adelaide Institute director's arrest, civil rights groups mobilised to denounce Fredrick Töben's arrest in Germany under "draconian free speech laws". John Bennett, a well-known Australian revisionist and activist who chairs the Australian Civil Liberties Union, urged people to go to German embassies and other institutions to protest. Bennett organised a fund to secure Töben's legal defence and release. Another group, Electronic Frontiers Australia (EFA), an independent group promoting online freedom of expression, also spoke out against the arrest and expressed anger that the German authorities treated the material posted on an Australian website as if it had been published in Germany. EFA president, lawyer Kimberley Heitman, accused the German government of trying to legislate in practice for the whole world. Mark Weber, director of the IHR, also protested indignantly at the arrest and remand of his Australian colleague, but nothing changed Töben's situation in Germany.

After seven months in prison without bail, he was brought before a Mannheim district court presided over by Judge Klaus Kern on 8 November 1999. On the first day of the trial, Töben announced that he would not defend himself against the charges against him because this would only serve to bring new charges against him for additional violations of German laws on 'Holocaust denial' and 'incitement to hatred'. He rejected, however, the German authorities' claim that the revisionists were dangerous neo-Nazis or anti-Semites. His lawyer, Ludwig Bock, also announced that he would not defend Dr. Töben either, as he risked being indicted as well. He therefore confined himself to reading a statement to the court in which he compared the persecution of Töben and other "Holocaust deniers" to the witch trials of the Middle Ages. He claimed that German laws against revisionism seriously violated the principle of freedom of expression. He justified his and his client's decision to a journalist: "If I say anything, I myself will go to jail, and if he says anything, he exposes himself to another trial.

Prosecutor Klein later confirmed that these fears were fully justified: "If they had repeated illegal things in court, I would have brought new charges". As has already been explained, the legal system in Germany renders defendants and witnesses defenceless and prevents lawyers from freely exercising their profession. Indeed, in November 1999, Ludwig Bock was awaiting the outcome of his appeal, because while defending Günter Deckert he had been convicted and fined DM 9,000 for having complained that political leaders and judges in his country prohibited debate on the subject of the Holocaust.

The trial ended on 10 November 1999. The court found Töben guilty of incitement to racial hatred, of having insulted the memory of the dead and of public denial of genocide because in his writings sent to people in Germany he had questioned the evidence of Holocaust extermination. Klaus Kern, the presiding judge, said that there was no doubt that Töben was guilty of "Holocaust denial" and that, as he showed no signs of rectifying his conduct, he should be sentenced to imprisonment. He was therefore sentenced to ten months in prison. Fortunately, Judge Kern took into consideration that the defendant had already spent seven months in prison and agreed to pay a fine of DM 6,000 in lieu of the remaining three months of his sentence. Frederick Töben's German friends immediately collected the money, and within 24 hours of the verdict he was released.

Particularly important in the ruling was the decision on the internet, as the consequences could be far-reaching. The Mannheim court declared that German law had no jurisdiction over Dr. Töben's writings and online publications, and therefore refused to enter into the evidence presented by the prosecution in relation to the Adelaide Institute's website. Judge Kern argued that the court could only consider material that Töben had emailed or physically distributed in Germany. As soon as he was released, Töben declared it a victory for free speech: "We have saved the internet," he said, "as a place where we can tell the truth without being punished for it. For his part, public prosecutor Hans-Heiko Klein was also aware that the court's verdict could set a dangerous precedent and immediately filed an appeal. This is the first time," he said, "that a German court has decided that some things said on the internet in Germany cannot be subject to German law. This is a very bad thing. It will weaken our legislation which is very important to ensure that history does not repeat itself in Germany."

Back in Australia, the struggle continued with a new battle. As we noted at the beginning, in 1996 the ECAJ (Executive Council of Australian Jewry), the most powerful of Australia's Jewish lobbies, had filed a complaint with the aim of banning the Adelaide Institute's website from the Internet. One year after Töben had won a victory for Internet freedom in the German court case, on 10 October 2000, the Human Rights and Equal Opportunity Commission (HREOC), under pressure from Australian Jewry, issued an injunction against the Adelaide Institute. HREOC Commissioner Kathleen McEvoy alleged that the Institute had violated Section 18C of the Racial Discrimination Act 1975 by publishing materials whose primary purpose was to denigrate Jews. McEvoy said the materials, "none of which were of sufficient historical, intellectual or scientific standard", should be banned because they were "intimidating, insulting and offensive". ECAJ vice-president Jeremy Jones was quick to reiterate that "Töben's Holocaust denialism was offensive, insulting and, as confirmed by HREOC, illegal". Jones added that the commissioner "had demonstrated that she understood the need to enforce laws that include the internet and had endorsed the view of other jurisdictions that anti-Semitism masquerading as pseudo-history is as pernicious as the worst form of racial hatred." Peter Wertheim, ECAJ's counsel in the legal proceedings and a Jewish community leader, referred to the case as "a landmark" because it "dealt with internet hate for the first time in Australia and most likely in the world."

Dr Töben's response was defiant: he claimed that he had no intention of complying with the HREOC (Human Rights and Equal Opportunity Commission) order and said he had no intention of apologising for the publication of "objectively correct material". Töben accused HREOC of considering only the interests of Jews and called its actions immoral. He said he had "no intention of doing anything" because the truth could not be considered an offence to anyone. In early November 2000 the Australia/Israel & Jewish Affairs Council joined ECAJ in petitioning the country's Federal Court to enforce HREOC's censorship order against Töben and the Adelaide Institute.

The attempted censorship of the Adelaide Institute set a shameful precedent for a country with a long tradition of respect for civil liberties and free speech. Terry Lane, a veteran columnist and television commentator, asked Commissioner McEvoy if she was "going to order every sincere person who dislikes one group or another to cease and desist and apologise." This journalist went so far as to say that Töben's claims about the gas chambers "could be proved or disproved by the evidence", so there was no need to censor them beforehand. If Töben is telling the truth," Lane added, "nothing can stop him. If he is a malicious writer, he will be ignored. We should check his claims, not ban them." Another author, civil rights advocate Nigel Jackson, referred to HREOC as a "pseudo-judicial" body and called its order "a victory of interests over principle". On 17 September 2002, the Federal Court, in response to the Jewish lobby's application, upheld the application of anti-racial hate laws against the Adelaide Institute's website. In 2003, in the case of Töben v. Jones, the Court issued Australia's first ruling in relation to racial hatred against religious groups. Töben failed to remove the materials in question and also refused to apologise.

In 2004, a Mannheim court issued a European Arrest Warrant (EAW) against Frederick Töben, who was accused of publishing anti-Semitic and/or revisionist material online in Australia, Germany and other countries. Despite the existence of the European Arrest Warrant, Dr. Töben travelled the world without any problems. In 2005 he gave an interview to Iranian state television in which he denounced the State of Israel, "founded on the lie of the Holocaust". In December 2006 he participated in the Tehran Conference with his revisionist colleagues. However, problems continued to arise in his own country as a result of his refusal to remove the censored texts from the Institute's website and, consequently, his confrontation with the Federal Court.

Jeremy Jones of the Executive Council of Australian Jewry (ECAJ) meanwhile continued his relentless pursuit in the courts. At the end of February 2008, Dr. Töben, summoned to the Federal Court in Sydney, made strong accusations against two Jewish judges of the High Court, Alan Goldberg and Stephen Rothman, whom he accused of "propagating the Jewish Holocaust" in order to "protect a historical lie". On 7 August 2008, the Australian newspaper *The Advertiser* reported that "Holocaust revisionist Frederick Töben could be jailed for criminal contempt of the Federal Court if he could not face a fine." He was accused of continuing to publish racist texts on the Adelaide Institute's website, despite a Federal Court order in September 2002 and a further injunction in 2007.

Two months later, on 1 October 2008, Töben was travelling from the United States to Dubai. When his plane landed at Heathrow airport for a technical stop, British police boarded the plane and, in application of the 2004 EAW, arrested the Australian revisionist on board. He was brought before a Westminster District Court on the 3rd and British magistrates decided to hold him in London's Wandsworth prison pending a decision on his extradition request. Töben stated that he was protected by the Schengen treaty and would not accept extradition, but the hearing was set for 17 October.

British revisionists mobilised against the outrage perpetrated against their Australian colleague. A group of supporters, including David Irving, demonstrated in front of the court. The press devoted considerable attention to the affair. *The Telegraph* reported the Töben case appropriately, calling the arrest "a brazen attack on free speech". In an editorial, it warned: "The arrest of Dr Frederick Töben should alarm us all". In Parliament, Liberal Democrat Party spokesman Chris Huhne reminded the House that "Holocaust denial" was not a crime in Britain, and called on the British courts to reject Töben's extradition. Simultaneously, Andreas Grossmann, the prosecutor of the Mannheim district court, welcomed the arrest and said that despite attempts to avoid extradition to Germany, he hoped to have Töben in court next year. Grossmann warned in statements to Australian media that the defendant's stubbornness and obstinacy could cost him five years in prison in Germany.

On 17 October 2008 there was anticipation. Journalists with cameras and microphones gathered in front of the City of Westminster Magistrates Court. Kevin Lowry-Mullins, Töben's lawyer, declared before entering that they would fight every issue. Also speaking to journalists was Lady Michèle Renouf, the Australian-born British revisionist model who runs the website *Jailing Opinions*, which has been assisting Töben since she learned of his arrest. A staunch supporter of freedom of research, expression and thought, Renouf stressed the importance of the court decision for freedoms in the UK. However, the hearing was postponed until 29 October. Lowry-Mullins explained on the way out the scope of the ruling, as it was a question of whether a state could request the extradition to the UK of any person, even if the crime charged was not a crime in the UK.

Finally on 29 October came the victory awaited by Töben, Lady Renouf and so many revisionists around the world. Daphne Wickham, the judge at Westminster Magistrates' Court, ruled before a packed courtroom of Töben supporters that the European arrest warrant was invalid because it did not sufficiently specify the offences: it did not mention the name of the website, where or when the materials had been published, but only said publications on the internet around the world. Melanie Cumberland, the lawyer representing the German authorities, argued that the requested information could be provided; but the district judge said: "The requirement, in my view, cannot be met with a drop-by-drop information as and when provided by the authority of the issuing country. I consider that the details are vague and imprecise. I consider that the order is invalid, and I therefore disqualify the defendant." In other words, without even going so far as to pronounce on whether the alleged crimes of opinion were extraditable offences, the judge dropped the charges against Dr Töben on the grounds of formal defects in the arrest warrant. Cumberland announced that he intended to appeal to the Supreme Court. Pending such an appeal, Judge Wickham, after prohibiting him from making statements to the press, granted Töben provisional release on bail of £100,000 on condition that he give an acknowledged address, which would be that of Lady Renouf.

Michèle Renouf stated on the way out that they were not afraid of ending up before the Supreme Court, as this would allow Dr. Töben's case to gain greater international impact. Finally, perhaps considering that the filing of the appeal could end up being detrimental to the interests of the Holocaust lobby, Töben's lawyers were informed on 18 November that the German authorities were waiving their appeal. On the evening of 19 November, while the

British Parliament honoured Zionist Shimon Peres with the Order of St Michael and St George, Fredrick Töben celebrated freedom with his friends. On 21 November Kevin Lowry-Mullins reported that his passport had been returned to him and that he was preparing to leave Britain. The lawyer regretted that his client had not received any compensation for the almost two months he had been held against his will in London.

By 3 December 2008, Töben was back in Australia; but far from enjoying a respite, he faced a continuation of the persecution that the Executive Council of Australian Jewry had initiated in 1996. In April 2009, Töben was convicted for ignoring a Federal Court order to remove material from the Adelaide Institute's website. Sentenced to three months' imprisonment, he argued that he did not have the money to pay a fine to avoid imprisonment, let alone the legal costs of such a lengthy court case, as demanded by Jeremy Jones, who had brought the case on behalf of Jewish organisations. Töben appealed the verdict in June.

The appeal hearing was held on 13 August 2009. Lawyer David Perkins told the court that the texts published on the Adelaide Institute's website were only "a drop in the bucket" compared to the amount of revisionist material available online. The judges insisted that the case was not about the Holocaust, the gas chambers or the execution of Jews during World War II, but about disobedience of Federal Court orders. Evidently, this was a quibble, i.e. a false argument put forward with sufficient skill to make it appear true. The Federal Court would not have ordered the removal of the material in 2002 without pressure from Jewish lobbies seeking the banning of texts that questioned the official version of history. The three judges of the Federal Court of Australia therefore rejected the appeal and upheld the committal to prison. "You follow orders blindly, gentlemen," Töben said to the judges as he left the courtroom.

Frederick Töben thus became the first prisoner of conscience in Australia's legal history. He initially spent a week in a maximum security punishment block at Yatala Prison in the northern suburbs of Adelaide, a prison where the worst criminals are held. He was subsequently transferred to a much less rigorous detention centre in Cadell, about 200 kilometres north-east of Adelaide, where he was able to receive the support of his friends, who kept visiting him. The

Adelaide Institute was taken over by Peter Hartung, a businessman and political adviser with a spirit of resilience worthy of his predecessor and friend.

As for the costs of the proceedings, Dr. Töben had to bear them. On 25 June 2010, Jeremy Jones, who behaved like a hound that does not let go of its prey, submitted a statement of costs and expenses amounting to 104,412 dollars. On 30 June, the Federal Court decided to request $56,435 as a provision and on 15 September 2010 issued a valuation certificate stating that the amount requested by the Court was correct. Thus began another complicated legal battle between Jeremy Jones and Fredrick Töben which lasted for more than two years, and the amount demanded kept increasing. On 27 February 2012, Jeremy Jones asked for a new assessment of costs. On 10 April, Dr Töben filed an application for an interlocutory injunction in which, inter alia, he requested that the assessment of court costs be removed or excluded. On 3 May 2012, Judge Mansfield rejected Töben's claim, and Töben also had to pay the costs relating to the interlocutory application. On 18 May 2012, Fredrick Töben wrote to Jeremy Jones in these terms:

> "Your claim against me in the matter of costs in excess of $175,000 is unjust and inadmissible. I have sold my house in which I had lived for twenty-seven years, the only asset I had, to satisfy your previous requests. I have no other funds or securities and will not be able to pay a penny. If necessary, you may petition for my insolvency. I have at all times exercised my right to freedom of expression. In order to demonstrate the injustice you have done me, I maintain a cross-claim against you in the Federal Court, claiming damages for breaches of sections 18 (1) and 20 (1) of clause 2 of the Competition and Consumer Act (we will not venture to translate the title of that Act). I also intend to bring an action for defamation. The grounds for this action go back to your article of 31 August 2009 ('The last word: contempt for the truth'), which you published on the internet and which is still there. If the lawsuits I am proposing are heard by the Court, I expect to receive a substantial amount in damages, sufficient to meet your claims for costs. However, I am prepared to waive my legal rights to sue you for the above actions, provided that you stay your claim for costs.
>
> I look forward to your advice".

These lines, taken from the documentary archives of the Adelaide Institute, which contain the texts of the court proceedings, reflect the unequal struggle of a humble man, lacking in resources, against the Australian Jewish lobbies, whose wealth is practically unlimited. After serving time in prisons in Germany, England and Australia, Fredrick Töben had lost all his material possessions and was ruined, but he had an exemplary conviction and greatness, which today makes him a paradigm for all those who strive in one way or another to ensure that future generations of young people study a true world history, in which the impostors are unmasked.

Without space for further details, we will add that after seventeen years of legal persecution by representatives of Australia's Jewish community, on 24 September 2012 Dr. Fredrick Töben was declared insolvent by the magistrates of the Federal Court of Sydney. After the legal deadline for appeal had expired, *The Australian jewishnews* broke the news at the end of October with the headline "Töben tied up". Under Australian law, the declaration of insolvency entailed the confiscation of his passport in order to facilitate the monitoring of his finances and income. Thus, "tied up", he was condemned to live as a pauper for the rest of his life as punishment for his "crimes".

9. Victims of persecution in the UK

Alison Chabloz sentenced in England for three songs

Alison Chabloz, the blogger from Charlesworth (Glossop), in the English county of Derbyshire, told *The Barnes Review* in 2018: "I am the only singer in modern British history to have been imprisoned for singing songs that no one is obliged to listen to". Chabloz wrote and performed songs that the untouchables, who initiated the persecution, did not like. The organisation CAA (Campaign Against Antisemitism), chaired by Gideon Falter, filed a complaint, which was later taken over by the CPR (Crown Prosecution Service). Many months before her arrest, Alison Chabloz had been receiving suspicious anonymous letters, which she regularly handed over to the Glossop police. The officer in charge had specifically asked Alison not to open them. However, although she had even received death threats, such as: "Be careful that someone doesn't push you under a train", the investigation incomprehensibly ceased when she was arrested for the first time in November 2016.

In the aforementioned interview with *The Barnes Review*, Chabloz explains that he was working as a singer on cruise ships when he became interested in politics in 2010. The suffering of the Palestinian people, permanent victims of international Zionism, was the key that allowed him to move towards the great space of intellectual freedom of revisionism. Along the way, she met the footballer Nicolas Anelka, a friend and defender of the Palestinian cause, and the French actor and comedian Dieudonné M'bala M'bala, who put her on the trail of the indispensable professor Robert Faurisson.

In 2014 he travelled to Germany, specifically to Hamburg, where he had six weeks of training before starting a three-month work contract on a ship. There she saw for the first time that the power of certain Jews is unlimited. The ship's captain called her into his office and showed her screenshots of tweets exchanged with a Zionist called Ambrosine Shitrit. In them she once again defended the Palestinians and used satire to criticise the Zionist state. Shitrit exposed Alison

Chabloz's messages on her website as an example of anti-Semitism. This was enough for her to be humiliated and fired by the captain himself. At nine o'clock in the evening of the first day of her contract she was standing on the dock without a job. She tried to negotiate with the company, a German branch of Costa Cruises, the European subsidiary of Carnival Group, the Anglo-American company that dominates the cruise market, which is run by Micky Arison, an Israeli-born American businessman. Of course, there was nothing to negotiate.

Instead of being frightened or demoralised, Chabloz remained active online and continued to read revisionist texts. In 2015, the Swiss company Uniworld offered her a new job. From April to October she was on contract on a ship sailing on European rivers, which did not prevent her from participating in August in the Edinburgh Art Festival, which she had attended in previous years. Soon the organiser let her know that they were under pressure to cancel her performances, as she was considered an anti-Semitic Holocaust denier who should not be allowed to perform in Edinburgh. Despite all the protests, the organisers withstood the downpour and Alison Chabloz was able to continue singing. On the last day, she was photographed in Edinburgh's Princess Street doing the quenelle salute, a gesture popularised by Dieudonné, which consists of extending one arm diagonally downwards with the palm of the hand facing downwards while the opposite hand touches the shoulder. Alison showed the photo on her Twitter account, a decision that was to trigger the process against her, since two days later the Campaign Against Anti-Semitism published it on its blog and announced the complaint to the police. A day later *The Times of Israel* joined the offensive against the singer.

Among the most heartwarming events of 2016 was her contact with Gerard Menuhin, author of *Tell the Truth and Shame the Devil*, whose performance in defence of Horst Mahler has been discussed above. Alison received as a gift a poem by Menuhin entitled *Tell Me More Lies*, to which she set to music. She also wrote the songs in 2016 that were to cost her a two-year prison sentence. In "Survivors" he directly alluded to the Holocaust. In another of the questioned songs, he referred to Auschwitz as "a theme park" and the gas chambers as "a fable". In a song entitled "Haavara" he denounced the Haavara Agreement, a subject to which we devoted ten pages in chapter VIII of our *Proscribed History*. As we know, it is the collaboration pact between Nazis and Jews, which involved a transfer from Germany to Palestine of more than 60,000 German Zionists with their entire fortune.

Apart from his arrest, the worst thing about 2016 was the impossibility of performing his alternative songs in Edinburgh again. Nevertheless, Chabloz performed in September at the London Forum, a nationalist rally. His Twitter account reached 3,500 followers; but in October it was suspended. Shortly before his arrest, he received a letter from the police informing him that the investigation into the provocations and anonymous threats he had received had been unsuccessful. Finally, one evening in November, she was arrested. After being interrogated, she was held for six hours in a cell while the police searched her house, where they seized her laptop, which was not returned to her until a year later. She was released on bail the following day. She was told that she was under investigation for distributing "racist" material through her songs and for harassing two women, one of whom was Shitrit, who had caused her dismissal in Hamburg. A week later she received a summons from Westminster Magistrates' Court for her song "Survivors". The Crown added further charges for three of the songs deemed highly offensive and joined the private complaint filed by Gideon Falter, president of the CAA, thus making it a public complaint.

Throughout 2017, Alison Chabloz saw her rights and freedom restricted. A series of hearings followed, during which she was again interrogated. Due to repeated transfers to London, she spent several nights in Derbyshire county cells. Finally, after challenging a judge considered to be an avowed friend of Israel and questioning two prosecution witnesses, the trial took place in May 2018. Outside Westminster Crown Court Alison Chabloz and her supporters were mobbed on arrival by groups carrying Israeli flags. On the day of the trial, on 25 May to be precise, a burly individual with two very visible tattoos: on his face the Zionist star and on his neck the word "Chosen" (a clear allusion to belonging to God's chosen people), oozing hatred from every pore, confronted a man and pushed him in front of witnesses with the intention of throwing him to the ground. Lady Michèle Renouf, who was also present at the hearing, was also rebuked on her way out. On 14 June, on her way to collect her sentence, Chabloz arrived with some friends from the National Front and was once again subjected to the usual insults: "scum", "Nazi", etc., uttered by several friends of freedom of expression when it is exercised by them.

Judges at Westminster Magistrates' Court found Charlesworth blogger Alison Chabloz, 54, guilty of disseminating seriously offensive material on YouTube. The conviction related to the lyrics of three songs in which, Judge John Zani said, she intended to insult Jewish people. Prosecutor Karen Robinson misrepresented the facts to the extent that they were not political songs, but "a disguise for attacking a group of people for their devotion to a religion". Lawyer Adrian Davis, meanwhile, warned the judge that his ruling would be critical, as it would set a precedent for the exercise of free speech. "It's hard to know," he said, "what right has been violated by Ms Chabloz's songs."

Alison Chabloz was given a two-year suspended prison sentence, i.e. conditional on her not reoffending. She was also banned from using social media for one year. In addition, she was required to provide 180 hours of service to the Derbyshire community, which had neither reported her to nor asked for compensation of any kind, and where there is no synagogue. In the judgment, the court found that there was no repentance in Ms. Chabloz and warned her that if she aspired to become "a martyr to her cause" and did not respect the terms of the suspended sentence, she would end up in prison. Complainant Gideon Falter expressed his satisfaction and declared that Alison Chabloz was a "relentless and repulsive" anti-Semite who incited hatred of Jews by claiming that "the Holocaust was a hoax perpetrated by Jews to defraud the world". As usual, it repeated the usual refrain: "This judgement sends a strong message that anti-Semitic conspiracy theories and Holocaust denial will not be tolerated in Britain".

Unsurprisingly, Chabloz lost the appeal. On 13 February 2019, Judge Christopher Hehir of London's Southwark Crown Court upheld the conviction. The court found that the singer had lost her sense of perspective by calling Jews "thieves, liars and usurpers". Gideon Falter, for his part, underlined the importance of the success of his lawsuit, noting that it was "the first conviction in the UK for Holocaust denial on social media". He warned that "other anti-

Semites who think they can mistreat the Jewish community online with impunity should take note".

10. Other victims of persecution for thought crimes

All Against Catholic Bishop Richard Williamson

The case of the English Catholic bishop Richard Nelson Williamson is internationally known because of the repercussions of his statements on the Holocaust. Bishop Williamson belonged to the Fraternity of St. Pius X and was excommunicated by John Paul II in 1988. In November 2008, Swedish television recorded an interview with him in Regensburg (Germany), which was broadcast on 21 January 2009, a few days before Pope Benedict XVI issued a decree lifting the excommunication of him and three other renegade bishops. The bishop's words produced a media scandal, unleashed by Zionist organisations, and came to jeopardise the Vatican's relations with Jewish religious leaders. The interview begins as follows:

> P. "Williamson, are these your words: 'Not a single Jew was killed in the gas chambers. These are nothing but lies, lies, lies'. Are these your words?
>
> R. - I think you quote me from Canada, yes, many years ago. I think the historical evidence is overwhelmingly against six million Jews having been murdered in gas chambers as a result of a deliberate policy of Adolf Hitler.
>
> P. - But you said that not a single Jew was killed.
>
> R. - In gas chambers.
>
> P. - So there were no gas chambers.
>
> R. - I think there were no gas chambers, yes".

The dogma of faith of the Holocaust had just been publicly denied by a Catholic bishop. Anathema! For the rest of the interview, Williamson turned to the revisionists and said that according to them between 200,000 and 300,000 Jews had died in concentration camps, but none of them in gas chambers. After asking the interviewer if he had heard of the *Leuchter Report,* Monsignor Williamson enlightened the journalist when he replied that he did not know it: the research at Auschwitz, the conditions in a gas chamber, the characteristics of

Zyklon B were the subjects explained by the priest. The interviewer reacted with a question: "If this is not anti-Semitism, what is anti-Semitism?" The answer was that historical truth could not be anti-Semitism.

The criticism of such a heinous thought crime was fierce and the demands immediate. As early as January, Regensburg's public prosecutor, Günter Ruckdaeschel, announced that an investigation had been opened against Williamson. Criticism extended to Pope Benedict XVI for lifting his excommunication. A Vatican spokesman immediately pointed out that the bishop's views were unacceptable and violated church teaching. In a front-page article, the Vatican newspaper *L'Osservatore Romano* reaffirmed that the Pope deplored any form of anti-Semitism and that all Catholics should do the same. Rabbi David Rosen of the American Jewish Committee, Rabbi Marvin Hier of the Simon Wiesenthal Center and the Jewish Agency, effectively the mouthpiece of the Israeli government, denounced the Vatican for pardoning a Holocaust denier.

Bishop Williamson, now back at his headquarters in La Reja, Buenos Aires province, thanked the Pope for his decision, which he described as "a step forward for the Church". On 26 January 2009, Cardinal Angelo Bagnasco, president of the Italian Bishops' Conference, defended the Pope's decision to rehabilitate Williamson, but criticised his views as "unfounded and unjustified". The president of the Bishops' Conference in Germany, Heinrich Mussinghoff, was also quick to "strongly condemn the explicit denial of the Holocaust". Monsignor Williamson issued a statement apologising to the Pope for having caused him "distress and trouble" because of his views on the Holocaust, which he himself described as "imprudent".

The outcry and pressure from Jewish organisations multiplied and exposed the Vatican's inability to respond other than obedience and docility. Charlotte Knobloch, president of the Central Council of Jews in Germany, announced that in these circumstances she was suspending her dialogues with Catholic leaders. On 3 February 2009, the Chief Rabbinate of Israel officially broke off relations with the Vatican and cancelled a meeting scheduled for 2 and 4 March with the Holy See's Commission for relations with Jews. Oded Weiner, director general of the Rabbinate, addressed a letter to Cardinal Walter

Casper, saying, "without a public apology and retraction, it will be difficult to continue the dialogue."

On the same day, 3 February, Angela Merkel, faithful to the voice of her masters, demanded that Pope Benedict XVI clarify the position of the Church: "The Pope and the Vatican," she said, "must make it unambiguously clear that there can be no denialism. In Germany the whole machinery for stoking the "scandal" fire was in full swing: The *Bild Zeitung* warned the Pope that "the extermination of six million Jews could not be denied" without a reaction. The *Süddeutsche Zeitung* applauded the chancellor's warning and recalled that a German pope could not "back a Holocaust denier" without offending the Jewish community. The *Berliner Zeitung* wrote that Williamson had not only mumbled in private, but had spoken publicly, calling on the Pope to excommunicate him again. In an attempt to contain the criticism, on 4 February Benedict XVI ordered Richard Williamson to recant "publicly and unequivocally."

The bishop had been living in Argentina for five years, but on 19 February he was declared "persona non grata". The Argentine Ministry of the Interior, through the National Directorate of Migration, urged the British bishop to leave the country within ten days. The note stated that it took into account "the public notoriety following his anti-Semitic statements to a Swedish media, in which he doubted that the Jewish people had been victims of the Holocaust". The Argentine government added in the note that Williamson's statements "deeply offended the Jewish people and humanity".

Monsignor Williamson, who travelled to England, nevertheless resisted all pressures and in an interview with *Der Spiegel* said that he had always sought the truth and therefore converted to Catholicism. He declared that he was convinced of what he had said: "Today I say the same thing I said in the interview with Swedish television: historical evidence must prevail and not emotions. And if I find other evidence to the contrary, I will retract it, but that will take time." The bishop drafted a written apology, but Federico Lombardi, Vatican spokesman, said he "did not meet the conditions for him to be admitted back into the Church". Of course, the Jewish community also rejected it. Marvin Hier of the Simon Wiesenthal Centre demanded: "If he wants to apologise he has to affirm the Holocaust".

Brigitte Zypries, Germany's Minister of Justice, eventually dismissed the possibility of issuing an EAW for the British authorities to arrest the bishop and extradite him to Germany. Finally, in April 2010, a trial was held in Regensburg at which Williamson did not appear. Nor did the three Swedish journalists who had taken part in the interview come to testify. Lawyer Matthias Lossmann applied in vain for acquittal. Monsignor Williamson was sentenced to a fine of 10,000 euros for "incitement to racial hatred". Following an appeal, in July 2011, again in absentia, Williamson was sentenced in the second instance to pay 6,500 euros, but due to procedural flaws, a review of the proceedings was forced. On 24 February 2012, he was acquitted. The court found that the charges had been brought incorrectly because the prosecution did not adequately specify the nature of the offence. The sentence was therefore quashed on the grounds of procedural errors,. Since the possibility of new charges remained open, he was convicted in absentia for the third time on 16 January 2013. This time the fine was reduced to 1,600 euros. Williamson refused to pay and appealed again.

As can be seen, what was important in the case was the monumental uproar, the unrelenting harassment, the disproportionate reactions against a Catholic priest just because he dared to speak his mind. In our opinion, what was really regrettable was not the usual condemnations and threats from international Jewish organisations or the demands made on the Pope by the German press and Chancellor Merkel, the daughter of a Polish Jew and remarried to a Jewish professor, but the Vatican's and the Church's capitulation. "I have come into the world to bear witness to the truth," Jesus replied to Pilate as he was about to be handed over. "You shall know the truth, and the truth shall set you free", he taught his disciples. Unfortunately, the Catholic hierarchy has long since given up speaking the truth as Jesus Christ taught. Both the Vatican and the Red Cross know very well what the truth is about the so-called extermination camps; but their present leaders have capitulated, preferring to lie and to abide painfully by the dogma of faith of the Holocaust.

On 25 March 2016, Good Friday, the Holy Father Francis presided over the Stations of the Cross in the Colosseum in Rome. The event was broadcast by numerous television stations to hundreds of millions of people around the world. The Pope commissioned Cardinal Gualtiero Basseti to write the meditations. For the Third

Station, Jesus falls for the first time, Basseti referred to the sufferings of today's world. In the first place of the meditation he wrote: "...There are sufferings that seem to deny the love of God. Where is God in the extermination camps? And a little later, before praying the Our Father: "...We pray to you, Lord, for the Jews who have died in the death camps...". It is obvious that there was no need to mention among today's tragedies and in pride of place a suffering of seventy years ago. Only servitude justifies this mention by Cardinal Basseti, who, by of course, forgot to write a single word for the unfortunate Palestinian people. Yes, like Monsignor Williamson, the Church knows that the death camps did not exist. It knows the truth, but it affirms the lie out of cowardice, because it is subservient to deception and ignores the words of Christ: "You shall know the truth, and the truth shall set you free".

Haviv Schieber, the Jew who slashed his wrists to avoid deportation to Israel

In *On the Wrong Side of Just About Everything But Right About It All*, Dale Crowley Jr. recounts attending Haviv Schieber's funeral with his close friends in a blizzard of snow, a fitting backdrop to the tormented and courageous life of this revisionist Jew. Dale Crowley quotes this line from Schieber: "My Jewish brothers love to hate. They do not know how to forgive. They are sick and they need the doctor, Jesus, and the medicine, the Bible." Schieber, then, was a Christian, and in his articles, interviews and statements he always expressed his desire for truth and justice. "Nazism," he once said, "made me afraid because I was a Jew. Zionism makes me ashamed to be a Jew." When asked if the Protocols of the Elders of Zion were authentic, he invariably replied, "It doesn't matter. It's all come true."

Ernst Zündel learned a great deal from Haviv Schieber, with whom he maintained a good friendship. Zündel regarded him as an extremely intelligent person. From him he obtained first-hand information about Zionism, as Schieber explained to him the reality of the State of Israel. In 1932 Schieber was a passionate Zionist who emigrated from his native Poland to live in British Mandate Palestine. He had Palestinian friends and lived and did business with them until 1936 when, disillusioned by the reality, he chose to return to Poland. There he saw how, instead of helping the neediest Jews, the Zionist organisations selected only young socialists who could be useful in their plans for the future state. In 1939, when the Nazis invaded Poland, he returned to Palestine, where he married, started a family and became the Jewish mayor of Beersheba,. His final disillusionment with Zionism came when he discovered its true nature during the 1948-1949 war of conquest. Fed up with murder and injustice, he flew to the United States from Israel on 18 March 1959.

The Zionists then began their persecution and pressured the US authorities to deport him. The legal battle to obtain political asylum lasted more than fifteen years. He was initially allowed to stay until 1 February 1960. On 4 April 1961 a court order ordered his deportation, but his claims that he would be physically persecuted in Israel were heard and deferred. Finally, on 5 August 1964, he was invited to leave the country voluntarily as an alternative to deportation, but was warned that if he did not leave the United States he would be deported. The asylum process lasted until the early 1970s. As late as 23 June 1970, an appeals court denied him indefinite political refugee status. When Zionist pressure was on the verge of succeeding, Haviv Schieber slit his wrists at Washington D.C. airport to prevent being put on a plane to Israel.

In the United States, Schieber became the admired Quixote of a group of Americans, Jews and Christians, who saw in him an indomitable idealist. Schieber became a whirlwind of activity in defence of the rights of the Palestinian people and in denouncing the imposture of Zionism. Haviv Schieber died in 1987. During the last years of his life, despite two serious operations in 1985, he continued his work at the head of his "Holy Land State Committee", set up to fight for a state in which Jews, Arabs and Christians could live in peace.

Hans Schmidt, the American imprisoned for four words

Emigrated to the United States in 1949, Hans Schmidt became a citizen in 1955. In addition to marrying and having two children, he became a businessman in the restaurant industry, but he had also founded and chaired the German-American National Political Action Committee (GANPAC), an organisation dedicated to protecting the rights and interests of the country's largest ethnic minority. In 1985, his offices in Santa Monica (California) were attacked and damaged to some extent. Schmidt, who was in contact with the IHR and had attended some IHR conferences, edited and published two hard-hitting newsletters, one in English, *GANPAC Brief*, and the other in German, *USA-Bericht*. A civil rights activist, he was outspoken in his revisionist views and opinions, including denouncing the falsification of history and the Holocaust campaign. He was also ruthless about the betrayal and capitulation of German political leaders.

On 9 August 1995 he was arrested at Frankfurt airport. He was 68 years old and retired. He had travelled to Germany to visit his elderly mother and was about to fly back to Florida. Schmidt was arrested on the basis of an arrest warrant issued on 28 March 1995 by a judge in Schwerin, which was replaced by a second arrest warrant dated 5 October. The 'crime' had been the sending of a copy of his newsletter *USA-Bericht* (*USA Report*) to the home of Rudi Geil, a member of the 'Bundesrat'. The newsletter contained an open letter he had written in response to an article published in *Die Zeit*. Offended by what he read, Geil filed the complaint that led to the arrest warrant. The offending paragraph that prompted the arrest alluded to "the left, the anarchists, the Jew and the Freemason infesting the political system, together with the controlled press." According to the arrest warrant the expressions "the Jew infested" and "the Freemason infested" were directed against these two population groups in Germany. The charges against him related to the famous paragraph 130 (I, 2) and were the usual ones.

For the first time an American citizen was arrested for something he had written in an e-mail sent from the United States, for expressing an opinion that was absolutely legal in his country. US political leaders, so quick to condemn violations of human rights and freedom of expression when it is in their interest, remained silent. When questioned, they dismissed the matter with the familiar "domestic issue". Protests came from American civil rights activists, who sent a flood of letters to German officials and journalists and took out newspaper advertisements denouncing Schmidt's treatment. On 22 August, for example, a group of citizens stood outside the German consulate in New York holding a large banner entitled 'Travelers Alert', warning Americans planning to travel to Germany that they risked imprisonment if they expressed 'incorrect political views'.

While in prison, Schmidt accused the US Embassy of providing false information to Germany to facilitate his prosecution.

Due to his delicate health, his lawyers managed to get him released on bail in January 1996. Thus, after spending five months in prison, he managed to return to the United States and was able to avoid further prosecution. There he wrote a book about his experience, entitled *Jailed in "Democratic" Germany*, which was published in 1997. Until his death in 2010, he continued to fight against the power of the Jewish lobbies and their influence in the United States and around the world.

Arthur Topham, convicted in Canada for "hatred" of Jews

Arthur Topham is a long-time revisionist fighter who in November 2015 was convicted in Canada of the crime of "hate". Topham maintains the website *The Radical Press*. For eight years now he has been resisting harassment from the enemies of free speech, so his fight has been long and heroic. The site has been sabotaged on several occasions. The first attack on the materials posted on the website, took place in 2007. Even then, charges were laid against Topham under the Canadian Human Rights Act. His first arrest and imprisonment, on 16 May 2012, coincided with further sabotage of the site. He was charged with "willfully promoting hatred against people of the Jewish race or religion". The two individuals who sued him are known to have acted at the behest of the Jewish Masonic lodge B'nai B'rith of Canada.

Topham himself has revealed that the text that contributed most to the filing of the lawsuit was a satirical article entitled *Israel Must Perish*, written in May 2011, in which Arthur Topham parodied Theodore N. Kaufman's famous *Germany Must Perish*, published in 1941. What he had done was simply to substitute the names in the sentences that exuded the most hatred for Germany. That is to say, where Kaufmann's book said "Nazis", Topham had written "Jews"; instead of "Germany", he had written "Israel"; instead of "Hitler", he had written "Netanyahu". He intended to expose the hypocrisy of Jews, who accused others of hatred. On 15 April 2014, a provincial court judge surnamed Morgan, emulating the practices of the Inquisition, prohibited the publication of the names of the two individuals who had filed the criminal complaint against Arthur Topham, publisher of *The Radical Press*, for "hate crime".

The trial against Topham began on 26 October 2015 and concluded on 12 November with a guilty verdict for Topham. At the time of writing, the sentence, which could be two years minus one day, is not yet known. Readers interested in more details about the trial can go to *The Radical Press* website, which contains a full transcript of the archives of each session of the trial. The jazz musician and Jewish revisionist Gilad Atzmon intervened in the trial and also published an excerpt on 8 November 2015. It explains that the Crown presented among the experts on Judaism and anti-Semitism Len Rudner, a "Jewish professional" who for fifteen years had been working for the Jewish Congress of Canada and its successor organisation, the CIJA (Center for Israel and Jewish Affairs). Prior to the start of the trial, he had tried to force the internet service provider to shut down the site. Rudner himself has filed civil lawsuits against Topham. As in the cases of Pedro Varela and the Europa Bookshop or Fredrick Töben and the Adelaide Institute website, most of the books and texts listed by Rudner can be obtained on the internet or freely purchased on Amazon and in bookshops.

Gilad Atzmon (see note 4), who is not only a musician but also a philosopher and author of several books, was the expert on Jewish issues presented by Arthur Topham and his lawyer Barcley Johnson to counter Rudner's arguments. Atzmon's competence in "Jewish identity politics" was recognised by the court. The jury listened with fascination to the precise and complex explanations of this unique Jew, who asserted that many of the apparently anti-Semitic writings were produced by early Zionists. Atzmon, a former soldier, experienced first-hand the perverse ideology of Zionism and the tribal mechanisms that are fanatically applied in Israel.

On Friday, November 20, 2015, having been found guilty in the previous trial, Arthur Topham appeared before the Supreme Court in Quesnel for a hearing related to the bail issue and also additional claims related to the publication in *The Radical Press of* a photo of the juror in front of the court building. Jennifer Johnson, the Crown prosecutor, requested a number of extremely harsh conditions. It appears that while Topham and Johnson appeared in person, Bruce Butler, the Supreme Court judge, and defence lawyer Barcley Johnson appeared via telephone from Vancouver and Victoria respectively. The judge ruled that the publication of the photo of the jurors, who were standing in the snow and photographed from a distance where their faces could not be clearly seen, could not be a danger to their safety. In any case, he demanded its withdrawal.

The latest we have learned about Topham, whose website *The Radical Press* is now censored, is that on 6 August 2018 he was re-arrested at his home by a specialist hate crime team. On the judge's orders, the home was searched. Files and computers were seized. Due to a court order expiring on 12 September 2019, he was deprived of the freedom to make public the names of the plaintiffs or the international organisations supporting them. At the time of writing, Arthur Topham remains under arrest at his home in Cottonwood.

11. Appendix on the ruthless persecution of nonagenarians

The persecuted people listed in this last section, which we write as an appendix, are no longer revisionists, nor have they committed thought crimes. They are people who would normally never enter history textbooks. They would perhaps form part of what Miguel de Unamuno considered intrahistory. Their names have made the headlines for a day or two and then disappeared forever. Precisely for this reason, so that they do not end up in oblivion, we have chosen to include them in our work, albeit concisely. They are nonagenarian victims of unspeakable persecution for the simple fact of having served as soldiers in the army during the Second World War. Normally, these elderly men who served their country as teenagers should be honoured and recognised, yet they are treated as criminals.

The famous case of John Demjanjuk, extradited, accused, tried and sentenced to death, has already been discussed in chapter XII of *Proscribed History*. Another well-known case is that of Frank Walus, Zündel's witness in the 1985 trial. Falsely accused by the Nazi hunter Wiesenthal of being the 'Butcher of Kielce', he suffered a vicious campaign in the US media, which led to his public beating. The German-born American mechanic was attacked seven times by Jewish henchmen, who almost killed him in an acid attack. In order to finance his defence, he sold his house and was ruined. He also lost his US citizenship. After a long and costly appeals process, he won, but his health was already very poor and after suffering several heart attacks he died. There are more cases like these that could be recounted, but we prefer to give space now to the anonymous ex-soldiers, of whom we will present only a few examples.

In April 2013, it became known in Germany that prosecutors had decided to carry out a "final effort" to find Nazi criminals. To this end, a list had been compiled of the names of 50 living Auschwitz and other camp guards who were to be investigated in order to give satisfaction to Holocaust survivors. "We owe it to the victims," said Kurt Schrimm, head of the Central Office of the Judicial Authorities for the Investigation of National Socialist Crimes, who reported that the Auschwitz Museum had forwarded the list of names of former guards to them.

Efrain Zuroff, a furious Nazi-hunter, director of the Simon Wiesenthal Centre in Jerusalem and one of the masterminds of "Operation Last Chance", declared that the fact that most of the names on the list are octogenarians or nonagenarians is no reason why "justice" should not be done. Author of *Operation Last Chance: One Man's Quest to bring Nazi Criminals to Justice*, the vigilante avenger states in his book: "Don't look at these men and say they look weak and frail. Think of someone who at the height of his strength devoted his energies to murdering men, women and children. The passage of time in no way diminishes the guilt of murderers. Old age should not afford them protection". The famous Deborah Lipstadt, the Emory University professor, supported the idea that there is no age limit for prosecuting criminals.

Laszlo Csatary

It is the first name to appear on the list managed by German prosecutors and the SWC (Simon Wiesenthal Center). In July 2012, shortly after the arrival of Zionist Laurent Fabius at the Foreign Ministry, a meeting took place in France between Fabius, the Nazi hunters and Jewish community groups. As a result of the meeting, France asked Hungary to arrest Laszlo Csatary, who was living in Budapest under his own name. A spokesman for the Ministry stated that there could be "no immunity" for those who had carried out the Holocaust. On 18 July 2102 the SWC reported that Csatary had been arrested. His lawyer Gabor Horwath said he was interrogated for three hours behind closed doors by a Budapest prosecutor, who accused him of anti-Semitism. No charges were brought against him, but he was placed under house arrest. According to his persecutors, he participated in the deportation of more than 15,000 Jews to Auschwitz in 1944. Csatary denied being an anti-Semite and cited examples of relations with Jews in his family and circle of friends. He also denied having been a commander of the Kosice ghetto in German-allied Hungary. Horwath said he "could easily have been mistaken for someone else". To apply pressure, vigilantes organised demonstrations outside the house with signs reading "Last chance for justice". A group from the European Union of Jewish Students, all wearing very indignant faces, formed a chain with their hands tied.

Two "activists" climbed up to the floor and stuck crossed-out swastikas and a sign with the slogan "We never forget" on the door. In August 2013, Laszlo Csatary died at the age of 98 while awaiting trial. In reporting the death, the lawyer recalled that Csatary had only been an intermediary between Hungarian and German officials and had not been involved in any crime.

Samuel Kunz

On 21 December 2010, Christoph Göke, spokesman for the Dortmund prosecutors, reported that a 90-year-old man, Samuel Kunz, a former guard in Sobibor who had helped exterminate 430,000 Jews, had been charged. According to press reports, Kunz admitted that he had worked between 1942-43 in the Belzec "extermination camp". When his flat was raided by the police, the old man denied that he had been personally involved in any crime. The news reported that a "flurry of arrests" was taking place among people in their nineties and that Nazi hunters were pleased with the zeal of the police. Alongside the bloodletting of people, the economic bloodletting continued: days before Kunz's arrest, on 9 December 2010, Rüdiger Grube, CEO of Deutsche Bahn, declared that the suffering of Nazi victims was not forgotten, so the state railway company was donating 6.6 million dollars to fund projects for survivors, handed over to the EVZ (Remembrance, Responsibility and Future Foundation).

Johan Breyer

As a result of an arrest warrant issued by Germany, in July 2014 Johan Breyer, an 89-year-old man who had emigrated to the United States in 1952, was arrested at his home in Philadelphia, Pennsylvania, accused of having acted as an accomplice in the murder of hundreds of thousands of Jews. Breyer admitted that he had been a guard at Auschwitz, but said he had served overseas and had nothing to do with the murders. Although his lawyer, Dennis Boyle, warned that his client was in too frail health to be jailed while awaiting an extradition hearing, the judge said the detention centre was equipped to care for him and refused any bail. The Associated Press reported statements in Jerusalem by Nazi-hunter Efraim Zuroff, who reminded the American public that in 2013 the German authorities had displayed posters in some cities with the slogan "Late, but not too late" that the decrepit Breyer should be extradited. Zuroff added that Germany "deserved credit" for "making a last-ditch effort to maximise the prosecution of those responsible for the Holocaust."

Oskar Gröning

The shameful poster campaign deserves comment, for Oskar Gröning was one of the thirty Auschwitz guards singled out in the context of the operation "Spät, aber nicht zu spät" (Late, but not too late). They depicted in black and white the main façade of Auschwitz in the background and the railway tracks over the snowy ground, which converged before the entrance to the camp. At the bottom, a red stripe with the inscription mentioned above. The SWC offered rewards of 25,000 euros for those who denounced the grandparents. The Wiesenthal Centre reported that six cases were located in Baden-Würtenberg, seven in Bavaria, two in Saxony-Anhalt, four in North Westphalia, four in Lower Saxony, two in Hesse and one each in Rhineland-Palatinate, Hamburg, Schleswig-Holstein, Saxony and Mecklenburg-Western Pomerania. All of them were former guards.

One of the four prosecuted in Lower Saxony was Oskar Gröning, who was arrested in March 2014. When he was formally charged in September 2014, Gröning, known as the "Auschwitz accountant", was 93 years old and charged with complicity in the murder of at least 300,000 people. "Oskar Gröning did not kill anyone with his hands, but he was part of the extermination machine," survivor Judy Lysy told retired judge Thomas Walter, who investigated Gröning in Toronto and Montreal. The trial began in April 2015, and Gröning's failing health forced the trial to be suspended for a few days. The verdict was made public on 15 July. Although the prosecutor had asked for three and a half years in prison, the Luneburg court, disregarding the fact that Gröning was already 94 years old and had not killed anyone, sentenced him to four years. Justice Minister Heiko Maas, a Social Democrat, said the trial had helped to alleviate the "great failure" of the German justice system, which had only managed to bring to justice about 50 of the 6,500 SS members at Auschwitz who survived the war.

Reinhold Hanning

In the summer of 2015, the court set to try Reinhold Hanning, a 93-year-old former Auschwitz guard accused of complicity in the murder of 170,000 people, was awaiting a medical report to determine whether the nonagenarian was mentally fit to stand trial. Anke Grudda, a spokeswoman for the Detmold court in North Westphalia, told the Associated Press that the trial could not begin until the neurological report was completed. The British newspaper *Daily Mail* reported that there was insufficient evidence to show whether Hanning had made decisions himself or had merely assisted others in the work. The case was supplemented by statements from an alleged grandson of victims, Tommy Lamm, 69, who from Jerusalem told the story of his grandparents, who were shaved and gassed shortly after arriving at Auschwitz, and linked Hanning to their deaths. Lamm said he was willing to go to Germany to hang him with his own hands. Finally, in November 2015, neurologists concluded that Reinhold Hanning could withstand two-hour daily court sessions.

Siert Bruins

Accused of killing a member of the resistance during the World War, Siert Bruins, a 92-year-old Dutch-born former security guard, was brought to trial in Germany in September 2013. The public prosecution, despite the fact that he was a nonagenarian, asked for life imprisonment. The prosecutor argued that Bruins had killed Aldert Klaas Dijkema, who in September 1944 was working for the resistance against the German occupation of the Netherlands. Surprisingly, the judge found that there was insufficient evidence that the accused was the perpetrator of the alleged crime, which took place seventy years earlier. Detlef Hartmann, the lawyer for Aldert Klaas' sister, who was allegedly seeking revenge, said that his client was upset by the court's decision. For his part, Siert Bruins left the courtroom with a walker and was unable to express an opinion.

A 91-year-old woman

Many of the detainees were usually ill, as it is impossible to reach the age of ninety without serious physical and especially mental deterioration. In most cases, the full names of these elderly people were not even revealed to the press. We will end, then, with an anonymous victim, who will serve as a symbol of so many unknown people who have suffered and suffer the insatiable hatred that, eighty years later, is still displayed by the eternal "victims"; but also as a symbol of the moral and political misery of the Federal Republic of Germany, whose Chancellor Angela Merkel cynically declares that her country must pay "eternally" for the Holocaust. A state that persecutes old men who served their homeland and carried out the orders of their superiors has neither credibility nor dignity.

On 22 September 2015, *Fox News* carried this news item: "German woman, 91, charged in 260,000 Auschwitz deaths". The body of the story reported that an unidentified 91-year-old woman had been charged by German prosecutors with involvement in the deaths of 260,000 Jews at Auschwitz. *The Times of Israel*, one of *Fox News'* sources, specified that the woman, a member of the SS, had been a radio operator under the commandant of the camp in July 1944. Heinz Döllel, a spokesman for the prosecutor's office, said it did not appear that the woman was unfit to stand trial, although the court would not decide whether to proceed with the case until next year. It is most likely that the court, considering that being a radio operator is an abominable crime, will eventually try her.

Other books

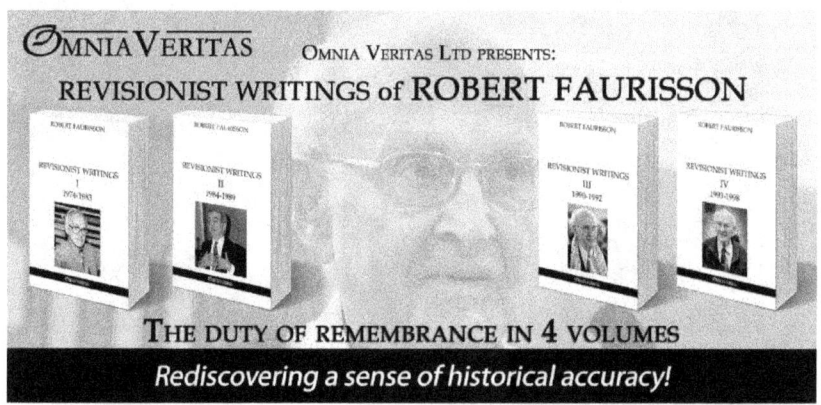

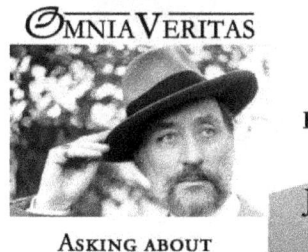
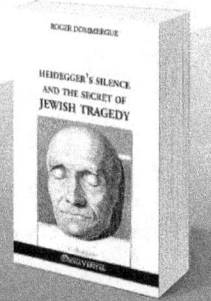

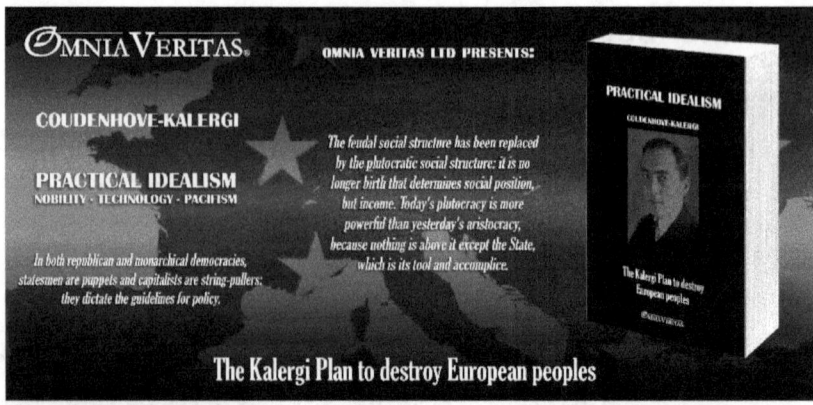

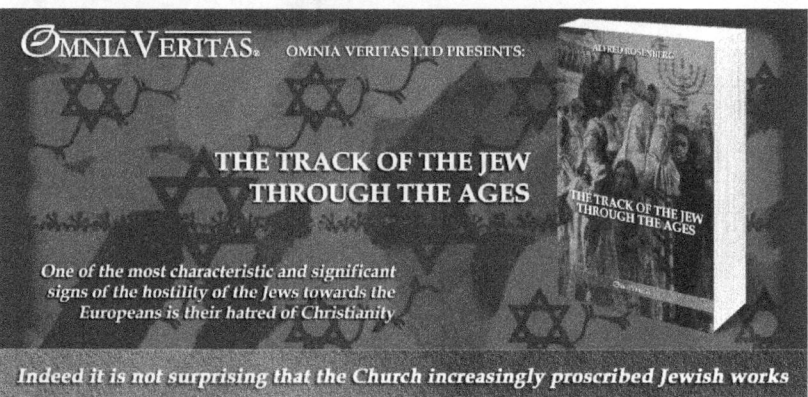

OMNIA VERITAS
OMNIA VERITAS LTD PRESENTS:
SOLZHENITSYN
The Jews Before the Revolution
"The purpose that guides me throughout this work on the life common the Russians and the Jews consists of looking for all the points necessary for a mutual understanding, all the possible voices which, once we get rid of the bitterness of the past, can lead us towards the future."
Aleksandr Solzhenitsyn
200 YEARS TOGETHER
The Jewish people is at the same time an active and passive element of History

OMNIA VERITAS
OMNIA VERITAS LTD PRESENTS:
SOLZHENITSYN
The Jews in the Soviet Union
"The revolution of 1917 provided a powerful impetus to Russian Jewry, so the essay naturally stretched into the post-revolutionary period. Thus, the title Two Hundred Years Together was born."
Aleksandr Solzhenitsyn
200 YEARS TOGETHER
The Jews in the Soviet Union
The uniqueness of Russian-Jewish entwinement disappeared during the new Exodus

OMNIA VERITAS
The Real Victors of the Second World War
Omnia Veritas Ltd presents:
The World Conquerors
THE REAL WAR CRIMINALS
by
LOUIS MARSCHALKO
The Betrayal of America by the Secret Power.

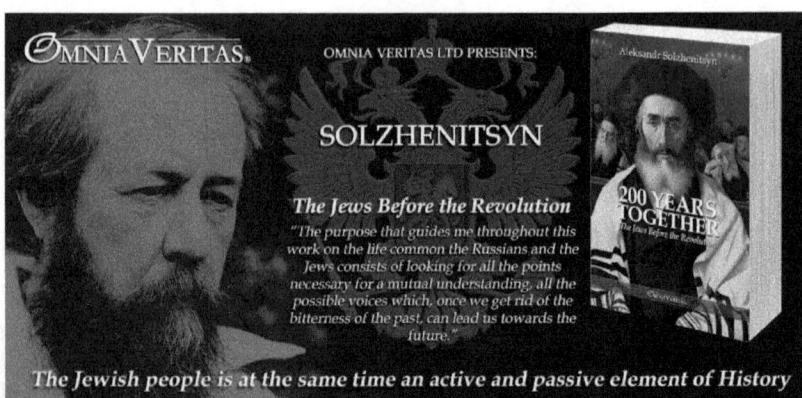

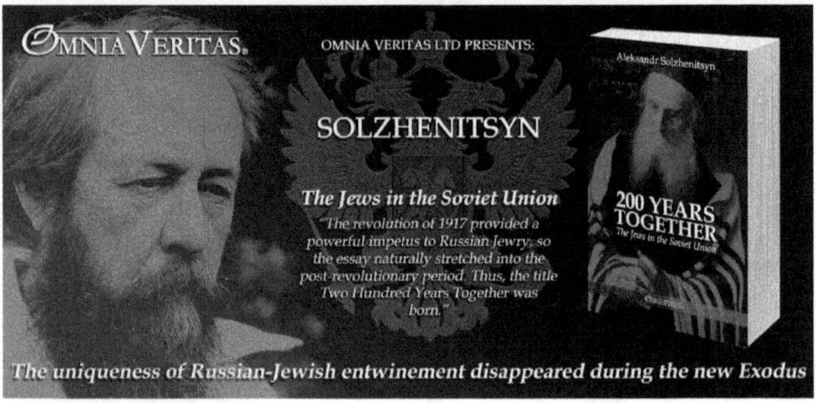

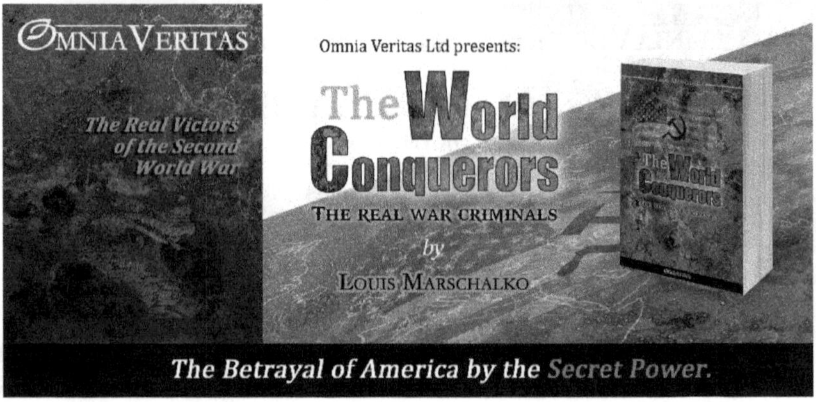

www.ingramcontent.com/pod-product-compliance
Lightning Source LLC
Chambersburg PA
CBHW050139170426
43197CB00011B/1900